Old Worlds

*Egypt, Southwest Asia, India, and Russia
in Early Modern English Writing*

JOHN MICHAEL ARCHER

Old Worlds

Egypt, Southwest Asia, India, and Russia
in Early Modern English Writing

STANFORD UNIVERSITY PRESS

STANFORD, CALIFORNIA

2001

Stanford University Press
Stanford, California

© 2001 by the Board of Trustees of the
Leland Stanford Junior University

Printed in the United States of America
on acid-free, archival-quality paper

Library of Congress Cataloging-in-Publication Data

Archer, John Michael.

Old worlds : Egypt, Southwest Asia, India, and Russia in early modern
English writing / John Michael Archer.
    p. cm
  Includes bibliographical references (p.) and index.
  ISBN 0-8047-4337-1 (alk. paper)
   1. English literature—Early modern, 1500–1700—History and criticism.
2. Egypt—In literature. 3. Shakespeare, William, 1564–1616. Antony and
Cleopatra. 4. Milton, John, 1608–1674—Knowledge—Asia. 5. Dryden, John,
1631–1700. Aureng-Zebe. 6. Middle East—In literature. 7. Russia—In literature.
8. India—In literature. I. Title.

PR129.E3 A73 2001
820.9'355—dc21

2001057658

Original Printing 2001
Last figure below indicates year of this printing:
10 09 08 07 06 05 04 03 02 01

Typeset by Publication Services in 10/14 Janson

For the members of my graduate seminars, 1987–1995

Contents

Acknowledgments

The following people have helped me during the writing of this book, without helping me to any errors, which are all my own: Ursula Appelt, Richard Burt, Madeleine Brainerd, Hunter Cadzow, Patricia Cahill, Joseph Cleary, Anthony B. Dawson, Frances E. Dolan, Fraser Easton, Margaret W. Ferguson, John Gillies, Christopher GoGwilt, Kim F. Hall, Richard Halpern, Jean E. Howard, David Scott Kastan, Ania Loomba, Joyce Green MacDonald, Fiona McNeill, Earl Miner, Zita Nunes, David Quint, Petar Ramadanovic, Stella P. Revard, Edward W. Said, Yumna Siddiqi, Jyotsna G. Singh, Gayatri Chakravorty Spivak, Peter Stallybrass, Paul G. Stanwood, Helen Tartar, Rachel Trubowitz, Dorothea von Mücke, Virginia Mason Vaughan, Priscilla Wald, and Paul Yachnin. My apologies to anyone I have inadvertently left out. I am grateful to David Hiley, Provost, and Marilyn Hoskin, dean of Liberal Arts, University of New Hampshire, Durham, for financial support toward publication. I would also like to thank the staffs of the Newberry Library and the Huntington Library, where I began my research into old worlds while holding short-term fellowships.

JMA

New York, Vancouver, Portsmouth

Para-Colonial Studies

In 1498, Christopher Columbus distinguished the lands he had visited as "another world from that in which the Romans and Alexander and the Greeks laboured to gain dominion," and, five years later, a letter attributed to Amerigo Vespucci and entitled *Mundus Novus* appeared in print to herald this "New World."[1] Our continued fascination with these acts of naming still distracts us from the full significance of the "Old World" in early modern thought after Columbus, the traditional three-part world of Asia, Africa, and Europe itself. Already "old," because it was the theater of classical antiquity, the three-part world was retrospectively and almost accidentally renamed as the Old World in another sense, by comparison with the New. The Old World was as much a European fiction as its rival, which was hardly new to its inhabitants. Africa and Asia, worlds in themselves in a sense, were themselves agglomerations of yet other societies, cultures, and economies, as was Europe. The imaginary borders of all three parts of the classical globe were porous, and they shifted slightly from one geographical description to another during and after antiquity. Places and cultures new to Europeans within the Old World were described in accounts by real and purported travelers throughout medieval and early modern times. Finally, the New World was almost always conceived as a lost part of the Old World, a fold in its global immensity and temporal endurance. In a period that venerated the past as a source of invention as well as tradition, the Old World remained a vital, and even novel and unsettling, space throughout the sixteenth and seventeenth centuries, its prestige strengthened rather than diminished by the renewal of antiquity that the New World promised.

To judge by the moderate number of books about the New World published during the sixteenth and seventeenth centuries in Europe, interest in America, as it also came to be called, was consistent and broad but neither all-consuming nor detached from the persistent curiosity about the Old World.[2] The English in particular remained more concerned with the Old than the New for much of the period. Richard Eden translated the writings of Peter Martyr and others under the title *The Decades of the Newe Worlde* in 1555, but his book was read largely for its material on Russia and the Far East.[3] When Richard Willes brought out a new version in 1577, he entitled it *The History of Trauayle in the West and East Indies*, chiefly adding Ludovico de Varthema's travels through Egypt, Arabia, and India. Richard Hakluyt's *Divers Voyages, touching the discouerie of America and the Ilands adiacent vnto the same* (1582) similarly became *The Principall Navigations, Voiages and Discoveries of the English Nation* (second edition, 1598–1600), the first two-thirds of which concerned the north and northeast (Russia and the passage to China) and the south and southeast (Africa, the eastern Mediterranean, and South Asia). In England's neighbor, France, 180 new books on Asia and the Turks were published to some 40 on the New World between 1480 and 1609.[4]

The desire for information about the Old World continued, and actually increased, in England well past the first recorded voyages to the New. John Gillies describes the spread of the new cartography of Abraham Ortelius and Gerhard Mercator during Shakespeare's time.[5] Prose writings of various sorts have received less attention. Two loosely constituted genres, the eyewitness travel narrative and the second-hand compendium of geographical and historical knowledge, competed for learned and unlearned readers alike. Yet a mutual dependence also linked the eyewitness narratives and classical sources such as Herodotus, partially translated into English in 1584, antiquarian surveys such as Walter Ralegh's *History of the World* of 1614, and global geographies such as Pierre Belon's in the sixteenth century and Peter Heylyn's in the seventeenth.

Why did England, on the verge of an Atlantic empire from our belated point of view, turn so resolutely toward both the East and the past during these early modern centuries? In *The Mediterranean and the Mediterranean World in the Age of Philip II*, Fernand Braudel provides an answer by relating early modern England to the larger world in which it was positioned. The Levant Company of merchant adventurers, chartered by the crown in 1581, and its offshoot the East India Company, founded in 1600, prospered because the Spanish and Portuguese had become preoccupied with America and with the route to India around the Cape of Good Hope:

> The old firm of the Mediterranean gained once more from the terrible battles of the Atlantic. Between 1583 and 1591 it was no coincidence that English agents should have made their way along the roads through Syria to the Indian Ocean, Persia, the Indies, and Sumatra. These wanderers have left us their fantastic travellers' tales of the routes in the Near and Far East. In Egypt . . . the English were out-manoeuvred by skillful and persistent competition from the French. The English therefore turned their attention to Syria and the roads through it.[6]

A double movement ensued, then, first to the eastern Mediterranean and soon afterward to the countries still known by the biblical names Mesopotamia and Babylon, and eventually to India.

England's eastward trajectory within the changing global economy of the sixteenth and seventeenth centuries also plotted an itinerary through cultural tradition. This is roughly the itinerary I have followed in this book, which deals with the various old worlds England attempted to reinterpret in the sixteenth and seventeenth centuries: Northeast Africa, Southwest Asia, Russia, and India. The claims of firsthand travel accounts challenged the assumptions of armchair geographers and world historians while continuing to rely on them; plays, poems, and narrative fiction drew on both. Gradually, an established history that linked Europe, and England within it, to the African and Asian pasts through both the Bible and classical antiquity was flattened to become what Edward W. Said calls an "imaginative geography," the ground-plot of the systematic orientalism of the eighteenth century.[7] Recent work on both the New and Old Worlds has left a fund of early modern writings about Africa and Asia relatively untouched, yet they speak as much to present-day concerns about culture, race, gender, and nationality.

The founding of the first successful American colony at Jamestown in 1607 came relatively late in England's uneven course of economic and cultural expansion. English ships had made tentative incursions into the Mediterranean since the fifteenth century.[8] At a certain level, of course, the settlement of North America was indeed a different enterprise from the commercial exploitation of the well-worn routes of the Old World. Viewed from a global perspective, however, England's territorial and commercial ventures appear as two parts of the same process. And the global view is often implicit in the careers and cultural productions of the times. Ralegh sponsored the abortive Roanoke colonies in Virginia during the 1580s and visited Guiana twice, and he also wrote an encyclopedic history of Old World empires; John Smith led the Jamestown colony and described its origins, and he authored a largely fanciful account of his earlier adventures in Asia and Africa, publishing it, along with an extension of the Virginia material, in 1630; George Sandys both served as treasurer in Jamestown and composed his mythographic commentary on Ovid there— eventually he published a narrative of his travels in Egypt and the Levant, as well. As Thomas Hahn has pointed out, the persistent use of the names "Indian" and "Indies" in New as well as Old World contexts, as in Willes's *History of Trauayle in the West and East Indies*, was not accidental: "What has often been labeled a simple error by Columbus actually reflects a major aspect of late medieval and early modern ideology."[9]

New and Old Worlds together made up the same "new world" within Europe's developing global consciousness. At the same time, the image of the new totality was also fractured from the start, confused at its paradoxical edges and even within its multiplying borders by blank spaces and monstrous conjectures, as an examination of Renaissance world maps shows.[10] The distinction of new and old calls for more critical examination than it usually receives, as I have implied above.[11] The naming of the New World was a virtual imposition of European power. But, at least in part, it was also a tacit acknowledgment in early modern times of what we would now call a *separate economy*, really a complex of separate economies and separate cultures—separate and hierarchically assimilable to that of Europe, of course, under a dawning racial system, but alien all the same. The newness of the New World marked a season of profound instability for Europe as well as an opportunity for violent conquest. At the very moment when European hegemony over the world is often supposed to have originated, we find two worlds—at least two—rather than one, in the European imagination.

It is true that Europe went on to attain a considerable measure of global influence by the eighteenth century despite the challenges presented by the New World and the new Old World. A partial explanation for Europe's virtual hegemony has been offered by the world-systems theory pioneered by Braudel and Immanuel Wallerstein. The vocabulary of world-systems theory—derived from its concentric model of core areas, semiperipheries, and colonized peripheries—continues to inform new historical and cultural materialist treatments of European power during the early modern period in literary studies. A brief consideration of the theory behind the terminology will help us determine its utility and limitations for the study of Europe's role in the Old World.

In part an economic and sociological historiography, world-systems theory takes the "long" sixteenth century in Europe (1450–1640) as its initial point of departure. A "world-system" is primarily a disposition of social relations across a geographical area, relations which alter over time, and eventually beyond recognition as a new system is produced.[12] The modern world-system does, indeed, cover all, or most, of the globe, but this is not the principal meaning of the prefix. "It is a 'world' system," Wallerstein writes, "not because it encompasses the whole world, but because it is larger than any juridically-defined political unit" (*World-System*, 1:15). The European world economy of the twelfth to fifteenth centuries was neither global nor alone, nor was it a particularly important economy in a field that included the Mediterranean, Indian Ocean, Central Asian, and immense Chinese systems. Samir Amin and Janet L. Abu-Lughod argue separately that, before the sixteenth century, Europe was located on the periphery of an extensive Mediterranean system controlled by an Arab-Islamic core.[13]

Wallerstein holds that world economies are dynamically structured within by an axial division of labor from core to periphery, what Marxists generally call the international division of labor:

> This division is not merely functional—that is, occupational—but geographical. That is to say, the range of economic tasks is not evenly distributed throughout the world-system. In part this is the consequence of ecological considerations, to be sure. But for the most part, it is a function of the social organization of work, one which magnifies and legitimizes the ability of some groups within the system to exploit the labor of others. (*World-System*, 1:349)

While the division of labor maintains the tension within each world economy, different world economies are connected through the exchange of luxury goods for gold and silver (*World-System*, 1:302). In the past, boundaries between systems shifted through the absorption of adjacent peripheries into the rising system's internal division of labor, sometimes by means of military conquest.

The modern world-system proper, initially centered in Europe, did, in fact, annex other areas in this way to become the sole world economy by the mid-nineteenth century. Wallerstein explains Europe's ascendancy by locating the onset of capitalism there in the sixteenth century, tying it, as Marx did in the first volume of *Capital*, to the eventual creation of a "world-embracing" market.[14] Nevertheless, there were precedents for wide-ranging and complex, if not capitalist, world economies elsewhere in the Old World. In her book *Before European Hegemony*, Abu-Lughod remarks that Wallerstein's writings "treat the European-dominated world-system that formed in the long sixteenth century as if it had appeared de novo," although it likely drew from the extensive world economies of China, South Asia, and North Africa in the thirteenth and fourteenth centuries that she goes on to describe (pp. x, 12). K. N. Chaudhuri has established the economic and social vitality of the Indian Ocean's world economies from the inception of Islam, tracing them beyond Abu-Lughod's terminus in the mid-fourteenth century to the intervention of the

Portuguese, Dutch, and English.[15] Without entering into the large questions of when and where capitalism arose and precisely how it is to be defined, I suggest that what is new about early modern Europe can only be appreciated if it is set within a wider Old World context.

Wallerstein's world-systems model assumes unfixed and dynamic economic relations rather than ecological and geographical advantages or historical fatality. Nevertheless, in its classic, and perhaps most influential, form, it can be taken to suggest that Europe's dominance by the eighteenth century was an unprecedented "rise" and that Asia's fortunes were a characteristic lapse into a cycle of obsolescence or decadence.[16]

Abu-Lughod proposes that changes within economic systems be ascribed to chaotic, and sometimes violent, restructurings rather than regular cycles. The integration of communications and transactions in one area was accompanied by their dispersal in others, as peripheral zones became centers of activity, while core areas and their semiperipheries were gradually defused or forcefully displaced. Thus the "rise of the West" and the "decline" of the East and the South should be conceived as a restructuring of preexistent world economies in a partly arbitrary and partly opportunistic fashion; trade routes and long-standing commercial practices became available, were taken over, and ultimately rearranged to serve new commercial groups (Abu-Lughod, pp. 361, 367, 369). Terms such as *core* and *periphery* are broad spatial designations that provisionally cover the complex and unstable economic effects of Europe's early modern engagement with the world, or worlds, it faced.

"There is surely no such thing as a model of decadence," as Braudel remarked. "A new model has to be built from the basic structures of every particular case." The Mediterranean was not in decline during the sixteenth century, "Nor above all should we talk of the irreversible decline of the Ottomans, although this was a phrase already to be heard in the West" (*Mediterranean*, pp. 1203, 1240). Early modern Europe set the familiar discourse of decadence in motion; by invoking the threat of degeneration and situating it outside their borders, Europeans reinterpreted their place in the Old World and managed their own anxieties about internal instability and decay.

Degeneration was linked, materially as well as etymologically, with gender. I will now turn briefly to the manner in which European women were associated with the consumption of foreign luxury goods in the early modern imagination. World-systems theory has obliquely influenced critics concerned with gender, sexuality, and the market. If the New World was feminized as virginal and for-the-taking in European discourse, the Old was saddled with a meretricious, corrupt, and sterile sexuality.[17] As it consolidated its holdings in America and its own eastern borders, Europe strengthened the "rich trades" it maintained with the separate economies based in Russia and the Indian Ocean, exchanging gold and silver for luxury goods like spices, perfumes, precious stones, silk, and other textiles.[18] And from the late sixteenth century on, the consumption of luxuries in Europe was increasingly attributed to women, first to court ladies and courtesans and then, in the private realm of the household, to bourgeois housewives.[19] As Laura Brown observes, "goods for female consumption and then women in general come to stand for the massive historical, economic, and social enterprise of English imperialism."[20] Complaints about the vanity and rapacity of all women signaled the production of consumer culture, rather than its repression, and covered up the role that men as well as women played in the spiral of demand that ultimately made much of Asia and its luxury goods peripheral or subordinate to the European economy by the eighteenth century.

European consumption and what would become the international division of labor were joined along gendered lines. During the thirteenth century, women were involved in many aspects of production and commerce in different locations, winding silk thread in China, preparing flax in Egypt, both spinning cloth and changing money in Bruges (Abu-Lughod, pp. 85, 92, 234, 330). This was hardly an Edenic and uniform past: different types of oppression and self-determination were experienced by different people in different economies and cultures. But by the early seventeenth century, a new hierarchy had come into being and begun to spread, one which sequestered European women in the household while making other women the tacit supports of colonizing and commercial ventures in a widening periphery and beyond. "Women's work" was devalued and misrecognized as nonproductive, inside and outside of the home.[21] Furthermore, as Maria Mies argues, "the colonial process, as it advanced, brought the women of the colonized people progressively down from a former high position of relative power and independence to that of 'beastly' and degraded 'nature.' This 'naturalization' of colonized women is the counterpart of the 'civilizing' of the European women."[22] Kim F. Hall contends that some European women themselves, such as the English writers Mary Wroth and Aemilia

Lanier, were partly complicit in this process, enhancing their status with white men by distinguishing themselves from the figure of the dark, corrupt, and foreign woman.[23]

The depiction even of noncolonized women in Asia and Africa as naturally degraded was part of the same complex in which the source of luxury was associated by male and female consumers alike with degeneration, and degeneration with the gendered, sexualized, and racially marked landscape of the "East." The modern world-system was accompanied by a modern racial system that was bound up with sexuality and gender. Wallerstein holds that race in modern times is the product and the expression of the international division of labor between core and periphery.[24] If we apply his terms to Europe's sphere of control and influence in the early modern period, we must recognize that the hypothetical core-periphery relation would have had implications for the way that inhabitants of external arenas were viewed, as well—the enslavement of Africans is the most pressing example. But the axial division does not adequately account for the many ways in which the stratified populations of different areas, particularly ones outside Europe, have been biologically and culturally typed since the fifteenth century. Michel Foucault offers a different narrative of Europe's transition from a society of aristocratic "blood" to one of bourgeois "sex" at the end of the early modern period: "Through the themes of health, progeny, race, the future of the species, the vitality of the social body, power spoke *of* sexuality and *to* sexuality."[25] This account, too, is insufficient on its own and should be set alongside Wallerstein's. Gender and race were linked across the expanse of the Old and New Worlds through the dialogue of power and sexuality.

Europe did not generate its obsession with degeneration solely out of its own social transitions; the fantasized cycle of rise and fall was laden with anxieties about its place within a vast prehistory and an unstable contemporaneity. Hemmed in by historical and economic circumstances in the Mediterranean and the Baltic during the late sixteenth and early seventeenth centuries, the English remained captivated by the Old World, even as they turned slowly toward America. A latecomer among the Europeans, early-seventeenth-century England may have possessed "an empire nowhere," as Jeffrey Knapp has aptly described it, but the very intangibility of its non-empire prepared the way for would-be global strategies in later times that overlapped and eventually superseded older imperial forms.[26]

Despite its limitations, world-systems theory provides the cultural critic with a historical perspective on current claims about "globalization." This term, which circulates in mass culture as well as academic circles, designates the worldwide integration of economic forces through the dissolution of trade barriers, the rapid electronic transfer of funds, and the interplay of uniformity and localism brought about by the expanded communications and entertainment media, including computers and the Internet. With the onset of the 1990s, it is often said, a fundamental break with capitalism's past has occurred. As Arjun Appadurai contends,

> It takes only the merest acquaintance with the facts of the modern world to note that it is now an interactive system in a sense that is strikingly new. Historians and sociologists, especially those concerned with . . . the world systems associated with capitalism . . . , have long been aware that the world has been a congeries of large-scale interactions for many centuries. Yet today's world involves interactions of a new order and intensity.[27]

There is no doubt that key changes in capital flows and mediatization are currently taking place in a manner that affects many parts of the world in similar ways. Yet, as Paul Smith explains, the claims made for globalization in the First World are excessive. Instead of the conquest of time and space and the global equalization of opportunity, we behold a world divided into the North and the unevenly developed South.[28] Amin adds that globalization as such is not only partial but fragile, beset by continued national disparities in the First World and a chaotic failure to address the problems of the Third, particularly Africa.[29]

Moreover, as Smith and others point out, the strictly economic developments grouped under the heading of globalization do not constitute a radical break with the past: "capitalism is in fact forging a mythological continuity with its deeper past, with the fundamental tenets of what we might call an Ur-capitalism, capitalism as it prepared itself for industrialization in the North after the centuries-long process of primitive accumulation described by both Adam Smith and Karl Marx."[30] There is a historical link, however mythologized and falsely glorified, between the cultural forms that accompanied early modern economic relations and the way globalization is represented in the present. In the context of Indian history, for example, Gayatri Chakravorty

Spivak remarks that the East India Company "prefigured the shifting relationship between state-formation and economic crisis-management within which we live today"; the company once again desires the role of the state, and so "in financial globalization the wheel has come full circle."[31] On the level of visual representation, as well, the inhabitants of the North are heirs to the fractured global image first crafted by the European cartographers of the sixteenth century.[32]

Even now, according to Smith, the project of globalization has not fulfilled its promise or threat—"But this project nonetheless has as a central stratagem: the annunciation of its own realization in the mythic or fundamentalist vision of the global."[33] The complex of issues around the visual representation of the globe suggests a second area of methodological and theoretical concern that informs the following chapters. Let me shift ground from claims about the systematic nature of global economic relations to what I shall generally refer to as *modeling*, the systematic imagining of the world, and of the old worlds of Africa, South Asia, and Russia, in European texts. A list of terms and concepts related to modeling and the model in this study includes the *museum*, the *monumental*, and the *performative*. The early modern words *antiquity*, *antiquities*, and *antiquarian* are also key, as are *description*, *travels*, and *prospect*. The ancient rhetorical commonplace of the world as a *theater* is foundational. Significantly, Ernst Robert Curtius' classic survey of the metaphor culminates with a hesitant evocation of Asia's turn on the world stage.[34] As Said has observed, "The Orient then seems to be, not an unlimited extension beyond the familiar European world, but rather a closed field, a theatrical stage affixed to Europe. . . . In the depths of this Oriental stage stands a prodigious cultural repertoire whose individual items evoke a fabulously rich world: the Sphinx, Cleopatra, Eden, Troy, Sodom and Gomorrah, Astarte, Isis and Osiris, Sheba, Babylon."[35] Recently, in *Culture and Imperialism*, Said has shown how Egypt in particular was modeled by the immense *Description de l'Egypte* commissioned by Napoleon and the pretend villages and stage-sets of European spectacle.[36]

The fifteenth-century proposal for a "conference" or staged debate between Christian controversialists and Islamic scholars stands as a provisional origin for the subsidiary theatricalization of the East in Said's account.[37] A variety of means for assembling evidence, opinion, and artifact preceded colonial and imperial formations without necessarily predicting or prescribing them. In a consideration of "Museums and Globalization," Martin Prösler remarks that the early modern prehistory of collecting "testifies to the manner in which the 'global perspective' is rooted within an institutional structure—not just geographically, but above all in the way that the sense of an ordered world is acquired."[38] It has become conventional, of course, to cast the Renaissance's *wunderkammern* or "cabinets of curiosity" as confused spectacles that generated a sense of the marvelous without objectifying the non-European fragments that they after all confounded with European oddities.[39] Yet the primitive accumulation of world culture by European power and knowledge was symbolically figured in the cabinets. The apparent disorder of most collections was really an earlier form of order we have learned to forget, one based on systems of resemblance and fully embodied in compartmentalized furniture, labeled shelves, and carefully situated chambers. This is an appropriate moment for me to acknowledge a general debt to the great scholar of *Asia in the Making of Europe*, Donald F. Lach. Long before current debates over wonder and objectification, Lach assessed the passion of the *virtuoso*:

> His cabinet of curiosities was not a haphazard collection of old objects but a systematic display which tried to transmit concretely the relations that were thought to obtain between the worlds of nature and art. . . . Virtuosity in the sixteenth century thus involved looking for a new certainty based on discovering the invisible ties which were assumed to link science with art, antiquity with modernity, and Europe with the rest of the world. The collection of curiosities was conceived of as such a synthesis in miniature, a tangible cosmography.[40]

What learned elites and princes competed to acquire and display was precisely an image of the newly perceived alignment of old and new worlds, a global image that European collectors were in a position to accumulate.

Johannes Fabian's book *Time and the Other* shows how the sense of an ordered world that Prösler describes was instituted through learned practices related to collecting and display. The modern discipline of anthropology derives from an older "political cosmology" in Europe that was imbued with the intricate spatial systems of rhetoric and the art of memory. "Conceiving outlandish images and moving in strange space, mostly imaginary," Fabian re-marks, "was a preoccupation of savants long before actual encounter with ex-otic people and travel to foreign parts, and for reasons to which actual encounter seems to have added very little."[41] Justin Stagl has established the link among early modern methodologies of information gathering for travel-ers, the rhetorical reforms of Peter Ramus, and the *ars memorativa*.[42] Fabian stresses the role of what he calls *visualism* in the later development of such forms of producing knowledge, the assumption that to visualize a culture is also to understand it. He considers "the exhibition of the exotic in illustrated travelogues, museums, fairs, and expositions. These early ethnological prac-tices established seldom articulated but firm convictions that the presenta-tions of knowledge through visual and spatial images, maps, diagrams, trees, and tables are particularly well suited to the description of primitive cultures" (pp. 106, 121). Visualism distances the observer from the observed in time as well as space, creating the category of the primitive and ascribing it to the ob-ject of observation. It contributes to a "denial of coevelness," the alignment of the observed along a different timescale than the European observer (p. 31).

It will be useful to explore some specific instances of the exhibitive ten-dency Fabian has uncovered in colonial modernity before returning to the early modern period. Timothy Mitchell makes the model Egyptian villages and miniature cities featured in European world exhibitions the starting point of his study of nineteenth-century Egypt. He shows in detail how the Egyptian state's educational and military regimes were formed by the ab-stract social planning of imperial powers such as France and England, schemes that the use of models and images already enacted in the seemingly innocent realms of leisure and entertainment. "Spectacles like the world ex-hibition and the Orientalist congresses set up the world as picture," Mitchell writes, inaugurating "the age of the world exhibition, or rather, the age of the world-as-exhibition. World exhibition here refers not to an exhi-bition of the world but to the world conceived and grasped as though it were an exhibition."[43] The last point is worth dwelling upon, for although Mitchell's qualification about nineteenth-century representation sets the modern period apart from the early modern, thinking it through jars our re-ceived ideas about representation in earlier centuries, as well.

The world-as-exhibition presents a paradox for colonial modernity in Mitchell's view. It is based upon a split between reality, that which is pictured or modeled, and representation, the model itself: "But 'reality,' it turns out, means that which can be represented, that which presents itself as an exhibit before an observer. The so-called real world 'outside' is something experienced and grasped only as a series of further representations, an extended exhibition" (p. 29). How, after all, does one know that something is real? To the extent that one can imagine representing it to someone else, or even to oneself. For the nineteenth-century traveler or official in particular, the reality of Egypt was always understood through prior models of various sorts—even to deny the accuracy of these earlier images or analyses was to perpetuate their presuppositions about accuracy, reference, and the visual essence of truth. It may seem as if the observer was under no such burden in early modern times, but as we shall see, an ancient textual and representational tradition partly determined judgments about the Old World even then, albeit in ways partially lost to us.

Bernard S. Cohn points to early modern beginnings where India is concerned, another Old World whose scholarly and theoretical treatment, like Egypt's, has mainly been confined to the nineteenth century. Cohn opens his essay on "The Command of Language and the Language of Command" with Sir Thomas Roe's embassy to the Mughal emperor in 1615. "Europeans of the seventeenth century," he remarks, "lived in a world of signs and correspondences, whereas Indians lived in a world of substances." Roe often interpreted Mughal social rituals as representations that expressed contempt for him as an ambassador. The concept of language itself formed a barrier: "Meaning for the English was something attributed to a word, a phrase, or an object, which could be determined and translated, at best with a synonym that had a direct referent to something in what the English thought of as a 'natural' world."[44] Attempts to describe the lived worlds of both Jacobean and Mughal people are necessarily uncertain, and distinctions between correspondence and substance risk the denial of coevalness that Fabian attributes to anthropology. Nevertheless, Cohn does show that something like Mitchell's relay between reality and representation, or nature and the word, was already present in English thought and practice in the early seventeenth century.

Cohn demonstrates, in effect, that the split between reality and representation gave birth to a range of "investigative modalities" in British India by the eighteenth century.[45] Chief among these means of gathering and presenting knowledge about India were the historiographic modality and the observational/travel modality—the relatively direct heirs, I would say, of the geographical-historical compendia and the travel narratives of the sixteenth and seventeenth centuries. The first modality underlay the others and was the most complex and extensive, because of the special place accorded history in British thought; it was concerned among other things with "the ideological construction of the nature of Indian civilizations" (pp. 6–7). The observational/travel modality similarly entailed "the creation of a repertoire of images and typifications that determined what was significant to the European eye." Travelers repeated generic accounts of ascetic holy men, widow burning, and historical sites, yet, despite their remarkable similarity over two centuries, "their representation changed through time. What is observed and reported is mediated by particular sociopolitical contexts as well as historically specific aesthetic principles," from the sublime to the realistic (p. 7). An early modern vantage point reveals the repertoire to be even older and more repetitive, although Cohn's caution about the changing currents of social and aesthetic mediation is still more necessary as we trace European travel's genealogy back in cultural time.

Another key modality in Cohn's list is the museological one, which, as we have seen, also bears genealogical traces from a recent past of accumulation and display. "For many Europeans India was a vast museum," he writes of the eighteenth century, "its countryside filled with ruins, its people representing past ages—biblical, classical, and feudal; it was a source of collectibles and curiosities to fill European museums, botanical gardens, zoos, and country houses" (p. 9). The later period Cohn describes adopted a retrospective view of India's relation to Europe that would have seemed strange to the early modern observer: in possessing India one laid claim to no more than one's own past, which was, after all, the narrative of a global or universal history crowned by European suzerainty. Nevertheless, early modern collecting had prepared this claim. Books as much as artifacts helped lay the groundwork; in fact, books were artifacts, hastily published, traded, and acquired for the libraries of antiquarians whose uneasy kinship with cabinets of curiosity has been remarked.[46] What Cohn says of the later museological impulse was partly true of the early bibliographical one, and of the considerable circulation in curiosities that Lach has evoked in profuse detail: "The objects . . . were found, discovered, collected, and classified as part of a larger European project to decipher *the* history of India" (p. 77; Cohn's emphasis). Or, as Lach writes of the sixteenth century, "The word 'wonder' no longer meant 'mystery' or 'miracle.' . . . Rather it had come to mean that which evoked astonishment, stimulated reflection, and provided visual aids to the investigation of the physical world."[47]

Is it anachronistic to ascribe motives of domination to the European project of decipherment and investigation of the physical world outside Europe? One difference between the study of the Old, as opposed to the New World, is the absence of large-scale European colonies, let alone successful European empires, in Africa and Asia. Yet it would be wrong to say there were no colonies in Asia, for the Portuguese and Dutch did establish territorial dominion over key trading outposts and considerable economic control over the routes they commanded. The development of land empires in the Americas also affected European interaction with the Old World, increasing Europe's economic confidence and, on a practical level, abetting its ability to navigate seas all over the world, including the Indian Ocean. Europe, of course, was not a monolith, and intra-European rivalry reduced the Europeans' ability to control the oceans or deploy, say, the Iberian peninsula's New World wealth toward the conquest of militarily advanced and politically sophisticated eastern powers. Rivalry in the Indian Ocean also drove naval encroachments and militarization, however, as K. N. Chaudhuri argues, spurring what he terms *armed trading* throughout the area.[48]

We need more categories like "armed trading" that defy the antinomies of current debate. The question of anachronism has been posed through artificially sharp distinctions, such as "encounter or exploitation," "exploration or empire," where the first term supposedly excludes any participation in the second. Serious consideration of the European presence in Africa and South Asia consequently begins only with the late eighteenth century in much current scholarship (the situation is somewhat better with Russia). To analyze antiquarian and travel discourses before the eighteenth century is, in most cases, not to engage in colonial studies—although the theoretical problems posed by *post*-colonial studies often prove surprisingly pertinent. It is vital to avoid the notion of "pre-colonial" studies, however, for the sixteenth and seventeenth centuries did not contain the germs of the inevitable colonization of the rest of the Old World by Europe; Russia and the Ottomans were never colonized in the conventional sense at all. A proper consideration of Europe amidst the Old World during the early modern period requires a concept like *para-colonial* studies, where the Greek prefix means "alongside of" without precluding either "before" or "beyond," and can suggest both "closely related to" and "aside from," as well. An understanding of the para-colonial, conversely, might help us to develop nontotalizing or nonessentialist understandings of colonial power in the New World and in the world of today.

There is a pressing sense, as Walter Benjamin asserted, in which one cannot responsibly avoid reading the past through the present, "For every image of the past that is not recognized by the present as one of its own concerns threatens to disappear irretrievably."[49] By this, Benjamin precisely did not mean that the historian necessarily fabricates or constructs a past that never existed. Yet the past is hardly an even, or easily accessible, ground for historiographers and their explorations, in Benjamin's opinion. Neither truth of correspondence nor the appropriation of past constructions of "truth" is at stake: we still lack a concept or term for the process by which the past is selectively recognized and reconstructed through the concerns of the present. One of Benjamin's best-known aphorisms, found in the "Theses on the Philosophy of History" (1940), suggests that a kind of everyday violence has governed the preservation of the past. Let me quote it through the passage in which it first appeared in print, a few years before the "Theses." "Would it not be true that the study of individual disciplines, once the illusion (*Schein*) of unity has been removed, flows together into the study of cultural history as the inventory which humanity has preserved to the present day?" Benjamin resists posing the question in this manner:

> whatever the historical materialist would survey in art or science has a lineage which cannot be contemplated without dread. The products of art and science owe their existence not merely to the effort of the great geniuses that created them, but also to the unnamed drudgery of their contemporaries. There is no document of culture which is not at the same time a document of barbarism. No cultural history has yet done justice to this fundamental state of affairs, and it can hardly hope to do so.

These words are from the essay "Eduard Fuchs: Collector and Historian" (1937).[50] It was when he wrote about collecting that Benjamin may first have contemplated the civilized barbarism that lies behind the "inventory" of culture.

Early modern collecting, as much a symbolic or cultural act of accumulation as an economic one, continued to inform the compulsive acquisitiveness of the bourgeois nineteenth century in Europe. In a fragment of his Arcades project, Benjamin mentions "the pathological aspect of the notion of 'Culture'" embodied in the detailed account of the antiques store found in Balzac's *La Peau de chagrin*.[51] The prefix *para-* can also mean abnormal or pathological, although Benjamin's awareness of the difficulties of recognizing the past cautions us against lapsing back into an organic or normalizing model in reconceiving the compulsive pathology on display in the wonder-cabinet.

The employment of the idea of modeling itself, no less than terms like *pathological*, requires self-critical care. Martin Bernal, we shall see in Chapter 1, finds differing models of global antiquity in European thought in a useful, if occasionally schematic, manner, as V. Y. Mudimbe has remarked.[52] A system is a type of model, and the world-systems theory I began by outlining is yet another way of modeling the globe over space and time. The critique of models by thinkers such as Cohn and Said that I have just examined forms a useful corrective to the systematic claims of Wallerstein and Braudel. The "world economy," Said writes, "more accurately was the loose agglomeration of *European* financiers, merchant bankers, loan corporations, and commercial adventurers."[53] I think that we can combine some aspects of world-systems theory with the critique of global models if we keep in mind that systems are constituted by such loose confederacies and the models they impose upon the world. Mitchell concludes that the exhibition's division of the world in two—real and image, West and East—was "an essential part of the larger process of its incorporation into the European world economy" (p. 166). Perhaps the term *system* should be reserved for ramifications of modeling that escape the immediate intentions of elites. In what follows, I assume that the analysis of models and systems in cultural theory can be used to expose the interests they inevitably perpetuate and partly serve.

My choice of Old Worlds has been necessarily selective, partly because there are particular gaps in current scholarship and cultural history that I wish to address. Though the smallest part of the three-part world, Europe generated enough material about its own antiquity and modernity to deserve a book in itself. In a sense it is the forest that has been rendered invisible by the continual growth of studies on every aspect of Renaissance culture and early modern society within its elastic borders. The Jews and the Turks both represent key worlds of their own with immensely important ties to Europe—in different senses it should be said "the rest of Europe"—during the period. The relation of both to the English context has been extensively treated in a range of recent articles and books, by David S. Katz, Avraham Oz, and James Shapiro on the Jews, and Nabil Matar and Daniel J. Vitkus on the Turks and the Ottoman Empire.[54] My approach would add little to on-going work on Jews and Turks, in part because I adhere to the method of early modern geographical compilations and investigate the European survey of discrete regions rather than peoples, cultures, religions, or civilizations. I am particularly interested in the intersection of two itineraries: an itinerary drawn from Graeco-Roman antiquity, which largely means Herodotus, and the routes of Old World English trade described by Braudel and figured in the travel accounts of the sixteenth through seventeenth centuries. The superposition of these itineraries extends the traditional sweep of the Fertile Crescent, from Egypt through Southwest Asia and India; Russia, the inheritor of Herodotus' Scythia, serves as counterpoint or frame. Sub-Saharan Africa and Persia would require separate studies: my treatment of Ethiopia gestures, however inadequately, toward a wider context for the Egyptian chapter, and references to Persia punctuate my treatments of ancient Mesopotamia, Egypt, and even early modern Russia. The vast subjects of China, Japan, and the Moluccas, it goes without saying, also demand separate treatment, and they effectively fall outside the overlap of early modern trade with the geo-historical itinerary of Mediterranean antiquity.

Egypt and Ethiopia, Southwest Asia, Russia, and India form the backbone of this book. Through four chapters, I address travel accounts, geographical works, and literary texts that rewrite European traditions about a plural antiquity from the English perspective, with consequences for developing notions of racial and sexual difference.

My first chapter deals with the changing view of Egypt and its antiquity in England from the late sixteenth to early seventeenth centuries. Egyptian learning was held in great respect by humanist scholars; a large part of this chapter consists in a preliminary account of geographical and travel writings from late antiquity to the Renaissance that offer a mixed view of Egypt and its history. Ethiopia was also venerated as the home of pictographic writing, asceticism, and godly living, although Heliodorus' *Ethiopica*, translated by Thomas Underdowne in 1587, provides a complicated assessment of the Ethiopian legacy. Shakespeare's *Antony and Cleopatra* coincided with an important moment in the shift from veneration of these areas to their association with decadence in the first decade of the seventeenth century. My reading of Shakespeare's play stresses how it both confirms and challenges the way Egypt was coming to be regarded during the period. Racial and sexual images are mediated by the onset of a museological way of perceiving Egypt in differing ways.

Travelers to the Levant during the seventeenth century visited the sites of the Mesopotamian and Assyrian empires as well as Egypt, and geographical accounts such as John Speed's *Prospect of the Most Famous Parts of the World* (1631) and Peter Heylyn's *Cosmographie* (1657) devoted many pages to the antiquities and current conditions of Southwest Asia. Heylyn served Milton as a major source for his description of the area's ancient civilizations and their fall in Books XI and XII of *Paradise Lost*. Chapter 2 analyzes several descriptions of Southwest Asia and the monuments that dotted its landscape, ruins that came to symbolize the inevitable cycle of grandeur and decay that Europeans associated with these biblical lands. I conclude with the controversy over the location of Paradise—Milton indirectly comments on this scholarly dispute and perhaps on James I's participation in it when he depicts the destruction of Eden during the Flood, "To teach thee that God attributes to place / No sanctity."[55] The vanity of human place and power is identified with the theater of Asia and its cycle of empires, a theater of war that parodies the destruction of Paradise and leaves only ruins and relics in its wake.

Milton takes us from Southwest to Northern Asia in Chapter 3, which begins with a consideration of his *Brief History of Muscovia*. Milton's text, heavily dependent on earlier sources, comes at the end of a tradition of English descriptions of Russia that dates from Elizabethan times. I will survey this material from the sixteenth to the seventeenth centuries, recapitulating the time span of the previous two chapters. The early modern view of Russia differs from that of Egypt and Mesopotamia; in a sense, Russia emerges as the opposite of these two ancient civilizations, an anti-civilization whose roots lie in the barbarous Scythia that Herodotus implicitly juxtaposed with Egypt in the fourth book of his *Histories*. To an Elizabethan such as Philip Sidney, Russia also signified slavery. Before the sixteenth century, the Mediterranean world drew its slaves largely from southeastern Europe and Russia—"slave" and "Slav" were once interchangeable names in the European vocabulary. With the exploitation of the Americas, various African peoples replaced Eastern Europeans and Russians in a greatly expanded slave system in which England came to play an important part. By reading Shakespeare's *Love's Labour's Lost* and John Fletcher's *The Loyal Subject* along with a selection of travel accounts, I chart how this change affected the representation of racial difference on the one hand, and of gender and sexuality on the other. The chapter concludes by returning to Milton's *Muscovia* and the later seventeenth-century outcome of the changing relationship between civilization and race.

England's representation of India against the backdrop of civilization and race is the subject of the fourth chapter. In the vast literature on India from classical to early modern times, admiration for ancient accomplishments in philosophy gave way to horror and consternation at the monstrous and barbaric by Milton's time. The earliest sources mention the asceticism of Indian "gymnosophists" and the conquests of the subcontinent by Dionysus and Herakles in tracing connections between Graeco-Roman and Indian civilizations. By the European Middle Ages, a fascination with the practice of *sati*, the burning of Hindu wives in their husbands' funeral pyres, takes hold of European narratives of travel to India: alluded to by Propertius and others as a sign of wifely constancy, *sati* was increasingly condemned in early modern accounts, some of which cite Mughal opposition to the practice as a model for European intervention and imperial control. The conflict between Islam and Hindu practice lies behind Dryden's confusion of the two cultures in *Aureng-Zebe*, a heroic play that freely adapts historical events and cultural images from the traveler François Bernier's *History of the Late Revolution of the Great Mogal*. The many references to *sati* in the play culminate in the madness of its woman villain Nourmahal, who imagines herself within the flames as she dies of poison in the last scene. Bernier's own descriptions of wife burning cast it repeatedly as a "tragedy," and Dryden's theatrical evocation of *sati* makes it the mark of a heroic, barbaric, but inevitably self-consuming world.

Often linked together in geographical and literary texts as well as the world system during the period, Egypt, Asia, and India constituted much of the Old World for Europeans during the sixteenth and seventeenth centuries. My book ends with the beginnings of the Enlightenment's attempt to distinguish between civilization and barbarism, but it will also suggest that the mixture of veneration and condemnation in the earlier tradition continued to inform later views of these non-European cultures, in part through the persistent influence of dramatic and poetic texts that complicate any simple judgment about a collective past.

ONE

Antiquity and Degeneration

The Representation of Egypt and Shakespeare's Antony and Cleopatra

In the first volume of *Black Athena*, Martin Bernal persuasively demonstrates that before the eighteenth century Egyptian learning and its antiquity were venerated by Europeans.[1] What he calls the "Ancient Model" of Egyptian colonization in Greece remained untouched by the "Aryan Model" of subsequent centuries; the racism of academic discourse had yet to eclipse the Hermetic Renaissance. His brief chapters confirm that the period understood classical antiquity to be broader than the Graeco-Roman paradigm that the nineteenth-century disciplines of classics and national literary history have left us with. Yet in his brilliant presentation of the evidence for the sixteenth century's veneration of Egyptian learning, Bernal overlooks a narrative of African degeneration that was also present in the European discourse on Egypt from early times, a counterdiscourse of disrespect that would become the mainstream view as the modern racial system developed in the wake of the slave trade during the seventeenth century. Bernal is aware of the sexual connotations in the later association of Egypt and the East with decadence and degeneration, but he does not devote particular attention to them, or to their roots in earlier formulations of Egyptian decadence such as we find, for instance, in parts of Shakespeare's *Antony and Cleopatra*.[2]

Notions of racial difference may not have been fully developed in early-seventeenth-century England, but Shakespeare's play is linked to their modern formation through its staging of what John F. Danby called "the vast containing opposites of Rome and Egypt, the World and the Flesh."[3] Although Danby's own reading of these categories is at times subtle and, as he claims, "dialectical," their broad sweep has helped perpetuate a stereotypical association of European Rome with reason and African Egypt with passion, femininity, and transgressive sexuality in much subsequent criticism. The role played by the "Flesh" in Danby's influential schema is part of this tendency. As Ania Loomba has shown, sexuality and sexual difference are closely related to the formation of race and racial difference in *Antony and Cleopatra*. The figure of Cleopatra blends sexual and racial differences in a paradoxical way: "She is the supreme actress, artifice itself, and simultaneously primitive and uncultivated."[4] Loomba's reading of Cleopatra anticipates Judith Butler's theory of performativity in *Gender Trouble*. Sexual difference is a kind of performance that dissimulates the natural, rather than a symmetrical structure based on the uncultivated or uncultured body; furthermore, the parodic repetition of gender categories can undermine rather than reconfirm them. Butler has amplified her notion of performance, casting the specifically theatrical as only one instance of a much wider complex of cultural and linguistic repetitions.[5]

Two questions come to mind. If racial categories, in Danby's words, function as "containing opposites," are sexuality and race "contained" in parallel ways in a text like *Antony and Cleopatra*? And if the representation of sexuality and gender resists containment through repetition and performance to some degree, are racial representations performatively subversive in the same way? Shakespeare's play participated in the unstable early modern discourse about Egyptian antiquity, in part by opening up the sexuality of the tradition. This chapter is a cultural study of the play in its shifting discursive setting, rather than a source study of its antecedents. Ultimately, I want to trace the relation between racial and sexual constructions during the period by reading Shakespeare's text in relation to a number of historical, geographical, and travel writings that became available roughly within a century of its publication.

The second book of Herodotus' *Histories* (ca. 450 B.C.) is the starting point for any discussion of the discourse of Egypt in European culture. The first two books appeared in a vigorous English translation in 1584. In the opening pages of Book 2 sixteenth-century readers learned of the claims made by the priests at Memphis, Thebes, and Heliopolis: "the Aegyptians first inuented and used the surnames of the twelue gods: which the Grecians borrowed and drew from them. The self same were the first founders of Aulters, Images, and Temples to the gods: by whom also chiefly were carued the pictures of beasts and other creatures in stone, which thing for the most part they proue and confirme by lawfull testimonies and good authority."[6] Herodotus does not always believe his Egyptian informants, but he certainly takes them more seriously than Greek ideas about the region. The Ionians, for instance, are wrong to maintain that "Egypt" is identical with the Nile delta, the product of alluvial deposits more recent than the evident antiquity of the people it currently sustains. "I my selfe am fully perswaded," Herodotus writes, "that the Aegyptians tooke not their beginning together with the place of Delta, but were alwayes since the first beginning and orig-inall of mankinde" (p. 73 recto). Even if the Ionians and other Greeks are right about the delta, they have misreckoned, "making but thrce partes of the whole earth, Europe, Asia, and Africa: whereas of necessity Delta in Aegypt should be accounted for the fourth, sithens by their owne bookes it is neyther ioyned with Asia, nor yet with Africa" (p. 73 verso). The Nile was the traditional dividing line between Asia and Africa (or Libya) in the three-part world, but Herodotus resists splitting Egypt between the two conti-nents. The passage is difficult, but in the end he does seem to hold that Egypt, the land on either side of the Nile below the delta as well as the delta itself, should be considered a separate and ancient part of the world, with Asia on one side and Africa on the other.[7]

Egypt is older than its delta; otherwise there would have been a time when Egypt did not exist, before the action of the river created the delta. Herodotus reasons, "wherefore if they had no country at all, what caused them so curiously to labour in the searching out and blazing of their aun-cient[r]y, supposing themselues to be the chiefe of all people, the knowledge and intelligence whereof, was not worth the two yeares triall and experi-ment which they wroughte in the children" (p. 73 recto). The reference is to the well-known story of the Egyptian King Psammetichus' attempt to discover if his people really were the oldest upon the earth, which Herodotus tells at the very beginning of his Egyptian book. The king commanded that two children be brought up in total isolation by a shepherd, who was never to speak to them. One day, when the children were about two years old, the shepherd entered the cottage to find "both the litle brats sprawling at his feete, and stretching forth their hands, cryed thus: Beccos, Beccos." Psammetichus, after making "curious search," discovered that *beccos* was the word for "bread" in Phrygia, a country in northern Anatolia beyond the Greek colony of Ionia. Henceforth, the Egyptians held the Phrygians to be a people even older than themselves (pp. 69 verso–70 recto).

Herodotus' use of the anecdote to introduce Egypt is puzzling, because he immediately goes on to the list of Egyptian "firsts," and he asserts the virtual priority of the Egyptians himself several times throughout the course of the book. In a sense the story bolsters the case for Egyptian wisdom, exchanging antiquity for a new basis of knowledge in "experiment." It becomes the mark of a truly civilized people to discover and acknowledge that other civilizations came before them, a lesson to the Ionians of Anatolia and a confirmation of the general fifth-century Greek belief that the Egyptians were in turn older than themselves. Psammetichus' method mirrors Herodotus' own as a historian or, etymologically, a "researcher": just as the king made curious search among known languages, so Herodotus tells us that he searched out different groups of priests all along the Nile to get his information as well as alternate versions of the tale. "Howbeit many fond fables are receited by the Grecian writers," he typically adds—for instance, that Psammetichus had the children tended by women whose tongues were cut off to ensure silence (p. 70 recto). There is a hint of skepticism in Herodotus' story of the experimental method and the inquiries to which it leads, despite his own implication in it. Herodotus openly rejects the outcome of another one of Psammetichus' experiments, an effort to prove the bottomlesss depths of the supposed springs of the Nile with a plumb line (p. 76 recto). Psammetichus, we later learn, was a relatively recent ruler, and the first king of Egypt in memory to admit a Greek community and establish ties with Greece (p. 113 recto). His mention at the start of the book prepares the reader for the philhellene King Amasis and the Persian invasion of Egypt at its end, but it may also suggest that "new" ways of thought have corrupted Egyptian learning.

In turning from Psammetichus to the priests of Egypt, Herodotus echoes what they told him about the Egyptian discovery of the pantheon, returning to this theme repeatedly. "True it is," he states later, "that the names by which the gods are usually called, are borrowed and drawne from the Egyptians," as his travels among foreign peoples have attested. Poseidon (Neptune), Hera (Juno), and a few other gods are the exceptions (p. 83 verso).[8] The Pelasgians, or original inhabitants of the Greek mainland, used to call the gods simply *theoi* or "disposers," and learned to differentiate them by name from the Egyptians; the name of Dionysus or Bacchus was introduced long afterward, evidence of sustained contact with the land of the Nile (pp. 84 recto–verso). Dionysus, central to the religious life of Herodotus' times, was brought to Greece by the shadowy culture-hero Melampus:

> Most euident it is that the picture of Phallum worne of the Greacians in the feast of Bacchus, was found out and deuised by him, whose discipline in this point the Greacians obserue at this day. This Melampus was a man of rare wisdom, well seene in the art of diuination and soothsaying, the author and first founder to the Graecians as well of other things which he had learned in Aegypt, as also of such statutes and obseruances as belong to the feast of Dionysius [*sic*], only a few things altered which he thought to amend. For why, to thinke that the Graecians and Aegyptians fell into the same forme of diuine worship by hap hazard or plaine chaunce, it might seeme a uery hard and unreasonable gesse, sithence it is manifest that the Greekes both use the selfsame custome, and more then that, they kept it of olde. (p. 83 verso)

In Egypt itself, Dionysus is the same as Osiris, and Demeter (Ceres) is Isis; different localities worship different minor deities, but all Egyptians are devoted to this sacred pair (pp. 81 recto, 86 recto).

"In the seruice and worship of the gods," in fact, "they are more religious and deuout then any nation under heauen" (p. 79 recto). This statement introduces a description of religious practices in the midst of a long list of Egyptian customs. Herodotus prefaces the list by praising Egypt because it has more wonders and its people have done more memorable things than any other nation. The inventory itself, however, stresses the differences between the Egyptians and other peoples, especially the Greeks:

In this countrey the women followe the trade of merchandise in buying and
selling: also uictualing and all kinde of sale and chapmandry, whereas con-
trarywyse the men remayne at home, and play the good huswiues in spinning and weauing and such like duties. In like manner, the men carry their
burthens on their heads, the women on their shoulders. Women make
water standing, and men crouching downe and cowring to the ground.
They discharge and unburthen theyr bellies of that which nature voydeth
at home, and eate their meate openly in the streetes. (pp. 78 recto–verso)

Herodotus does not return to the evident importance of women in Egyptian
society (he was told of only one woman ruler, the vengeful Nitocris, p. 95
recto), but his description looks forward to the reputation of Cleopatra and
her court, and it heavily influenced the early modern image of Egypt as well.

The Egyptians consistently transpose Greek gender roles, from the disposition of the body to economic activity. Yet the book strives to bring
Egypt closer to Greece as it progresses. Herodotus' technique consists of
gradually undoing these radical reversals through describing the uncanny
familiarity of Egyptian religious custom: "Let it stand also for an euident
and undoubted uerity, that assemblies at festiuals, pompes and pageants in
diuine honour, talke and communication with the gods by a mediator or in-
terpretour, were inuented in Ægypt, and consequently used in Greece.
Which I thinke the rather, for that the one is old and of long continuance,
the other freshe and lately put in practice" (p. 85 verso). In a later section,
Herodotus marvels that the Egyptians worship the dying-god figure Linus
in song just as the Greeks and other Mediterranean nations do. He adds that
they also resemble the Lacedaemonians or Spartans at least in having their
young men step aside for the elders in public places, although the Egyptians
bow rather than greet one another by name in the street. Their linen clothing, however, conforms to the garments prescribed by the Bacchic or
Pythagorean cult known in Greece (p. 90 verso). The Egyptians also invented astrology and perfected the art of divination (p. 91 recto).

Herodotus goes on to remark that the people of Egypt refuse to accept
foreign customs, with one exception: the city of Chemmis has instituted
Greek games in honor of Perseus, who visited Egypt with the Gorgon's head
on the way back from Libya, and who was descended from two earlier heroes

born in Chemmis—Danaus and Lynceus ("Lynaeus" in the 1584 version: p. 92 verso). Danaus, the twin of Aegyptus, is linked to Egypt in other sources. He and his brother were descendants of Io, who fled to Egypt after her impregnation by Zeus. Danaus' fifty daughters married and murdered all but one of Aegyptus' fifty sons. Danaus came to Thebes in Argos along with his daughters as a suppliant or perhaps a conqueror, and later assumed the rulership of that Greek city. Lynceus, the remaining son of Aegyptus, eventually succeeded him as king of Thebes.[9] Toward the end of Book 2, Herodotus ties the tradition of an Egyptian presence in the Argolid to the belief that central Greek rituals were derived from Egypt. Athena has a temple at Sais in Egypt next to which nocturnal ceremonies are practiced. This reminds Herodotus of the worship of Ceres or Demeter in the Thesmophoria:

> This is certayne, that the Daughters of Daneus [*sic*] were the firste that brought this custome oute of Aegypte, and made it knowne to the women of Pelasgos [the Pelasgians or earlier inhabitants of Greece]. But afterwardes mislyked of the Dores [the Dorians], it was utterly abolyshed and lefte off in all the Countrey of Peloponnesus, sauinge of certayne Arcadians, whom the people of Peloponnesis lycensed to contynewe in the Countrey, by whome the same order was retayned. (p. 116 verso)

Demeter, it will be recalled, is the Greek version of Isis.

Herodotus refers to the shared cultural and religious past of Greece and Egypt through the Danaus tradition a number of times. He thinks that the western delta city of Archandropolis ("Archandry" in 1584) was named after Archander, a Greek son-in-law of Danaus (p. 94 verso). Book 2 comes to a close with King Amasis' marriage to a Greek wife and his gifts to several Greek communities in North Africa and Anatolia: "But to the city of Lyndus [in Rhodes], why he should shewe hymselfe so franke and liberall, no other reason serued, sauing that the fame wente that the great temple of Minerua in Lindus was builded by the daughters of Danaus after they were knowne, and had escaped the daungers intended against them by the sonnes of Aegyptus" (p. 119 verso). *The Histories* is a carefully structured work of foreshadowings, echoes, and parallels. In setting up the invasion of Greek lands by Persia under Darius and Xerxes, Herodotus gives us the earlier invasion of Amasis' Egypt by the mad Cambyses. The march on

Egypt was essentially the beginning of a Persian campaign against a common Egypto-Greek culture.

Diodorus Siculus, who flourished around 49 B.C., adopted a more skeptical stance than Herodotus, but he drew on many lost sources to augment his remote predecessor's account of the Egyptians' evidence for their cultural priority. The opening books of his *Library of History* were readily available to educated readers during the Renaissance, who were evidently very interested in what it added to the Herodotean tradition.[10] Diodorus begins his history with "the barbarians" in Book I, not because he believes them to be older than the Greeks, as some do, but because he wishes to distinguish their acts from the Greeks' accomplishments. Nevertheless, he frequently notes Egypt's reputation for priority, and turns to its written records in charting Egyptian claims. I quote from the English translation of 1653: "The *Egyptians* affirm, that they were the first inventers of Astrology, Geometry, and many other Sciences; and that the best Laws and ordinances were instituted by them. . . . Howbeit (omitting such things as *Herodotus*, and others, writing the History of the *Egyptians*, have fabulously devised for their pleasure) we will follow the books of the Priests of *Egypt* which we have diligently sought out and perused."[11] Diodorus acknowledges plausible traditions about Egyptian colonizations in Argos and Colchis, but draws the line at an Egyptian origin for Athens: "They say moreoever, that the *Athenians* are they alone of all the *Greeks* that swear by *Isis*, and that do represent the form and manners of the *Egyptians*, affirming many other such like things, out of ambition, rather than the truth" (p. 16). It is but a step from accusations of Egyptian pride to laments over Egyptian degeneration from whatever past glories the country of the Nile possessed. Plutarch would take this step later down the road in the second century A.D. in "Of the Malice of Herodotus," despite his apparent celebration of Egyptian religion and its ties to Greece in another *Moralia* essay, "Of Isis and Osiris." Despite skepticism or outright contradiction, the tradition of Egyptian learning and precedence remained strong. Diodorus' marked distrust of Herodotus and the Egyptians does not prevent him from preserving Egyptian knowledge about the past that was very much alive in late antiquity and would otherwise have disappeared.

Diodorus devotes much space to Isis and Osiris, and describes the Egyptian invention of five other gods based on five elements. Homer borrowed his knowledge of various gods' transformations into human form from the Egyptians (pp. 4–5). Osiris is, of course, equated with Dionysus, and stories about Bacchus' conquest of Asia reflect the military campaign of a historical Osiris, who was deified after his victories. The later conquests of Sesostris sketched by Diodorus echo this tradition as well as Alexander's world empire (pp. 7–9, 38). Of Isis we learn that she was a great ruler who assumed control of Egypt after Osiris' death; her example led to reverence for all women, "And there to this day among the common sort the wife is master over the husband, the men confessing when they assign a dowry to their wives, that they are bound to obey their pleasure" (p. 14). The Greeks call Isis "law-giver," and Egyptian laws predate and excel Greek myth: "Now the *Greekes*, who in their devised fables, and incredible relations of their Poets, have set forth the rewards of the good, and the paines of the wicked, could not induce men to vertue by their writings, but contrarily have been derided and contemned by them for it; whereas it is otherwise with the *Egyptians*, who visibly, and not fabulously, distribute punishment to the bad, and praise to the just" (pp. 6, 64).

Many Greeks traveled to Egypt to learn from its ways, including Orpheus, Homer, Solon, Plato, and Pythagoras. "Certainly all these Philosophers, learned in *Egypt*," Diodorus writes, "whatsoever made them worthy of admiration amongst the *Greekes*, for *Orpheus* (as the *Egyptians* say) brought from thence divers Hymns of the Gods, the Celebration of the Orgies of *Baccus*, and the fiction of Hell" (pp. 65–66). He stresses the latter connection, demonstrating at length that the Homeric notion of the underworld is derived entirely from Egyptian beliefs about life and death. Diodorus traces the use of funerary statues to the Egyptians, and records the claim that the Greeks borrowed their statuary techniques in general from the people of the Nile (pp. 66, 68).

Diodorus seems finally to bow before the pressure of tradition in allowing Egypt some precedence over Greece. In his third book, however, he trumps the Egyptian claims with those of a more southerly group of peoples, the Ethiopians.[12] The ancient material on Ethiopia merits a study in its own right; here it is worthwhile to pause and consider its relation to the discourse of Egypt in Diodorus and the *Ethiopica* of Heliodorus, a Greek romance from the third century A. D. that popularized the Diodoran image of both places in the new millennium.

According to Diodorus, the Ethiopians claim that they were created before anyone else in the world:

> They of *Ethiopia* affirme further, that the *Egiptians* are descended of them, from the time that *Osiris* planted a Colonie of them in *Egypt*, which before was not firme Land, nor habitable, but was at the beginning covered with the Sea, and that afterwards with the slime and mud, which the inundation of *Nilus* brought along out of *Ethiopia*. . . . They say moreover that many Lawes of *Ethiopia* were transported into *Egypt*. . . . Besides, the use of great Statues, and the formes of Letters, were taken from them; for although the *Egyptians* use proper and particular Letters, which the common people study and learne, yet have they for all that, such as they call sacred Letters, knowne onely to their Priests, which have been privately taught them by their Parents; but in Ethiopia all the Men use the same Figures and Characters of sacred Letters. (pp. 113, 114)

Here the art of statuary is traced to Ethiopia, and with it the culturally charged art of writing. A marginal note to the 1653 translation underlines the claim that "Hieroglifique Letters" originated not in Egypt but in its neighboring land. The corresponding passage reads,

> The *Ethiopian* letters are made to the resemblance of divers Creatures, of the members of Men, and of sundry instruments and tooles of Artificers; neither do they express their words by the composition of Letters and Sillables, but by the formes of Images, the signification whereof through use hath remained in the memory of Men; for they write downe a Kite, a Crocodile, a Serpent, the Eye of a man, an Hand, a Face, and other such like things. . . . In like manner the figure of other parts of the body, and of certaine instruments, doe shew some other thing amongst the *Ethiopians*, who retayning the same, do presently, and at first sight understand what those Figures meane. (p. 115)

Unlike Egypt, where pictographic writing is part of religious mystery, in Ethiopia meaning is somehow open and immediately available to all through the forms of images.

Nevertheless, Ethiopia is a priestly culture like Egypt, and its religious ways were imitated by other peoples: "The *Ethiopians* maintaine also, that the worship of the Gods was first of all found out and observed by them; as also the Sacrifices, Pompes, Solemnities, and all other things, whereby honour is done unto them by Men; so that it is apparent by the common fame of their Piety and Religion spread over all the World" (p. 113). The rhythm of originary avowal in this statement parallels that in numerous passages on Egyptian priority in the wider tradition. But Diodorus also invokes the authority of Homer in the Ethiopians' favor, citing *Iliad* 1:423, where Zeus feasts with the "blameless Aithiopians."[13] At the start of the *Odyssey*, Poseidon is likewise visiting with them, "most distant of men, who live divided/some at the setting of Hyperion, some at his rising."[14] The idea of the Ethiopians as a nation divided in half runs throughout European representations of them.

The split image is duly present in Diodorus. "There are other *Ethiopians*," he notes,

> and those very populous, whereof some live on either side of *Nilus*, and in
> the Islands thereof; others in the *Mediterranean* Regions, lying toward
> *Arabia*: The most part of which, especially they that dwell upon the river,
> are black of colour, all alike in Face, have curled Haire, a dreadfull looke,
> leade a savage Life, are strong of body, with long Nayles like to wild Beasts;
> the pronunciation of their speech is shrill, and in their manner of Life and
> feeding they have nothing in common with us, but are altogether differing
> from other men. (p. 116)

In later antiquarian and travel writing, "Ethiopia" remains an unstable geographical signifier, floating among eastern Africa (indeed, all of sub-Saharan Africa in some sources), through Arabia, to the Indian subcontinent.[15] This placelessness, although an attribute of all utopias, is more than a matter of location, and less than ideal, as the passage just quoted shows. Not only are the "other" Ethiopians split by the Nile; they are ontologically different from "us." There is no mention of shared pictographic writing or influential religious beliefs, only shrill speech and total alterity. They are black and have curled hair. Later, Diodorus names the cave-dwelling Troglodites as Ethiopians as well (p. 131).

The germs of a modern system of ocular racial difference only quicken when claims for unitary cultural origins are rendered uncertain or untenable in Diodorus' text. Something similar happened in Herodotus. The city of Elephantine divides the northern segment of the Nile from the southern; southward there are nomadic groups of Ethiopians, then their great city of Meroe, which betokens settlement and civilization. A partial explanation for this slight inconsistency is provided by the "Asmach," descendants of an Egyptian garrison that went over to the Ethiopian king, and who live as far south of Meroe as Meroe is south of Elephantine. Because of their influence, "the people of Aethiopia were brought from a rude and barbarous kind of demeanour, to farre more civill and manlike behaviour, being instructed and taught in the manners and customes of the Aegyptians."[16] Herodotus typically stresses Egypt's priority in his second book. Yet he also describes the piety of the Ethiopian King Sabbacus, who conquered Egypt but limited his reign to fifty years (pp. 107 verso–108 verso). Later, the Ethiopian king is made to appear considerably more civilized than the Persian invader Cambyses, although Herodotus also describes the Troglodites, who live in holes.[17] In Herodotus, in fact, the Ethiopians already effect a greater split, that between Egypt and Ethiopia itself across the lower and upper Nile. In Diodorus it becomes clear that Ethiopia represents a *mise en abyme*, a picture within a picture and a lineage within a lineage. Moreover, within "Ethiopia" itself, the split image continues; claims of origin are simultaneously undermined in Diodorus, through geographical, customary, and bodily displacements that hint at infinite regress when the originary claims recorded by the detached, perhaps ironic historian are pressed too far.

The *Ethiopica* further embosses the pattern. Heliodorus' romance seemingly bequeathed the almost wholly laudatory tradition about the blameless Ethiopians to later times. The action, which opens *in medias res* with a series of pirate adventures and the false death of the heroine Chariclea, concerns an Egyptian priest's attempt to restore Chariclea to her parents, the Ethiopian king and queen. Exposed by her mother at birth because of her white skin, Chariclea was rescued by the Ethiopian Sisimithres and handed over to Charicles, a Greek visitor to the source of the Nile, who took her back to Delphi, where she became a priestess of Artemis. When she falls in love with the Thessalian youth Theagenes, Calasiris, the Egyptian priest, helps them elope, only to suffer with them through a series of misadventures. After Calasiris' death and a period of captivity in Persian-controlled Egypt, the pair are captured by the Ethiopian king and taken to the island city of Meroe, where they are destined for human sacrifice. Sisimithres, now the leader of the Ethiopian sages, confirms Chariclea's story of her birth, and Chariclea and Theagenes are spared and married. The *Ethiopica* was translated into French by Amyot in 1547 and into English as *An Aethiopian Historie* by Thomas Underdowne in 1587, an edition that influenced both versions of Philip Sidney's *Arcadia* and several of Shakespeare's late plays, among other works.[18]

Although human sacrifice is abolished altogether at the end of the tale at the behest of the sages or "gymnosophists," its role at court already tarnishes the luster of Ethiopian civility. Nevertheless, Heliodorus implies that Ethiopian wisdom exceeds Egyptian knowledge: Calasiris goes to Ethiopia to study, and the Ethiopian king reminds the Egyptian celebrants of the feast of the Nile "that Aethiopia bringeth this floodde to you," a statement of some symbolic weight.[19] As I show in Chapter 4, the gymnosophists ("naked philosophers") entered European discourse with the conquests of Alexander the Great, and they come down to Heliodorus with a considerable reputation for gentleness, sagacity, and principled resistance to kingly authority that he confirms in their opposition to human immolation (Heliodorus, pp. 266, 288). Yet the gymnosophists inhabited India, where Alexander first encountered them. Their presence in Heliodorus' romance attests once again to the geographical lability of Ethiopia. The gymnosophists are offset by the Troglodites, whose role in capturing the young couple is closely followed by the first mention of sacrifice (pp. 229, 233–34). The king announces that he rules over "the East and Weast [*sic*] Aethiopians," but the geo-ethnic diversity of his kingdom renders it increasingly incoherent to the reader (p. 238).

Ethiopian wisdom is also hinted at through the "fascia" or belt that serves as a token of Chariclea's true identity, "wherein were Aethiopian letters, not common, but suche as the princes use, which are like the letters that the Egyptians use in their holy affayres" (p. 107). Calasiris construes the characters, written by the Ethiopian queen to her lost daughter, and uncovers the mystery behind Chariclea's birth, somewhat garbled in Underdowne's translation: "thou werte borne white, which couler is strange amonge the Aethiopians: I knewe the reason, because I looked upon the picture of Andromeda naked, while my husband had to do with me (for then he [Perseus] first brought her [Andromeda] from the rocke, [and I thus] had by mishappe ingendred presently a thing like to her)" (pp. 107–8; additions mine). Perseus and Andromeda are chief gods among the Ethiopians and tableaux of her rescue from the sea-monster and subsequent marriage to the hero adorn the queen's chambers. We have seen how Perseus is claimed by the Egyptians in Herodotus; Heliodorus follows Apollodorus and Ovid in making Andromeda the daughter of an earlier Ethiopian king and queen, Cepheus and Cassiepeia.[20] The Ethiopian letters in Chariclea's belt hardly explain her whiteness, then. Why was Andromeda white in the first place? Why was her picture, with its mysterious influence, a picture of a white woman? Perseus and Andromeda remain figures from Greek mythology, and Andromeda's story is Chariclea's *en abyme*. Both daughters were exposed through their mothers—Andromeda to the sea-monster because Cassiepeia claimed to be more beautiful than the Nereids, Chariclea to the elements because of the queen's fear of an adultery charge. More pertinently, the whiteness of the later Ethiopian princess simply reflects, and is reflected by, the whiteness of the earlier one, in a potentially endless mirroring. A fundamental—or perhaps bottomless—whiteness grounds the supersession of barbaric human sacrifice in both main and inset stories. Writing of Diodorus and other Graeco-Roman authors on Ethiopia, V. Y. Mudimbe shows how African space is similarly defined by European reference points in the earlier classical tradition, a kind of mapping that requires vision, contrast, and the differentiation of darkness by means of light.[21]

It is Egypt that emerges as the real subject of the *Ethiopica*, despite the title by which it is known and the ostensible goal of its heroine. Egypt and its varied landscape is the setting for most of the action, and Calasiris, the self-exiled priest of Isis, its only compelling character. While visiting Delphi, Calasiris answers the usual frequently asked questions on his homeland, concerning Egyptian gods, their animal forms, the building of the Pyramids, and finally and most pleasingly to him, the source and nature of the Nile, "For the Grecians eares are woonderfully delyted with tales of Egypt" (p. 68). At this point Charicles tells him of his own visit to the Nile's cataracts and his adoption of Chariclea there. Much later in the story, at Syene near the cataracts themselves, the festival of the Nile and its mythology are described. The Egyptians hold the river to be the greatest of all the gods because he waters their land without clouds or rainfall every year:

> And this is the common sorts opinion. . . . Marry their divines say that the earth is Isis, and Nylus is Osiris, geving to either a new name. Therfore the Goddesse is very desirous of his company, and rejoyceth when he is with her, but loureth when he is absent, as if some unhappy blast of lightning had touched her. This tale have the skilfull men in natures secretes devised, because as I thinke, they would not make prophane persons privie of their secrecies conteyned therein. (p. 241)

Through the image of the Nile, Heliodorus expands upon the influential idea that there is a split between the common and the elite or Hermetic interpretations of ancient Egyptian wisdom. Earlier, Calasiris distinguishes mere necromancy from "the true wisedome, and from whence the other counterfet hath degenerated, which wee priestes, and holy men doo practise from our youth" (p. 92). Degeneration is exemplified in an Egyptian witch who conjures the body of her dead son to speak and is suitably punished (pp. 170–71).

The episode in which the Sycnians show the Ethiopian king how the Nile is measured is fraught with unspoken significance: "They shewed him a deepe well, which shewed the manner of Nylus, like unto that at Memphis, made of hewed free stone, wherein were lines drawen an elle one from an other, into the which the water of Nylus brought under the earth by a spring, and falling into these lines, declareth to the inhabitaunts the ebbes and floodes of Nylus" (p. 250). It is here that the king asserts that Ethiopia is in fact the source of the great river the Egyptians worship. The same measuring techniques are used at Meroe; its island location, one might presume, associates the city and Ethiopia itself even more closely with the sacred Nile. Yet Meroe is also the site of human sacrifice, compared with which the ceremonies at Syene, however misunderstood by the common people, appear pious and civil.

The frequent avowal of hidden meanings behind vulgar practices and stories in Egypt suggests some sort of lost subtext for the *Ethiopica* itself. Hints about the preeminence if not the priority of Egyptian wisdom may have formed part of the romance's purpose. Calasiris simply assumes that Homer was born in Egypt:

> but to tell the troth, he was our Countryman, an Egyptian, born at Thebes. . . . His father was supposed to be a prieste, because that the God [Mercury or Hermes] lay with his wife doing certain sacrifices after the manner of the countrie, and fell on sleepe in the temple, and there ingendered Homer, who had about him token of unlawfull generation, for on both his thighes there grewe from his birth a great deale of haire whereof as he travelled, as well in Greece, as in other countries, and made his poeme, he gained his name [for Homer supposedly means "the thigh"]. (p. 91; additions mine)

Homer probably became a wandering poet because his hairy thighs suggested he was illegitimate, Calasiris adds; like Chariclea, a bodily attribute made him an exile. Homer also resembles Calasiris himself, an Egyptian who passes as Greek because of his clothing and demeanor (pp. 61, 115). Homer and Calasiris are cross-cultural agents in the *Ethiopica*. The Ethiopian priest Sisimithres gave Chariclea to the Greek priest Charicles, but it is Calasiris who brings her back to Africa with her Greek consort through Egypt, despite the whiteness of her appearance. Egypt's role as a mediating civilization ensures its continued prestige at the end of the classical tradition, although it is whiteness that emerges as the supposedly neutral ground upon which reconciliation takes place.

Early modern Europe rediscovered the ancient belief in Egypt's cultural precedence over Greece along with the rest of classical learning. In the preface to "Of Isis and Osiris" in his translation of Plutarch's *Moralia* (1603), Philemon Holland observes,

> The wisdome and learning of the Aegyptians hath bene much recommended unto us by ancient writers, and not without good cause: considering that *Aegypt* hath bene the source and fountaine from whence have flowed into the world arts and liberall sciences, as a man may gather by the testimony of the first Poets and philosophers that ever were: But time, which consumeth all things, hath bereft us of the knowledge of such wisdome: or if there remaine still with us any thing at all, it is but in fragments and peeces scattered heere and there.[22]

The Renaissance was as dedicated to the Isis-like collection of these ruins and fragments as it was to the recuperation of Graeco-Roman culture.

Yet an ancient ambivalence toward Egypt was becoming evident once again as well, informed by the conflation of classical descriptions and reports of its current state in late-sixteenth- and early-seventeenth-century travel accounts in England. Johannes Boemus' *Omnium gentium mores* of 1520, a compilation of customary behavior throughout the known world, was a popular example. It was first translated in 1555 as *The Fardle of Fashions*; here I will refer to the 1611 translation, *The Manners, Lawes, and Customs of All Nations, Collected out of the Best Writers*. As the later title indicates, Boemus was an armchair anthropologist who mixed classical, travel, and geographical sources to amuse and instruct his readers with a compendium of exotic behavior. Boemus takes the link between Egypt and Greece for granted, duly noting that it "was so called of *Aegiptus* the brother of *Danaus* King of the Argyues."[23] And he gives precedent to the Egyptians, while recording that many aspects of their culture were derived in turn from the Ethiopians. "The Egyptians were the first that fained the names of the twelue gods," we read, in a tacit citation of Herodotus that later texts would often echo,

> they erected Altars, Idols, and Temples, and figured liuing creatures in stones, all which things doe plainely argue that they had their originall from the Aethiopians, who were the first Authors of all these things (as *Diodorus Siculus* is of opinion). Their women were wonte in times past to doe businesse abroad, to keepe tauernes and victualling houses, and to take charge of buying and selling: and the men to knit within the walles of the citty, they bearing burthens vpon their heads, and the women vppon their shoulders: the women to pisse standing, and the men sitting; all of them for the most part ryoting and banquetting abroad, in open wayes, and exonerating and disburdening their bellyes at home. (p. 18)

Through the blending of two passages from Herodotus, the mixed nature of the tradition resolves itself into a narrative of decline from the invention of the pantheon ("fained" in two senses, however), through the reversal of European expectations about gender roles in public, to the disburdening of bellies at home. This is contradicted somewhat by Boemus' subsequent translation of a passage from Diodorus Siculus (uncredited) praising the

Egyptians' strict regulation of behavior and disparaging the mythology of the Greeks, who "could not with all their writings draw men to vertue, but were rather derided and contemned themselues" (p. 37). Nevertheless, the expansion of Herodotus' simple statement that the Egyptians liked to eat outdoors into rioting and banqueting in the streets leaves a negative impression with the reader.[24]

A full account of contemporary Egypt was provided by Leo Africanus, a convert to Christianity from Islam, whose *History and Description of Africa* of 1526, translated by John Pory in 1600, has long been recognized as a source for many of Shakespeare's references to the continent. In what may be a distant echo of Herodotus, Leo also depicts Egypt as the scene of gender trouble. He provides an etymology of the name of Cairo, deriving it from "El Chahira, which signifieth an enforcing or imperious mistress."[25] Its women, he claims, "are so ambitious & proud, that all of them disdaine either to spin or to play the cookes: wherefore their husbands are constrained to buie victuals ready drest at the cookes shops" (p. 883). There may be something of this lean-cuisine society in the Ptolemaic and urban Egypt of *Antony and Cleopatra*. According to Leo, men and women alike "in their common talke vse ribald and filthie speeches," and wives often complain to the judge of their husbands' sexual inadequacy (p. 884), yet he also notes the harsh physical punishments of Egypt's legal system in a way that parallels Boemus' depiction of ancient Egypt (p. 887). On the whole Leo's sketch is fairly sympathetic: "The inhabitants of Cairo are people of a merrie, iocund, and cheerfull disposition, such as will promise much, but perform little. They exercise merchandize and mechanicall artes, and yet trauell they not out of their owne natiue soile. Many students there are of the lawes, but very few other liberall artes and sciences. And albeit their colleges are continually full of students, yet few of them attaine vnto perfection" (p. 882). Leo's Cairo sounds a lot like early-seventeenth-century London. He reverses the order of most European geographical descriptions by beginning with the urban flux of present-day Egypt and only then turning to its antiquities, affording them scant description at that. But unlike many later European travelers he does not make an implicit equation between the fallen monuments of the past and the declining fortunes of Egypt under the Ottomans during his own time.[26] Surveying what are for him merely ruins, the cultivated Islamic, and soon to be Christian, observer finally notes that at Aswan "are to be seene many buildings of the ancient Egyptians, and most high towers, which they call in the language of that countrey Barba" (p. 904). The relation between civilization and barbarism is as unstable here as in Boemus, although in a different, perhaps unexpected, manner.

Yet Boemus' and Leo Africanus' early and influential accounts of Egypt were combined within the somewhat confused discourse of Egypt and the Egyptians in early-seventeenth-century England. George Sandys acknowledges the many inventions of the ancient Egyptians in his *Relation of a Iourney*, yet he claims that "The *Aegyptians* of the middle times, were a people degenerating from the worth of their ancestors; prone to innouations, deuoted to luxury, cowardly cruell; naturally addicted to scoffe, and to couill, detracting from whatsoeuer was gracious and eminent."[27] The geographer Peter Heylyn plagiarizes this passage in his *Cosmographie in Four Bookes*, with one significant alteration: "such as have observed the nature of the Modern *Egyptians* affirm them to have much degenerated from the worth of their Ancestors; prone to innovations, devoted to luxury, cowardly, cruel, addicted naturally to cavill, and to detract from whatsoever is good and eminent."[28] The middle times of the Ptolemies become modern times in Heylyn's later, second-hand description of Egypt.

Fittingly, this mixture of antiquity and modernity can likewise be seen in Shakespeare's Ptolemaic Egypt. *Antony and Cleopatra*, set in a period of transition in ancient history, was also bound up with the economic and cultural transitions of its own time. The symmetry between sixteenth-century London and Leo Africanus' Cairo, for instance, was not coincidental—in a sense, the two cities were meeting each other halfway. London was increasing in economic power and metropolitan centrality while Cairo was becoming less and less important, hampered since the fifteenth century by European competition and a chronic shortage of bullion.[29] Cairo had dominated the Eastern Mediterranean and Southwest Asian regions for some forty years at the start of the fourteenth century. Under the Mamluk sultans, Egypt profited from a restructured world-system in the wake of the sack of Baghdad by the Mongols in the thirteenth century. One feature of the Mediterranean wing of Egypt's influence was the establishment of a longstanding relationship with Italy, specifically with Genoa and, more crucially, Venice.[30] Even after the Ottoman conquest of Egypt in 1516–17, Venice maintained a foothold in its still-profitable economy, moving its merchants from Alexandria to Cairo itself in 1552 and gaining trading concessions from the Turks in 1599.[31] Venice and Egypt were paired in the sixteenth century just as Rome and Egypt are in Shakespeare's *Antony and Cleopatra*. The English were well aware of the old association between Italy and Egypt; they were unsuccessful in a three-way competition with Italian and French traders for the Cairo textile markets at the end of the century. But the Egyptians, stuck with too much European cloth and not enough gold and silver, were perhaps the biggest losers.

The growth of the modern system of racial difference was a major part of these developments. Egypt's economic hardship contributed to the picture of decline painted by European travelers such as Henry Blount: "whatsoever little memory of *old Ceremonies*, might have beene left in *Egypt*, hath utterly perished in their frequent *oppressions* . . . which beside the change of *ceremony*, have corrupted all the ingenious *fancy* of that *Nation* into *ignorance*, and *malice*."[32] The enslavement of sub-Saharan Africans in the colonies of the New World added dark skin to conquest and degeneration in Europe's growing racial lexicon, with wider, para-colonial consequences. It was the monopoly of Venice and Egypt over the eastern routes that led the Iberian monarchies, and eventually England, to incorporate America into the European world economy.[33] A metro-politan culture's slaves generally come from outside its world economy (the great exception here is early modern Russia, as we shall see in Chapter 3). As the leading role shifted from the Mediterranean to the Atlantic theater in early modern times, slaves were drawn from Africa rather than the Balkans for work in America.[34] It became necessary to "other" and demean all African civilizations, including Egypt—despite the veneration in which its antique and Hermetic traditions were held, and despite the mixture of colors and cultures along the Nile that ancient and modern documents attest to.

This mixture was in fact enlisted in the process of othering. In 1605 the Puritan divine George Abbot, a future archbishop of Canterbury, granted the original Egyptians their reputation for learning in an ambitious quarto entitled *A Briefe Description of the whole WORLDE*. But he merges past and present in emphasizing skin color and the unstable figure of Cleopatra:

Although the Countrie of Egypt do stand in the selfe same Climate, that *Mauritania* doth, yet the inhabitants there, are not black, but rather dunne, or tawnie. Of which colour, *Cleopatra* was obserued to be: who by entice- ment, so wanne the loue of *Iulius Cesar*, and *Anthonie*: And of that colour do those runnagates (by deuices make themselues to be) who goe vp and downe the world vnder the name of *Egyptians*; being in deed, but counter- faites, and the refuse, or rascalitie of many nations.[35]

The opening lines of *Antony and Cleopatra* are part of the same discourse:

> Nay, but this dotage of our general's
> O'erflows the measure: those his goodly eyes,
> That o'er the files and musters of the war
> Have glow'd like plated Mars, now bend, now turn
> The office and devotion of their view
> Upon a tawny front: his captain's heart,
> Which in the scuffles of great fights hath burst
> The buckles on his breast, reneges all temper,
> And is become the bellows and the fan
> To cool a gipsy's lust.[36]

Historically a Ptolemy, Shakespeare's Cleopatra is described as the queen of Ptolemy and Egypt's widow, ambiguous designations that leave her color open (1.4.6, 2.1.37). Philo calls her tawny; Cleopatra says, "Think on me,/ That am with Phoebus' amorous pinches black,/And wrinkled deep in time" (1.5.27–29). These lines evoke her identification with Egypt's antiq- uity as well as her complexion, darkened by the sun. Yet the Abbot passage suggests that tawniness and antiquity can both be the deceptions of a run- nagate; darkness is dissociated from ancient wisdom and made suspect, and Egyptians are replaced by "gypsies."[37] A lost originary knowledge is juxta- posed with diaspora and counterfeiting, a demonic version of Holland's fragments and pieces scattered here and there. Instead of a purely Manichean division of black from white, Abbot pictures an intermediate zone in which light-skinned people darken themselves by "devices" and cir- culate like vagabonds. And Shakespeare amplifies the sexuality of this hybrid mixture, dissolving strict battle lines with the breeze from Antony's fanlike heart in lines that look forward to Enobarbus' "pretty dimpled boys . . .

whose wind did seem / To glow the delicate cheeks which they did cool, /And what they undid did" in the barge set piece (2.2.202–5). Cleopatra's color comes and goes in this trope in a manner that links race and sexuality without the stabilizing mediation of heterosexual lineage.

Walter Ralegh's *History of the World*, like Abbot's a global project with a Europeanizing and culturally conservative cast, pushes the association of Egyptian learning with degeneration and dissemination through the figure of the gypsy to its logical conclusion. Ralegh supports the traditional attribution of the pantheon to the Egyptians, but twists it by blaming them for falling away from monotheism under the influence of the devil. This tendency began with the Egyptian priests and has continued to our own times: "the Trade of riddles in Oracles, with the Deuils telling mens fortunes therein, is taken vp by counterfait *Aegyptians*, and cousening *Astrologers*."[38] Thomas Browne's speculations on past civilizations are gentler than Ralegh's, but they likewise associate the largely non-European world of antiquity with an inevitable cycle of growth and decay. In *Religio Medici* (1643) he notes a specific link between the wisdom of the Egyptians and the practices of their latter-day mimics in palmistry, a form of divination that also figures in *Antony and Cleopatra*:

> I carry that in mine owne hand, which I could never read of, nor discover in another. *Aristotle*, I confesse, . . . hath made no mention of Chiromancy, yet I beleeve the *Egyptians*, who were nearer addicted to those abstruse and mysticall sciences, had a knowledge therein, to which those vagabond and counterfeit *Egyptians* did after pretend, and perhaps retained a few corrupted principles, which sometimes might verifie their prognostickes.[39]

The Soothsayer, who is probably an Egyptian in Shakespeare's play as he is in Plutarch's life of Antonius, can read a little in nature's infinite book of secrecy (1.1.9–10), but he is principally a palm reader, like Browne's counterfeit Egyptians. "There's a palm presages chastity, if nothing else," Iras says in extending her hand to him. "E'en as the o'erflowing Nilus presages famine," counters Charmian, "if an oily palm be not a fruitful prognostication, I cannot scratch mine ear" (1.2.46–47, 49–50). This exchange links the soothsayer's art with a dissolute yet vital female sexuality, but also with the pyramid, another symbol of ancient Egyptian knowledge, which is used to predict the level of the river (2.7.17–23). Later in the action, the soothsayer, poised uneasily between hieroglyphic chiromancy and the cozening of the market, abruptly alters the course of the plot, and world history, by frightening Antony back to Egypt. The deceptive world of the marketplace and its gypsies, where Antony and Cleopatra first met and continue to display themselves (2.2.215, 3.6.3), is recalled in Antony's violent condemnation of Cleopatra in Act IV:

> Betray'd I am.
> O this false soul of Egypt! this grave charm,
> Whose eye beck'd forth my wars, and call'd them home:
> Whose bosom was my crownet, my chief end,
> Like a right gipsy, that at fast and loose
> Beguil'd me, to the very heart of loss. (4.12.24–29)

Antony himself assumes the Roman discourse that renders Cleopatra whore and trickster, a darkened remnant whose false soul turns antiquity into a conjurer's cheat, like the rigged game of fast and loose.

Antony and Cleopatra, then, clearly registers the tendency toward degeneration in the early-seventeenth-century discourse of Egypt. But it is important to recognize the signs of the other, still mainstream version of Egypt and its antiquity in the play. John Gillies has called attention to the "Herodotean character of Shakespeare's Egypt" as the source of the play's concern with cultural translation; the tradition of Herodotus also carried the veneration of Egyptian antiquity down to Shakespeare's time.[40] The anxiety about decay is mostly ascribed to the Roman characters. And by the end of the drama, the laudatory view of Egyptian culture seems to win out, if we take Cleopatra as a representation of Egypt in her final nobility. When she says she is "wrinkled deep in time" in Act I, Cleopatra is identifying herself, however playfully, with a notion of antiquity that is also personified in the female figure of Isis, whose name, Diodorus Siculus says, means "ancient, deriving the name from her eternity and ancient beginnings" (p. 4). Her greatest affront to the Romans is her appearance in the marketplace of Alexandria "In the habiliments of the goddess Isis" (3.6.17) with Antony by her side. The frequent and sometimes ribald invocations of Isis by Charmion and others throughout the text may rob this image of its dignity

(1.2.61), yet after all, as Plutarch tells us, "*Isis* is the president over amatorious folk" and deity of the errant moon.[41] By the end of the play, Cleopatra seems determined to out-Roman the Romans in doing a noble deed: "now from head to foot / I am marble constant; now the fleeting moon / No planet is of mine" (5.2.238–40). Edward Capell, the eighteenth-century editor, saw these lines as a reference to her earlier imitation of Isis.[42] Yet Cleopatra's reduction of herself to a statue also has something Egyptian in it: she is preparing herself for entombment in terms that evoke the Hermetic association of Egypt with the afterlife, as in her subsequent call for robe and crown, her "Immortal longings," and her vision of her "husband" Antony beckoning her onward: "I am fire, and my other elements/I give to baser life" (5.2.279–90). She seems determined to mount a performance both of Egypt and its supposed antithesis in Roman culture; Cleopatra remains a composite construction to the end.

Rome itself, however, is also a composite construction in the play, as it was in contemporary historical, geographical, and travel accounts. This is best seen through an examination of Antony and the mythological references out of which his public persona is largely assembled.[43] His climactic rejection of Cleopatra in Act IV brings to a head a chain of associations linking Antony to Hercules:

> The shirt of Nessus is upon me, teach me,
> Alcides, thou mine ancestor, thy rage.
> Let me lodge Lichas on the horns o' the moon,
> And with those hands that grasp'd the heaviest club,
> Subdue my worthiest self. (4.12.43–47)

There was a broad context for Antony's evocation of Hercules in the Renaissance knowledge of Graeco-Roman and Egyptian antiquity, and more particularly in what was known of the historical Marcus Antonius. According to Plutarch's life of Antonius, the immediate source of Shakespeare's play in North's translation,

> it had beene a speeche of old time, that the familie of the Antonii were descended from one Anton, the sonne of Hercules, whereof the familie tooke name. This opinion did Antonius seeke to confirme in all his doings: not

onely resembling him in the likeness of his bodye, as we have sayd before, but also in the wearing of his garments. For when he would openly shewe him selfe abroad before many people, he would alwayes weare his cassocke gyrt downe lowe upon his hippes, with a great sword hanging by his side, and upon that, some ill favored cloke.[44]

The self-dramatization of Plutarch's Antonius here is of a piece with his notorious sponsorship of actors and mountebanks both at home and abroad (Plutarch, "Life," pp. 10, 22–23).

It is when Shakespeare's Antony spurns Cleopatra, seemingly once and for all, that he reclaims his identity by reminding himself of his familial and cultural lineage. But even at his most self-obsessed and self-mythologizing, Antony throws in a reference to the moon of Cleopatra and Isis by recalling the fate of Lichas, the servant who brought Hercules the fatal shirt and was tossed sky-high for his pains. And there is something of Plutarch's Antonius, the actors' friend, in this histrionic retreat to a mythological identity. Already in Act I, upon hearing of Fulvia's death, Cleopatra challenges him:

> Then bid adieu to me, and say the tears
> Belong to Egypt. Good now, play one scene
> Of excellent dissembling, and let it look
> Like perfect honour.
>
> . . . .
>
> But this is not the best. Look, prithee, Charmian,
> How this Herculean Roman does become
> The carriage of his chafe. (1.3.77–80, 83–85)

Founded on the example of his putative ancestor, Antony's self-construction appears ultra-Roman in a masculinist mode, the authentic performance of a cultural past in which, for instance, Greek religion and society were totally subsumed by an empire that successfully asserted its historical priority. Cleopatra responds by exposing the self-stagings that constitute any claim of cultural integrity. She calls attention to the performative mechanism of Antony's mythology, sexualizing Antony's performance in a manner that breaks down the gender barriers upon which Roman ideas of honor and conquest were also founded. Cultural and sexual difference are differently "contained," or rather produced and managed, when the characters Antony and Cleopatra encounter one another on stage. Ptolomy's widow has Hellenistic roots but is identified with Egypt, particularly through the figure of Isis; moreover, her role is embodied on stage by a boy player. Antony's character seems unitary by comparison, yet the scene in which Cleopatra recalls cross-dressing him both implicates the Roman in the artifice of the Jacobean theater and exposes an unacknowledged strand in his personal mythology, the submission of Hercules to Omphale through the hero's adoption of women's clothes. "I drunk him to his bed," Cleopatra boasts, "Then put my tires and mantles on him, whilst / I wore his sword Philippan" (2.5.21–23). Gender difference is maintained here, it is true, however reversed the positions may be. The sword remains "his," a relic of a past conquest at Philippi; she only wears it, its ambiguous status as the phallus strengthened, not challenged. The lines may also recall Hercules' love for the boy Hylas, thoroughly yet excessively masculine.[45] Nevertheless, Antony's Roman masculinism is undercut somewhat through both the reversal and intensification of gender roles, and in a way that opens up his Herculean performances to reinterpretation from within.[46]

Omphale was the daughter of the queen of the Lydians in Asia Minor, as Diodorus Siculus, the earliest surviving source of the story of Hercules' subjection to her, records (p. 187; he does not include the cross-dressing episode). Cleopatra's various dressings, undressings, and manipulations of Antony reenact his ancestor's unmanning in Egypt rather than Asia; they extend an encounter with the racial and sexual other that was always paradoxically within as well as without the Graeco-Roman world, or rather the world of an antiquity that until the seventeenth century in Europe comprised a wider field of both cultures and sexualities than later scholarship allowed. Hercules or Herakles himself, as sources from Herodotus onward acknowledge, possessed a complicated lineage with roots in Africa as well as Asia and Europe; the tradition attempted to untangle it by claiming that there was more than one hero of the name. Herodotus commends those Greeks who worship him both as an Olympian god and as a hero, and records ancient versions of his cult in Phoenicia and Thrace (*Famous Hystory*, p. 82 recto). But the historian's most notorious claim is that the original Hercules came from Egypt: "This name I suppose to have come first from Egypt into Graece, and to have been borrowed of them, howsoever the Graecians dissemble the matter, to make the invention seeme their owne: whereupon I grounde wyth greater confidence, for that the parents of Hercules, Amphitrio and Alcmaena are by countrey and lynage Aegyptians" (pp. 81 recto–verso). For Herodotus, the actual birthplace of any historical Hercules who may have existed is less important than the issue of cultural influence, of where the name and attributes of the seemingly most Greek, and later Roman, of heroes actually came from.

Herodotus' influence was, as usual, pervasive later in the tradition. Writing in the first century B.C., Diodorus Siculus agrees that the Greeks are wrong to claim Hercules as theirs. He recounts how Osiris left his kinsman Hercules in charge of Egypt's armies when he went on his expedition to bring culture to the world; when the river Nile, also called the "Eagle," overflowed the province of a governor named Prometheus, Hercules restored it to its course, "whereupon some *Greek* Poets (turning true History into a fable) have written that *Hercules* killed the Eagle which fed upon the liver of *Prometheus*" (pp. 12, 7–10). Cicero urbanely lists six Herculeses in *De natura deorum* 3:42, including an Egyptian and Indian Hercules as well as three sons of three gods named Jupiter, "since, as I shall explain, we have traditions of several different Jupiters as well."[47] Plutarch's much later essay "Of the Malice of Herodotus," of course, rejects the Egyptian origin of Hercules altogether, extrapolating three heroes from Herodotus' account:

> the captaines and leaders of the Dorians (saith he) seeme to be descended in right line from the Aegyptians, . . . striving to make, not onely the other two *Herculees* Aegyptians and Phoenicians, but also this whom himselfe nameth to be the third, a meere stranger from Greece, and to enroll him among Barbarians, notwithstanding that of all the ancient learned men, neither *Homer*, nor *Hesiodus* . . . do make mention of any *Hercules* an Aegyptian or Phoenician, but acknowledge one alone, to wit, our Boeotian and Argien. (*The Morals*, p. 1230)

But Bernal is right in contrasting this piece with Plutarch's favorable account of Egyptian antiquity in "Of Isis and Osiris": both essays were rhetorical exercises "moralizing" on competing interpretations of past Greek culture from a shifting late Hellenistic perspective in the second century A.D.[48] Furthermore, Plutarch's rhetorical attack on Herodotus did not stop the spread of the tradition he transmitted during later centuries hungry for knowledge, any knowledge, about the sources of civilization in remote antiquity. Even Ralegh accepts the existence of the Libyan or Egyptian Hercules, although he identifies him with a biblical figure named Lehabim, a grandson of Ham (Ralegh, pp. 240–41; see Genesis 10:6, 13). Annius of Viterbo, a fifteenth-century Dominican monk who professed to have transcribed the lost writings of the Babylonian chronicler Berosus, forged or naively transmitted a fabricated account of world history since the flood in which Hercules figured prominently. Annius' English popularizer Richard Lynche published a book in 1601 entitled *An Historical Treatise of the Travels of Noah into Europe*. Lynche follows Varro and Servius in maintaining that there were forty-three men named Hercules in antiquity, only two of whom were renowned: the Greek Hercules, whom he dismisses as a mere robber or pirate, and the Libyan or Egyptian Hercules, son of Isis and Osiris, the authentic Hercules who conquered Europe and ruled in France, Italy, and Spain.[49]

Even more conservative versions of the tradition attest to a hero who traveled to numerous countries and fathered lots of children. With so many Herculeses and their offspring about in so many parts of the globe, Antony's claim of descent from Anton seems a little less impressive.[50] What does it mean, then, to act a Herculean part in Shakespeare's play—or a Roman one for that matter? Lynche, for instance, records that Rome itself was actually founded by one Rhomanessos. A grandson of Atlas whose name means "great height" in Aramaic, Rhomanessos called the city after himself; contrary to popular legend, "*Romulus* (being himselfe found hard by that cittie by wondrous accident) tooke his name of Roma, and not Roma of *Romulus*" (L1 verso). Whether or not stories such as these were believed in the early seventeenth century, they were preserved and circulated as fragments of a diverse tradition about the African and Asian origins of Graeco-Roman, and hence European, civilization. Behind Antony's performance as Alcides and the English audience's enjoyment of it there lies a sort of racial panic, a repeated denial of Egyptian and other influences through the very mythological materials that could just as easily be cited to affirm these influences.

The cultural instability of the myths surrounding Hercules provides one context for Antony's seduction by and of a racially ambiguous woman, the Omphale-like Cleopatra. She is a Ptolemy, perhaps, but one who has adopted the Egyptianism that may always have lurked within

Hellenistic, and before that classical, Greek culture. According to Diodorus, after all, the Ptolemies' homeland of Macedon received its name from Macedon the son of Osiris, who accompanied his father on his culture-bringing expedition and ended up ruling the northern region that took his name (p. 7). It is tempting to explain Cleopatra's acculturation, or reculturation, and its effect on Antony as a lapse into the watery state of decay that Danby associates with Egypt and its Nile.[51] But the Roman people themselves harbor such labile decadence within them, as Octavius is the first to complain:

> It hath been taught us from the primal state.
> . . . .
>   This common body,
> Like to a vagabond flag upon the stream,
> Goes to, and back, lackeying the varying tide,
> To rot itself with motion. (1.4.41, 44–47)

"Rome" and "Egypt" in *Antony and Cleopatra* are simply not antithetical in the way much criticism persists in declaring them to be. As Jyotsna Singh remarks, "Inherent to such readings is the tendency to naturalize patriarchal stereotypes that often equate Rome with reason and public duty and Egypt with sensuality and emotional excess."[52] The naturalization of racial as well as gender stereotypes is also at stake here.[53]

It is not only commoners in Rome itself who threaten to revert to the primal depths that Octavius' paranoia often invokes. The triumvirs on Pompey's galley at Misenum drink deeply with differing effects: "These quick-sands, Lepidus," Antony warns as Menas conspires with Sextus Pompeius, "Keep off them, for you sink" (2.7.58–59). "This is not yet an Alexandrian feast," Pompey goads, while Enobarbus proposes that "we dance now the Egyptian Bacchanals,/And celebrate our drink" (2.7.102–3). It is significant that their celebration of Bacchus is specifically ascribed to Egypt, for Bacchus or Dionysus, more clearly than Hercules, was often identified as an Egyptian deity.[54] Herodotus says that the Egyptians think Bacchus is the same as their chief god, Osiris, the consort of Isis or Ceres, and goes on to parallel the Greek worship of Dionysus with Egyptian processions, meetings, and sacrifices to Osiris (*Famous Hystory*, p. 81 recto).

Diodorus Siculus' influential account of Osiris' travels throughout the known world is presented as the true explanation behind the myth of Dionysus' conquest of the East; it was Orpheus who spread the story that Dionysus was born of Semele and Zeus in order to make his cult more palatable to the Greeks (pp. 7–11). In "Of Isis and Osiris" Plutarch himself describes how Osiris reduced the earth to civility by "sweet perswasions couched in songs, and with all manner of Musicke: whereupon the Greeks were of opinion, that he and *Bacchus* were both one" (*The Morals*, p. 1292). Lynche, following Annius of Viterbo, extends the conquest tradition backward to make Noah the first culture-hero and world traveler. Osiris is said to be the son of Cham (Ham) and his sister Rea, and the father of the real Hercules. He left many traces while establishing Egypt's empire over Europe; the Hapsburg dynasty, Lynche claims, derived its name from Apis, another of his titles (B2 recto–E2 verso). This combination of biblical, Egyptian, and classical antiquities seems far-fetched even by early modern standards, but it brings out and develops connections that were readily available within a complicated and rich tradition.

In their drunkenness, the Romans on Pompey's galley are honoring Dionysus, or Osiris, through their Egyptian bacchanals in the half-decadent, half-ritual manner that Shakespeare associates with the mysteries of Cleopatra's court, a mixture emphasized when they grasp hands and perhaps dance during the boy's drinking-song to the god (2.7.106–16). Shakespeare subtly recalls this scene later in the play when music invades the stage once more and the soldiers conclude, "'Tis the god Hercules, whom Antony lov'd, / Now leaves him" (4.3.15–16). In Plutarch's life of Antonius, however, it is Bacchus, not Hercules, who was supposed by the general's followers to have deserted him before the final battle: "it is said that sodainly they heard a marvelous sweete harmonie of sundrie sortes of instrumentes of musicke, with the crie of a multitude of people, as they had bene dauncing, and had song as they use in Bacchus feastes, with movinges and turninges after the maner of the Satyres" ("Life," p. 78). Earlier we read that Antonius was descended from Hercules but followed Bacchus in his way of life, and so was called the new Bacchus (p. 63).

But Shakespeare's linking of the two gods is part of a long tradition that antedates Plutarch. Herakles and Dionysus, as Bernal points out, are paralleled in *Iliad* 14:321–25, where Zeus compares his affairs with their respective mortal mothers.[55] They were frequently paired, not always to Herakles' advantage, in Greek comic drama.[56] Later on, the two figures were coupled as dual conquerors, as in Diodorus Siculus' material on India: "The learned of those dayes have written, That *Dionysius* came into *India* with his Army from the western parts. . . . The *Indians* doe hold moreover, with the *Greekes*, that *Hercules* passed also even unto them, armed with a club, and a Lyons-skinne, that he surpassed all other men in force of body and virtue; That he tamed the monsters both of Sea and Land" (p. 96). This association was taken up closer to Shakespeare's time by Spenser in Book 5 of the *Faerie Queene*:

first was *Bacchus*, that with furious might
All th'East before vntam'd did ouerronne,
And wrong repressed, and establisht right.

. . . .

Next Hercules his like ensample shewed,
Who all the West with equall conquest wonne,
And monstrous tyrants with his club subdewed.[57]

Book 5 also contains the mysterious episode in the temple of Isis, where the myth of Osiris and his queen serves as the prime allegorical representation of the book's theme, the virtue of justice.[58] Shakespeare's echoes of the parallel between Bacchus and Hercules as imperial victors, and his references to the Isis cult, offset Spenser's moralizing use of the Graeco-Egyptian allegorical tradition and remind us of its messy origins.

Hercules is not exclusively a Roman, or even a Greek, hero. He is not a unitary figure, and one of his many incarnations, perhaps his oldest, is Egyptian. He was a conqueror, yes, but so was Bacchus, the Dionysus of the Greeks and the Osiris of the Egyptians, his double—in one source his father, and perhaps his fate. For if Cleopatra is Isis, then Antony, as Bacchus, is her Osiris, a dying god whose destruction and display will purify Octavius' Rome of Egyptian corruption and prepare it for empire.

The bacchanals scene is underlain by racial panic, enunciated typically by Octavius—here a participant-observer, but comically objectified in the figure of Lepidus. "Lepidus is high-coloured," we are told (2.7.4)—an appropriate condition for the nominal ruler of Africa, which, along with Octavius'

Europe and Antony's Egypt and Asia, formed one-third of the traditional three-part division of the globe. "The third part, then, is drunk," as Menas remarks (2.7.90). Skin color was a less stable marker of racial difference in early modern Europe than it is taken to be today: at a time when many Europeans believed that the sun lent a dark tone to equatorial peoples and threatened northerners in those climes as well (recall 1.5.27–29), the flushed complexion of the drunkard functioned as a less serious, but feasible, emblem of racial and moral degeneration.

"It's monstrous labour when I wash my brain/And it grow fouler," Octavius worries (2.7.97–98), clearly playing upon the proverbial example of fruitless work, "to wash an Ethiope white."[59] And he makes the comparison with the familiar explanation for dark skin color explicit when he takes his leave after the song to Bacchus:

> Gentle lords, let's part,
> You see we have burnt our cheeks. Strong Enobarb
> Is weaker than the wine, and mine own tongue
> Splits what it speaks: the wild disguise hath almost
> Antick'd us all. (2.7.119–23)

These bacchanals are Egyptian indeed, and Octavius fears their effect upon his appearance, his speech, and his brain or core sense of identity. For it is not only the physical signs of drunkenness, but also the way they mark the foreign god's power over his subjects, that provoke Octavius' panic. He has almost been "antick'd," both made into a figure of foolery and submerged in an antiquity whose kinship he refuses to acknowledge.

The combination of respect for antiquity and fear of contagious decadence in European writing about Egypt has prepared us for both Cleopatra's final performance and its partial appropriation in Shakespeare's play. In Act I Antony wishes he had never seen Cleopatra, and Enobarbus replies, "O, sir, you had then left unseen a wonderful piece of work, which not to have been blest withal, would have discredited your travel" (1.2.151–53). Antony, like Enobarbus himself in his orientalist fantasy of the "Rare Egyptian" in her barge, is a European sightseer in Egypt whose travel account would lack credibility without reference to its chief wonder. Cleopatra is this "piece of work," like a building or statue, marble constant but also a little touristy. Antony, sounding like a travel writer, will later tell Lepidus

> they take the flow o' the Nile
> By certain scales 'i' the pyramid; they know,
> By the height, the lowness, or the mean, if dearth
> Or foison follow. The higher Nilus swells,
> The more it promises: as it ebbs, the seedsman
> Upon the slime and ooze scatters his grain. (2.7.17–22)

Antony's traveler's tale may be a distorted version of Leo Africanus' description of the measurement of the Nile by means of a "piller" set in a cistern within a "house"; Shakespeare could also be conflating pyramids and obelisks.[60] The passage likely recalls the wells of Syene and Memphis in Underdowne's translation of the *Ethiopica* too, another story about a woman whose color bears an uncertain relation with her country. The direct association of pyramids with the flow of the Nile in *Antony and Cleopatra* certainly ties them to Cleopatra herself, who is constantly identified with the fertile effects of the river's encounter with the land that she embodies as Isis.

It is useful to juxtapose Enobarbus' comparison of Cleopatra with a monument, echoed several times later in the play, with the image of the pyramids in the traditional descriptions of Egypt. Although some early modern sources maintained that they were storehouses for grain, Leo Africanus and others held them to be pharaonic tombs (p. 896). Their association with death goes back to Herodotus, who claims the priests told him that the great pyramid of Cheops and its smaller companion were built from the proceeds of royal prostitution. The 1584 translation embroiders the basic story of how Cheops

> made sale of his daughters honestie, willing hir to entertayne tagge and ragge all that would come, in case they refused not to pay for their pleasure, sithence Venus accepteth not the devotion of such as pray with empty hands and threadbare pursses. The Lady willing to obey the hestes of the King her father, devised also the meane to prolong the memorie of herselfe, and to advaunce her fame to the notice of all ages that should ensue,

wherefore she made request to suche as had accesse unto her, to give her a stone to the building and erection of a worke which she had determined, wherewith (as the brute goeth) she gave so many stones as served to the framing of a whole pyre, situate in the middest of the three former, in full view and prospect to the greatest pyrame, which is every way an acre and a halfe square.[61] (p. 104 verso)

The elaborate sexual etiology of the pyramids was frequently repeated by European authors well into the seventeenth century.[62] To the Scottish traveler William Lithgow the great pyramid was built by "that effeminate *Cheops*, who . . . did prostitute his daughter to all comers."[63] The excessive and feminizing sexuality of pyramid building also found expression in another story discounted by Herodotus but taken up by Pliny and others, that a pyramid made partially of dark Ethiopian stone was built wholly at the charge of the famous courtesan Rhodopis.[64] Sandys repeats the story, and immediately adds his own interpretation of the nearby Sphinx. It is "wrought altogether into the forme of an *Aethiopian* woman," he reports, "and adored heretofore by the countrey people as a rurall Deity," although it is also supposed to be the tomb of the pharaoh Amasis. Once again, Ethiopia is placed *en abyme* within the Egyptian material, this time to darken rather than lighten or neutralize it. "By a *Sphinx*," Sandys continues, "the *Aegyptians* in their hieroglyphics presented an harlot: hauing an amiable, and alluring face; but withall the tyrannie, and rapacity of a Lion: exercised ouer the poore heart-broken, and voluntarily perishing louer. The images of these they also erected before the entrances of their Temples; declaring that secrets of Philosophy, and sacred mysteries, should be folded in enigmatical expressions, separated from the vnderstanding of the prophane multititude" (pp. 131–32). This passage distills the complex relationship among sexuality, race and signification in the European tradition about the monuments of Egypt, and deserves a closer look.

Plutarch similarly describes the Egyptian priests' reliance on fables and mysteries: "this themselves seeme to signifie and give us to understand, by setting up ordinarily before the porches and gates of their temples, certaine Sphinges: meaning thereby, that all their Theologie containeth under aenigmaticall and covert words, the secrets of wisdome" (*The Morals*, pp. 1290–91). "Aenigmaticall," Ralegh explains, "is a composition or mixture of Images or Similitudes: in which sense, the monstrous Image of a Lyons body hauing a Mans head, was grauen on their Temples and Altars, to signifie, that to all men all diuine things are Aenygmaticall and obscure" (p. 324). Writing about the same time as Ralegh, Sandys also reads the sphinx as a hieroglyph. The Renaissance fascination with Egyptian hieroglyphs as the repositories of ancient wisdom began with the discovery and translation of Horapollo's fifth-century work *Hieroglyphica* in 1419. A flood of emblem books and manuals depicting the various pantheons of antiquity followed, with a special emphasis on the gods of Egypt, whose animal forms, long derided by the Romans, were now justified through moral allegory.[65] As Walter Benjamin remarks, "in the mystic and natural-historical respect the baroque is descended from antiquity: Egyptian antiquity, but subsequently Greek antiquity as well."[66] Sandys' sphinx is first a hieroglyph for the harlot, who presents an alluring face that hides the rapacity of a lion, located fittingly in her hindquarters. But images of the sphinx, he goes on to tell us, were also placed before the temples, as both signs and examples of how religious beliefs should remain enigmatic or double-meaning.

The sphinx, in other words, is not just a hieroglyph of the prostitute, but a hieroglyph of all hieroglyphs, of the hieroglyphic principle. Because prostitutes are different from what they appear to be, they lend themselves to hieroglyphic signification; conversely, all signification through images, whether performative or monumental, has something of the harlot about it. Prostitution is the paradigm for writing, which distances and hides meaning from the vulgar onlookers while revealing it to the initiated. The cult of emblematic meaning and of Egypt in general seemingly revealed sexuality as the basis for cultural representation through the pyramids and other hieroglyphic monuments and images. Yet however liberating such transgressive monumentality may have been for early modern Europeans, it was licensed under a developing system of racial difference. The alluring face of Sandys' sphinx, worshiped as a rural god, bears the features of an Ethiopian woman—a black Athena, perhaps, but also a harlot, an example of the long-standing European association of dark-skinned Africans with ungovernable sexual desire.[67] In Sandys' account, the pyramid-Sphinx complex is given an added accent of contemporary degeneration by his anecdote of a nearby holy woman whom the Christians claim prostituted herself in order to convert men to Islam (pp. 135–36).

The same play among sexuality, race, and the monumental is evident in *Antony and Cleopatra*. It is hard not to notice the similarity between Sandys' "voluntarily perishing lover" and Shakespeare's Antony; the play may have affected the travel tradition as well as been affected by it. Cleopatra, a dark if not Ethiopian woman like the one supposedly represented in the sphinx, unites antique meaning and sexuality just as Sandys' hieroglyphs do. She refuses to leave her monument, bizarrely drawing Antony up its "other side" to comfort him in his death (4.15). Called a whore and gypsy by the Romans in the play, Cleopatra is also "Egypt." Following Horace, Sandys says she was "a fatall monster unto Rome."[68]

Antony is monumentalized by his death, literally hoisted upon a monument, and then compared by Cleopatra to a sort of colossus:

> His legs bestrid the ocean, his rear'd arm
> Crested the world . . .
>   to imagine
> An Antony were nature's piece. (5.2.82–83, 99)

Dying as "a Roman, by a Roman/Valiantly vanquish'd" (4.15.57–58), Antony finally becomes the performance of Rome he had tentatively resumed in Act IV. He is now the piece of work, surveyed by Cleopatra and held up to her Roman enemies. In the same scene, however, she envisions the degrading specularization of herself and Egypt's monuments:

> Shall they hoist me up,
> And show me to the shouting varletry
> Of censuring Rome? Rather a ditch in Egypt
> Be gentle grave unto me, rather on Nilus' mud
> Lay me stark-nak'd, and let the water-flies
> Blow me into abhorring: rather make
> My country's high pyramides my gibbet,
> And hang me up in chains. (5.2.55–62)

The final image combines obelisk as gallows with pyramid as tomb.

Cleopatra wants to avoid performing the role of Egypt for a Roman mob in a triumphal procession, and being performed as Egypt in its accompanying theater. She warns Iras that "Thou, an Egyptian puppet shall be shown / In Rome as well as I," where

> The quick comedians
> Extemporally will stage us, and present
> Our Alexandrian revels: Antony
> Shall be brought drunken forth, and I shall see
> Some squeaking Cleopatra boy my greatness
> I' the posture of a whore. (5.2.207–8, 215–20)

The parody of Alexandria's transgressive sexuality in Rome's theaters does not so much "contain" as perform it, doing what it undoes, to borrow Enobarbus' formulation. If Cleopatra's vivid picture is at all accurate, the "boying" of her greatness also evokes the instability of Roman desire that Octavius reads as a sign of Rome's decay, but from which he profits (1.4.44–47). She might have attained a limited revenge, perhaps, in going to Rome after all and helping it enact its own monumental subversion.

Critical differences over the representation of sexuality and gender in *Antony and Cleopatra* have assumed monumental proportions themselves. Carol Thomas Neely sees Cleopatra's evocation of an Antony whose "legs bestrid the ocean" (5.2.82) as the completion of a symmetrical structure of gender in the play: Antony's masculine power complements its "reciprocal opposite" in Cleopatra's femininity, and the intensification of gender pushes the tragic genre, associated with a masculine and barren Octavius, to its limits. Jonathan Dollimore, however, finds different sexualities where Neely locates sexual difference: "Antony becomes statuesque in a way which recalls that the statue is a literal, material embodiment of a respect for its subject which is inseparable from the obsolescence of that subject. And isn't this the apparent destiny of Antony in the play, one with which he colludes, self-sacrificially and pleasurably?"[69] Cleopatra's monumental fantasy of Antony commemorates the masochistic failure of his homosocial competition with Octavius: his world has been well lost, but not for a symmetrically heterosexual love. According to Dollimore, Antony's subversive pleasure in his own obsolescence escapes both Octavius' effort to manage his image after his death, and Neely's attempt to contain it in a repressive structure of gender opposition.

Monuments, statues, and tombs are related to the vicissitudes of gender performance described by Butler, in early modern times no less than in our own. To monumentalize oneself or someone else is to strike or unveil a pose. Sexual difference is not a symmetrical structure but a complex of such performances. The repetition of gender categories, in fact, betokens the obsolescence of cultural, and primarily familial, positions: "gender identity would be established through a refusal of loss that encrypts itself in the body and that determines, in effect, the living versus the dead body."[70] Recalling Dollimore's definition of the statuesque in her discussion of another play, however, Valerie Traub reminds us that Shakespeare's construction of gender does not lend itself readily to subversion through monumental performance: "The logic crucial to *The Winter's Tale*, I submit, is respect *because* obsolete. . . . To the extent that a statue's function is commemorative, Hermione-as-statue safely re-members, but does not em-body, the threat of female erotic power."[71] The "encryption" of the dead body in the living is not essentially transgressive. More often than not, it performs the reaffirmation of sexual difference and the containment of whatever subversive potential it possesses. This, after all, is what Butler herself calls "the situation of duress under which gender performance always and variously occurs."[72]

In early modern travel and geographical accounts, as in *Antony and Cleopatra*, ancient Egypt was figured as a land of monuments as well as a place where gender relations were inverted. Two recent volumes, Lucy Hughes-Hallett's *Cleopatra: Histories, Dreams and Distortions* and Mary Hamer's *Signs of Cleopatra: History, Politics, Representation*, take up the figure of Cleopatra in Europe since antiquity and trace its career primarily as a monumental marker of sexual rather than cultural or racial difference. Hamer's study in particular casts Cleopatra as a "sign" that simultaneously affirms and resists male power: like Neely, Hamer often contends in effect that images of Cleopatra disrupt the generic codes of masculine representation; like Dollimore, she sometimes depicts this subversiveness as realized in performance and bodily display.[73] Useful as all these approaches are, there is something missing in the history they reconstruct that the example of Shakespeare's play can help us to supply and understand. For if the narrative of degeneration does not entirely contain sexual transgression in *Antony and Cleopatra*, it nevertheless leaves the text open to appropriation by the developing racial, and ultimately imperial, system of European modernity. Cleopatra's alternative to specularization in Octavius' triumph is to become a monument in another sense, hung on the pyramids or encased in her tomb. She will be preserved as either Rhodopis or Isis, rendered a museum piece, even as Antony is scapegoated for Rome's own covert Egyptianism and current decadence.

Both the triumph and the double funeral that Octavius in fact plans for Cleopatra and Antony assimilate them to the model of a vanquished and obsolescent past, like the models of ancient Egypt in nineteenth-century French Egyptology that Edward Said relates to the staging of Verdi's *Aida*:

> Egypt had to be reconstructed in models or drawings, whose scale, projective grandeur . . . and exotic distance were truly unprecedented. . . . The most striking pages of the [Napoleonic] *Description* [*de l'Egypte*] seem to beseech some very grand actions or personages to fill them, and their emptiness and scale look like opera sets waiting to be populated. Their implied European context is a theater of power and knowledge.[74]

Antony and Cleopatra mounts a similar puppet show. It is uncertain in Plutarch's life of Antony how, or even whether, Cleopatra killed herself. Significantly, Shakespeare's version is close to the one "which it seemeth Caesar him selfe gave credit unto, because in his triumphe he caried Cleopatraes image, with an Aspicke byting of her arme" (Plutarch, "Life," pp. 87–88). A similar game with sources is played at the end of *King Lear*, only in this play the chronicle accounts of Cordelia's suicide that follow Edmund's secret message are implicitly refuted by her political murder in the drama.[75]

Shakespeare allows history to be written by the victor in *Antony and Cleopatra*, for Octavius Caesar, unlike Edmund, was a survivor. Cleopatra's performance of her death enacts the very scene that Caesar's dreaded triumph will later depict in tableau: she has become a statue, a piece of work. If we consider only the interplay between gender and sexuality, it is tempting to follow Loomba's argument that "The narrative of masculinity and imperialism regains control but Cleopatra's final performance, which certainly exposes her own vulnerability, not only cheats Caesar but denies any

final and authoritative textual closure."[76] But what if masculinity and imperialism are two separate, if related, narratives? Hamer similarly collapses
them, optimistically asserting that "the formal celebration of the Roman
state in the triumph may be reread as momentarily subverted . . . into a procession of the Egyptian goddess Isis." "It seems clear," as Hamer concludes,
"that fantasies of the body played their part" in the story of Cleopatra, but
bodily fantasies of sexual and racial difference are produced and consumed
in sharply dissimilar ways in both Shakespeare's play and the representations
of Egypt that intersect it.[77] Gender and sexuality challenge the idea of "containment" by placing its workings on display through performance, but the
performance of cultural differences consolidates the fantasy of race, rendering it monumental, making it history. Even the veneration of cultural precedence and ancient wisdom looks forward to an imperial, if not quite an
Aryan, model of Egyptian antiquity.

TWO

Milton and the Fall of Asia

The modeling of empire and monumentalizing of the past in seventeenth-century English culture were not restricted to Egypt. Models came before empires and emporiums; they bespoke an ambition that exceeded England's actual holdings or spheres of influence, and that also extended backward to the very beginning of time. In 1661, one I. H. authored a pamphlet entitled *Paradise Transplanted and Restored, in a Most Artfull and Lively Representation . . . Shown at* Christopher Whiteheads *at the two wreathed Posts in Shooe-Lane, London.* The pamphlet describes several tableaux, evidently set up in Whitehead's inn, that depicted, among other things, Adam's naming of the animals:

> The Design, is a Model, or Representation of that Beautiful Prospect *Adam* had in Paradice, when the whole Creation of *Animals*, were together subjected to his imperious eye, and from his mouth received their several names, distinguished by them to those particular subservient Offices whereunto by Nature they were Ordained.[1]

The model of Paradise, restored along with the Stuart court, offered to any paying customer the latest "researches and enquiries after Foraign, Outlandish Creatures, whose names are not so well known to these Quarters of the World . . . that every man may be as wise as *Adam*, and read their names and qualities in their Aspects" (p. 2). Eve's encounter with the serpent and the apple was also represented: the masculine domination of the world through language was counterpointed by another form of orality, the feminine consumption of its temptations.

The display included realistic figures of the members of its target audience: "On the left side of the Room, are five beautifull Ladies seated, beholding these curiosities, a person of quality standing by them, attended with three Blackmore Lacquees in rich blew Liveries" (p. 4). The seated ladies and the black footmen in their rich cloth signify that England's gradual incorporation of the world was accomplished through hierarchies of gender, class, and race, and that it was fueled through the growth of a culture of consumption.[2] The show at Whitehead's inn anticipates on a small scale the vast nineteenth-century panoramas and exhibitions described by Walter Benjamin: "In the panoramas the city dilates to become a landscape. . . . The world exhibitions glorify the exchange of commodities. They create a framework in which the commodities' intrinsic value is eclipsed. They open up a phantasmagoria that people enter to be amused. . . . They submit to being manipulated while enjoying their alienation from themselves and others."[3] *Paradise Transplanted* and the exhibition it commemorates or advertises are part of the para-colonial rationality, both aristocratic and commercial, that informed learned works on antiquity and popular travel accounts consumed by a domestic audience, all intended "to please the wandering eyes of the Spectators" (p. 2).

John Milton, blind and recently released from the custody of Parliament's Serjeant at Arms, could not have shared in the wonderment that Whitehead's spectacle apparently aroused in the inhabitants of Charles II's London. Although *Paradise Lost* did not appear in its initial ten-book version until 1667, the epic's title might be read as an admonition to the new regime's projectors, and perhaps to Whitehead in particular. And Milton's description of the destruction of the garden of Eden in the Flood extends this critique; I quote here from a text based on the twelve-book edition of 1674:

> then shall this Mount
> Of Paradise by might of Waves be mov'd
> Out of his place, push'd by the horned flood,
> With all his verdure spoil'd, and Trees adrift
> Down the great River to the op'ning Gulf,
> And there take root an Island salt and bare,
> The haunt of Seals and Orcs, and Sea-mews' clang.
> To teach thee that God áttributes to place
> No sanctity, if none be thither brought
> By Men who there frequent, or therein dwell.[4]

Paradise, unlike Charles, cannot be restored and transplanted, in Shoe Lane or anywhere else.

There is a vast literature on the exact location, past and present, of Eden and its garden or Earthly Paradise, dating from antiquity. But before we can understand the place of *Paradise Lost* both in this tradition and its own times, it is necessary to examine the way it constructs Mesopotamia, Assyria, and neighboring places in general. Milton's depiction of the garden of Eden, which once "gave prospect large" over Adam's "nether Empire" (4:144–45) but which now survives as an island salt and bare in the Persian Gulf, is bound up with a wider European discourse on Southwest Asia. Asia is a holy land, the seat of human community and civilization, but also a land condemned to a perpetual cycle of imperial rise and fall heralded by the primal Fall itself. Throughout *Paradise Lost*, Milton locates the decadence of empire in the East while simultaneously criticizing the imperial ambitions of the restored Stuart monarchy in the growing metropolis of London.[5]

I

This chapter, like the previous one, is about a wide range of historical and travel writings as much as it is about a particular literary work. In the following section, I intend to outline a framework of European texts that progressively model Southwest Asia in European culture up to the seventeenth century, rather than provide a narrow array of sources and analogues for *Paradise Lost*. Contemporary travel accounts and a geographical tradition rooted in antiquity both stress the centrality of Babylon and its supposed heir, Baghdad, to the narrative of secular glory and decline that Milton's epic also shares in. The Egerton translation of the fourteenth-century book of travels attributed to John Mandeville contains an account of Babylon that serves as a paradigm for the fallen and faulty empires of the postlapsarian landscape he traverses. Here we read of

> the great Babylon, where the confusion of tongues was made, when the Tower of Babylon was in making; the walls of the which were sixty four furlongs high, and it is in the deserts of Arabia, as men go toward the kingdom of Chaldea. But it is long since any durst come near that wretched place; for it is waste and so full of dragons and nedders [adders] and other venomous beasts. . . . This ilk tower made Nemprot [Nimrod], that was king of that land; and men say that he was the first earthly king that ever was.[6]

Mandeville is recalling Isaiah 13:19–22, where the fall of Babylon and its occupation by dragons and wild beasts is prophesied. The destruction of the Tower of Babel and the later overthrow of the Babylonian empire in the Bible are conflated here and further juxtaposed with Cyrus' conquest of the city.[7] The biblical and classical traditions both ascribe the rise and fall of Asia's empires to a cycle of vainglory and destruction, whether militarily or divinely accomplished.

There are two Babylons in Mandeville and other early modern texts: in a doubling typical of medieval geography, Cairo and the Mesopotamian city were both known by the same name, a parallel that maps the Egyptian and Asian cycles of empire and decay onto each other. To make matters even more complicated, the Mesopotamian Babylon was often confused with Baghdad—founded relatively recently, in the eighth century, by the 'Abbasid dynasty that ruled Southwest Asia until the fall of its capital to the Mongols in 1258.[8] Henri de Feynes, for instance, insisted on identifying the two places despite their different locations: "This Citty, which now the Turkes call *Bagdat*, is at this present scituate vpon the Riuer *Tigris*, and not vpon *Euphrates*, as aunciently it was; though it bee still the selfe same stuffe and rubbish, which the *Babilonians* carried foure leagues further, to rebuild their CITTIE."[9] Mandeville keeps Babylon and Baghdad apart, and Marco Polo does not even mention the ancient metropolis. Polo attests that Baghdad is a very great city, but he goes on to tell a story about the Mongol invasion, also found in Mandeville, in which the Great Khan Hulagu starved the Caliph in a tower filled with his own gold.[10] We are far from the Babel story here, but this legend about another tower extends the ancient association of the region with fabulous wealth and inevitable conquest.

Herodotus serves as the father of this association as of so much else. In his first book he tells how Cyrus reduced Babylon: the Persian king partially diverted the Euphrates, reducing its level as it flowed through the city so that his troops could enter where the river did. The city was so large that its suburbs were secured long before the people at the center received the news.[11] Herodotus provides the measurements of its walls and the temple of Bel, the Zeus of the Babylonians, whose priestess, it is rumored, shares her bed with the god at the apex of its stepped pyramid. Despite his skepticism about this, the historian goes on to condemn the more visible practice of temple prostitution among Babylonian women (p. 57 recto). He records the role played by women rulers in the construction of the city, mentioning Semiramis and dwelling on Nitocris, whose tomb above one of its mighty gates was inscribed with an invitation to future rulers to raid it for money in time of need. Darius did so and only found another inscription mocking him for violating the dead (pp. 58 recto–59 verso). As in his influential account of the Egyptian pyramids, monumental structures are closely affiliated with women's bodies in Herodotus' descriptions of non-Greek cultures. Nitocris, as he recounts elsewhere, was also the name of an Egyptian queen associated with underground spaces (p. 95 recto).

Diodorus Siculus makes Semiramis the founder of Babylon and the builder of its temple to Jupiter Belus.[12] He links one of the city's wonders to another woman as well: "There was also near to one of the Castles or Palaces, a Garden hanging as it were in the Air, not made by *Semyramis*, but afterwards, by a King named *Siris*, at the request of a Concubine of his, who being a *Persian*, and desiring to see Meadows on Mountains, after the manner of her Country, perswaded the man to frame a Garden by Art, that might in trees and Meadows represent the Region of *Persia*" (p. 76). The Hanging Gardens, long an emblem of extravagant Asian power, represent the incorporation of the country in the city, or colonial space in the metropolis. They are a monument to empire, and a model of empire as landscape—a feminine landscape in Diodorus' anecdote. A woman's desire is revealed behind the wonder; moreover, the woman is a concubine rather than a queen, and a gendered narrative of decline has already set in.

Subsequent authors would question Semiramis' own role in Babylonian history, depicting her as the very type of feminine oriental luxury. Among the moderns, however, Walter Ralegh continued to sing her praises in his *History of the World*, the immense work that crowned both his life as a voyager and the period's subgenre of global chronicles and geographical descriptions. "*Ninus finished Niniue, Semiramis Babylon*," he wrote, "wherein shee sought to exceed her husband by farre."[13] To Ralegh, she was a vigorous and expansive ruler as well as a builder of cities. Semiramis represents the drive toward imperial totality that Ralegh himself had experienced in his Guiana ventures—not wholly admirable according to his Christian lights, perhaps, but justified through the force of his prose:

> Indeed in the first Age when Princes were moderate, they neither thought how to inuade others, nor feared to be inuaded: labouring to build Townes and Villages for the vse of themselues and their people without either Walles or Towers. . . . But *Semiramis* liuing in that age, when Ambition was in strong youth: and purposing to follow the conquest which her husband had vndertaken, gaue that beauty and strength to *Babylon* which it had. (p. 213)

With a backward glance at Queen Elizabeth, Ralegh boldly allegorizes empire through a female figure. His allegory looks to the future too. Semiramis beautifies as well as reinforces her city, making it into a metropolis that turns outward from itself and its immediate needs. European women, cast in the ambiguous role of consumers, were similarly enlisted in the imperial project throughout the seventeenth century. Luxury becomes the beauty that accompanies strength in the exemplary figure of Ralegh's Semiramis; "for her vitious life," he remarks, "I ascribe the report thereof to the enuious and lying *Grecians*" (p. 215).

Ralegh not only denigrates the Greeks, early losers in the game of world domination; he also gives Semiramis' people cultural precedence over the Egyptians, whose pyramids, he asserts, were imitations of the temple of Bel, from which the Babylonians observed the heavens (p. 216). Despite the continued esteem for Egyptian learning, respect for Mesopotamia was also a feature of Europe's plural notion of antiquity before the eighteenth century. According to Johannes Boemus' popular compendium of strange customs,

> those auncient Philosophers of Greece and Italy, which were first founders of sundry sects wherin they instructed their Disciples & Schollers, . . . and many others which wee see haue set down to their people diuers prescript ceremonies & ciuil disciplines: inuented not of those seueral sects, disciplines and lawes, within their city walles, but learned and brought them from the Caldeans themselues (beeing the most wise men of the world) from the Indian Philosophers, the Brackmans & Gymnosophists, and from the Aegiptian Priests, with whom sometimes they were conuersant.[14]

The order is important: Boemus places the Chaldeans before the Indians and the Egyptians in this passage. They were often credited with the invention of arithmetic and astronomy in particular; Diodorus attests to the expertise and antiquity of the Chaldean priests in the study of the stars, but also notes the Egyptian claim to have established their priesthood as a colony in Babylon (pp. 99, 14–15).

For Christian authors like Boemus and Ralegh, the advantage of recognizing the Chaldeans' priority lay in Mesopotamia's position in biblical history. The patriarch Abraham, of course, had come from the Chaldean town of Ur, and Lodowick Lloyd builds much on this in his world history *The Consent of Time*:

> for the *Egyptians* and the *Phoenicians* long after the flood, were taught by the *Chaldeans* of the flood, and of the former time, and after more perfectly instructed by *Abraham*, which in the time of famine trauailed from *Canaan* into *Egypt*, where for a time hee read Arithmeticke to the *Egyptians*, then rude and ignorant of any great knowledge, that hearing of these things, they beganne very obscurely and darkely to set down many things which they then not perfectly knewe, and yet are vnperfect, for that they were ignorant of the Genesis.[15]

In his *Briefe Description* of the world, George Abbot credits the Chaldeans with the invention of astronomy, and reasons that Isaiah condemned them only when their knowledge of the stars was corrupted by superstition.[16] Robert Stafford, another describer of the world, writes of Asia in general,

"The inhabitants of it, are generally very wittie, for from hence sprang all the Sciences which the Greekes haue learned of the Hebrewes."[17] Lloyd explains: "in the last years of the kings of *Assyrians* histories, the *Grecians* began: for this vnderstand, that the *Caldeans, Assyrians, Egyptians*, and all the East part of the world, which were first inhabited after the flood, were euen consumed with sworde and fire, before the *Grecians* or the *Romanes* were acquainted with the world, and therefore the lesse to be spoken of the olde auncient people for want of authorities" (pp. 124–25). In other words, an immense, partly lost history antedated the very beginnings of Graeco-Roman memory, a history that early modern authors strove to recover and control, through a sort of Renaissance of antiquarian scholarship within the Renaissance.

Why did Chaldean history come to an end? Lloyd's "sworde and fire" is confirmed by Diodorus, who writes that Babylon was left in ruins by the Persians (p. 76). But why should Babylon remain in decline? A century later, Pliny offers a different reason for its condition: "the cittie of Babylon, the capitall citie of all the Chaldean nations, for a long time carried a great name over all the world. . . . As yet to this day the temple of *Iupiter Belus* there standeth entire. This prince was the first inventer of Astronomie. It is now growne into decay and lieth wast and unpeopled, by reason that Seleucia the cittie standeth so neere it, which hath drawne from it all resort and traffick."[18] Built by one of Alexander's generals, Seleucia weakened and eventually replaced Babylon within the region's economic system. Commercial competition from a new city, rather than simple conquest, is responsible for Babylon's continued ruination, despite its antiquity and wisdom. Pliny's explanation delineates the economics of empire in a manner that European writers would take up much later.

Before we can understand the economics of empire in early modern Europe, however, we must appreciate how it was tinged by a new sense of religious difference alien to the ancient world. The sevententh-century chronicler John Speed ties economic prosperity to religion in his *Prospect of the Most Famous Parts of the World*. "The method propounded in our generall description of the world, giues *Asia* the prerogatiue, as well for worth as time," he writes, noting that the first people came from Mesopotamia, where God himself deigned to walk and the earliest empires also sprang up. "Howeuer," Speed continues, "now it is left (for her Infidelity) to the pun-

ishment of a Propheticall curse that long before past vpon her: & is deli-
uered vp into the hands of *Turkes* and Nations that blaspheme their Creator;
and therefore doth not flourish in that height as heretofore."[19] Southwest
Asia, in fact, was hardly in economic crisis under the Ottoman Turks during
the sixteenth and seventeenth centuries, a period in which its population almost doubled. Even Baghdad, eclipsed since the tenth century, remained
relatively prosperous despite the diversion of trade to the Red Sea and Cape
of Good Hope routes.[20]

Speed paints a very different picture. Although Asia is the origin of
human life and larger than Europe and Africa combined, "to which shee was
the Mistresse for Arts and Sciences," the continent is underpopulated and
overrun with savage animals and serpents due to God's righteous anger, who
"hath suffered (as it were) her own creatures, ouer which at first man had
the rule, to turne head vpon their Lords, and possesse their habitation." But
if Asia is an unfaithful and barren woman under Islam, she remains fertile
and inviting to Europeans: "In this though the Nation suffer for their monstrous irreligion: yet the earth which did not offend reserues her place, and
abounds with many excellent Commodities, not els-where to be had,
Myrrhe, Frankincense, Cinnamon, Cloues, Nutmegs" (Speed, p. 3).

Speed's expansion of Isaiah's curse upon Babylon to include all of Asia
nevertheless does not fall upon its valuable commodities, which remain to
tempt his readers with images of potential wealth. Asia is depicted as an un-
derexploited territory with a glorious past. Its record of conquering and
being conquered, closely intertwined with Christendom's own prehistory,
serves as an examplar of imperial domination; the area's current economic
and cultural decline, real and imagined, may turn the cursed barrier of Islam
into a blessing for those willing to lay claim to a lost paradise.

For the cycle of conquests that traditionally defines and delimits empire in
the European prospect of Asia can be extended to include Europe's conquest
of the continent. Lloyd expresses the commonplace of cyclical destruction in
a passage whose cadences will become familiar in seventeenth-century surveys
of the region:

> Thus *Assyria* sometime subiect to *Chaldea*, and *Chaldea* to *Assyria*: *Nineui* to
> *Babylon*, and *Babylon* to *Niniue*, vntill both were subdued by the *Medes*, and
> after by the *Persians*: so God doth appoint, and God doth disappoint states

and common wealthes, according to the decree of his eternall will, sinne being the onely cause of Gods anger and wrath, his wrath the cause of all calamities, destruction, and subuersion of kingdomes. (p. 103)

Another writer, John Cartwright, echoes some of Lloyd's moralizing but extends the chain of conquest closer to the present in his book *The Preachers Travels*. He concludes his description of Babylon by asking,

what is become of this proud city, which once held the world in awe? Where are her conduits, the rarenesse of her bathes, the hugenesse of her towers, the greatnesse of her Temples, the beauty of her princely palaces, & a number of other monuments of her kings vanities? Alas! time hath worne them out. . . . For first she was subdued by the *Medes*, then by the *Persians*; after by the *Grecians*, then by the *Saracens*; then by the *Tartars*, after that by the *Persians* againe: & now by the *Turkes*. So Go doth appoint, and God doth disapoint states and commonwealthes.[21]

The passage continues with the same words found in Lloyd's much earlier text. Cartwright also echoes, or is echoed by, Ralegh, who writes of Nineveh that "it is agreed by all prophane writers, and confirmed by the Scriptures, that it exceedeth all other in circuit, and answerable magnificence" (Ralegh, p. 213). In Cartwright the sentence runs "It is agreed by all prophane writers, and confirmed by the Scriptures, that this citty exceeded all other citties in circuit, and answerable magnificence" (Cartwright, p. 89). Ralegh's *History of the World* was published after Cartwright's *Preachers Travels* but entered in the Stationers' Register before it, early in 1611; both books were printed by Stansby, and some cross-pollination of manuscripts may have occurred. A common source could be responsible for their shared phrasing, but just as the traveler Cartwright borrowed from the historian Lloyd, so the historian Ralegh could well have borrowed in turn from Cartwright. Whatever the explanation, the interpenetration of these several texts demonstrates the mutual dependence of travel writing and antiquarianism during the period.

The criterion of eyewitness veracity in Cartwright's epistemology of travel causes him to rearrange some elements in the antiquarian tradition. Assyria was the location of the first monarchy in the world, "yet since, it hath endured so many mutations and changes by the outrage of armies, . . .

I will be sparing to write thereof, least I should write many things rather fabulous then true, and therefore laying aside the danger of lying, I will passe vnto those townes and ruines which I haue seene" (p. 87). History and landscape are altered; some features are emphasized and others repressed as Cartwright picks out the ruins of a region that "hath lost her ancient name." The continual warfare attributed to Assyria and Southwest Asia in general creates an anxiety about historical truth that justifies the deformation of traditional knowledge about the past in a blur of serial conquest.

The deformation or defacing of traditional knowledge in Cartwright's travel narrative is figured through the assimilation of the region's monumental antiquities to the vulnerable human body. In his description of a ruin known to Christian pilgrims as Daniel's castle, he describes how "time hath worne it out, it faring with buildings as with mens bodies, they waxe old, and are infeebled by yeares, and loose their beautie: neuerthelesse *Ecbatana* now called *Tauris* remaines in great glorie vnto this day" (p. 43). In the similar case of Nineveh, once "the Lady of the East, the Queene of Nations," biblical prophecy is cited to explain its current state: "now it is destroyed (as God foretold it should be by the Chaldaeans) being nothing else, then a sepulture of her self, a litle towne of small trade, where the *Patriarch* of the *Nestorians* keeps his seate, at the deuotion of the Turkes" (pp. 90–91). The body of Nineveh has become its own tomb, doubly violated by heretical Christianity and the invasion of Islam.

It is significant that Nineveh's disfigurement has also made it "a litle town of small trade." This is the language of commercial observation and appraisal; Cartwright may have entitled his book *The Preachers Travels*, but he often sounds more like a merchant. As occurs so often in both historical and travel accounts, the Babylon-Baghdad complex draws forth the most intricate mixture of historical and economic description:

> *Bagdat* is very aboundantly furnished with all kinde of prouision both of corne, flesh, fowle, fish, and venison of all sorts; besides great store of fruit, but especially of dates, and that very cheape. This citty by some is called new *Babilon*, and may well be, because it did rise out of the ruines of old *Babilon*, not farre distant, being nothing so great, nor so faire: for it conteines in circuit but three English miles; . . . In a word, this towne was once a place of great trade and profit, by reason of the huge Carauans, which

were wont to come from *Persia* and *Balsara*: but since the *Portugalls*, *Englishmen*, and *Hollanders*, haue by their traffique into the *East-Indies*, cut off almost all the trade of Marchandize into the gulfs of *Arabia* and *Persia*, both *Grand Cairo* in *Egipt*, and *Bagdat* in *Assyria*, are not now of that bene-fit, as they haue beene, either to the merchant, or great Turke. (p. 96)

The passage merits lengthy quotation as an example of how commercial ob-servation overlays traditional knowledge, turning history into a palimpsest.

Like Speed, Cartwright begins by noting the resources of the place he de-scribes, converting Baghdad into a list of exploitable commodities, including its inexpensive dates. And like Pliny long before, he ends by attributing the decline of the region's metropolis to the economic vicissitudes of imperial competition. Texts such as Cartwright's mark a growing perception that empire was potentially a matter of commercial influence, of markets and trading networks, rather than absolute territorial control and military occu-pation. Unlike Pliny, who found a neighboring city's rise enough to eclipse Babylon, Cartwright uncovers a more elaborate tableau, in which the im-proved technology of European navigation outpaces the economic culture of the caravan routes, diminishing Cairo at one end of the Ottoman Empire and Baghdad at the other while Portugal, England, and Holland compete for the Indian market. In this context, Cartwright's granting of the name "New Babylon" is almost ironic. Built from the ruins of an increasingly irrelevant past, Baghdad is scarcely three "English" miles in circumference; formerly the center of Asia, and of the Old World's leading economic system, it has been subsumed by new economic conditions and the discourse that accom-panies them—becoming, like Nineveh, a town of small trade.

A similar mixture of homely observation and commercial rationality is found in the writings of another author, Thomas Herbert, who during the 1630s published two quite different versions of his travels through the Ottoman Empire. In the first, he describes Baghdad as a city "of no great wonder, her circuit and building equall to a *cazbeen*, rage and time giues her nothing to boast of, but her memory, but the Bridge is eminent in her, so is her *Buzzar* and the *Sultans* Palace and Gardens, more large then louely, of more Quantitie than vse, shewing no more artificiall strength, wealth, or beautie then neighboring and late start-vp-townes about her."[22] Baghdad has been reduced to her citadel and her market through rage and time. In the rewritten account Herbert familiarizes the city rather than emphasizing its foreignness: "*Bagdat*, at this day scarce equalls *Bristow* in bulk or beauty: the circuit may be three miles and better, including fifteene thousand families. It is watered by *Tigris* call'd *Diglat* and *Dyguilah*, somewhat broader than the Thames, but not so navigable nor gentle."[23] The later version compares Baghdad with Bristol and London rather than the local towns that compete with it for trade and commerce. Herbert is beginning to link English and Asian trading centers in a system, as symbolic or discursive as anything else, that makes English cities the metropolitan standard against which the "start-up" economies of Asia are measured.

Herbert's depiction of the culturally old as economically new presages the ideology of underdevelopment in the modern world. In the later edition of his travels he describes the ancient city of Persepolis, but breaks off his enumeration of its wealth and grandeur in bygone days to ask "why stand we gaping at these prodigious sums. . . . For my part (by Gods help) I intend rather to admire the Anatomy of this glorious ruine, . . . the only Monument of the world, without imposture." Herbert typifies a shift in interest from antiquity, whose marvels one can gape at only metaphorically, to its ruins, visible in the present even if "Miserable in my poore description" (*Travels*, p. 144). Long before the Romantic Era, Europeans cultivated a fascination with ruins, increasingly valued for the nostalgic aura they seemingly presented rather than as documents of past civilizations. Herbert imagines a painting of Persepolis as he saw it: "But such at this day it is, that a ready Lymner in three moneths space can hardly (to do it well) depict out all her excellencies. Pitty it is, it is not done, the barbarous people every day defacing it and cleaving it assunder for gravestones and benches to sit upon" (*Travels*, p. 146). The traveler fears that the ruins will be ruined and desires a simulacrum of them, a portrait that will compensate for their "defacing" by the local inhabitants. The "barbarous" people make practical use of past materials, recycling them as part of a living, if discontinous, cultural history in the region; they also obliterate the traces of the past in the process of living it out into the present. To Herbert they "little know or value memory," a universal memory or world history for which the European observer claims to act as a custodian (*Relation*, p. 60).

The travel narratives of the seventeenth century add both ruins and ruinating "peoples," native but also somehow illegitimate, to the antique landscape that we find in the various books of geographical, customary, and historical knowledge. The protective idealization of ruins for their own sake casts the contemporary cultures of the area in a barbaric light, while allowing the traveler to stake out the global past for economic development in the present. But with idealization there came anxiety about the origins and authenticity of the monumental traces that travelers discovered and rediscovered.

Significantly, one of the central monuments in the traditional descriptions of the area makes a disappointing appearance in Herbert's accounts. The supposed remains of the Tower of Babel are recalled as "a grosse confused Mount, which Tradition only assures vs of, was part of *Nimrods* Tower the [*sic*] place seemes bigger at distance then neere at hand, slimy bricks and morter are digged out of it: which are all the liuing testimonials of this monument" (*Relation*, p. 139). In the second edition, Herbert doubts that the pile was the famous tower at all, and conjectures that it might be "the ruine of that monstrous Temple, which was erected by *Semyramis* in honour of *Bell* or *Iupiter Belus*" (*Travels*, p. 220). Ralegh writes, "By beholding the ruines of this Tower haue many Trauailers beene deceiued; who suppose that they haue seene a parte of *Nimrods* Tower, when it was but the Foundation of this Temple of *Bel*: (except this of *Bel* were founded on that of *Nimrod*)" (p. 216). One traveler who was not deceived was Cartwright, from whom Ralegh may again be borrowing here. Cartwright provides a comparable meditation on the sense of historical instability that monumental ruins paradoxically foster: "many trauellers haue bin deceiued, who suppose that they haue seene a part of that tower which *Nimrod* builded. But who can tel whether it be the one or the other? It may bee that confused Chaos which we saw, was the ruines of both, the Temple of *Bel* being founded on that of *Nimrod*" (p. 101). The putative site of Babel is more gross and confused than the lost original might have been, a simulacral ruin whose slimy bricks are sanctified only by tradition. As the Italian Cesare Federici and other travelers also noticed, the ruins seem larger the farther you are from them, a visual trick that serves as a figure for tradition and its distortions.[24]

II

The travelers' doubts about Babel show how skepticism toward a ruined past accompanied the veneration of antiquity in the historical and geographical material, a familiar pattern that suited Milton well. The Tower of Babel is the paradigm of all monuments and their ruins in *Paradise Lost*. The Babel tradition was renewed in Peter Heylyn's *Cosmographie in Four Books*, which went through six editions between 1652 and 1670 and exercised a considerable influence upon Milton. The *Cosmographie* was an encyclopedic compendium of antiquarian and travel descriptions of the continents and was heavily dependent upon many of the geographical writings I have already discussed in its treatment of Asia. According to Heylyn, "immediately after the Universal deluge, *Nimrod* the Son of *Chus*, the son of *Cham*, perswaded the people to secure themselves from the like after-claps, by building some stupendious Edifice. . . . The major part prevailing, the Tower began to rear a head of Majesty, 5146 paces from the ground."[25] In Heylyn's account, the Tower's "head of Majesty" becomes a figure for sovereignty and ultimately for empire. Nimrod's military power was established through a system of lesser towers: "By these strong forts he curbed the native, and assured his power; being the first that altered the Paternall form of Government, and drew unto himself the government of severall. Nations [*sic*], not having any dependance upon one another. The foundation thus laid by him, his successors soon raised the building to a wondrous height; advancing the *Assyrian* Empire, from the *Mediterranean* Sea, to the River *Indus*" (p. 792). Babel might have been destroyed, but it lives on as a metaphor of empire, by which "the native" is curbed and monarchy established. Yet the compositor's error unknowingly marks an unexpected ambivalence toward such an archetype of "the Paternall form of Government." Does empire consist in the government of several nations, or are nations and their peoples properly independent of one another in a fallen world?

In establishing Milton's extensive debt to Heylyn, Robert Ralston Cawley remarked, "It may be taken as another example of Milton's broadmindedness that he was willing to accept Heylyn as an authority in matters of geography when he disagreed with him about so many of the fundamental issues in life."[26] But Milton may precisely have been attracted by the turbulence surrounding the origins of domination even in such a frankly royalist and imperial project as Heylyn's *Cosmographie*.

Heylyn recurs to the cycle of imperial rise and decline several times in his chapter on Southwest Asia. He begins by paying tribute to the honor of its antiquity as the site of the garden of Eden and the first great monarchies of the world, but progressively emphasizes its degeneration (p. 640). "As is the Countrey, such the People, the most *Adjective* of any we have met with hitherto," Heylyn asserts of the Mesopotamians, able at no time to stand by themselves, but still requiring the addition of some neighbour Nation to be joyned unto them. Nothing that they can call their own, their Name, their Language, nor their Countrey. . . . Their Countrey successively subjected to the *Babylonians, Assyrians*[,] *Medes,* and *Persians.* From them first conquered by the *Romans,* under the conduct of *Pompey*; reduced into the form of a Province, by the Emperour *Trajan*; more fully setled and confirmed by *Aurelianus.* But being recovered by the *Persians,* they fell together into the power of the *Saracens,* and are now commanded by the *Turks.* (p. 789)

The Persian conquest of Assyria established an overly absolute form of rule that weakened subsequent generations: "never endeavoring to assert in the way of war, or opposition, either their ancient reputation, or their native liberties; but suffering themselves to be won, lost, fought for, and again recovered by their quarrelsome Masters, as if they had not title to their own Countrey, but were born to follow the fortunes of all Pretenders" (p. 749). The subjection of "the native" is really self-imposed, the abdication of an ancient reputation for civilization and liberty that only an outside observer can partially reclaim through scholarship and travel.

Heylyn's twist on the conquest cycle and his invocation of native liberties may have caught Milton's attention. The virtual panorama of Book 12 of *Paradise Lost* brings a number of issues in the tradition to a head. After the Flood, Michael tells Adam, people will live "Long time in peace by Families and Tribes / Under paternal rule" (12:23–24). Here it is Milton who seems to prefer the paternal form of government, even though his bucolic picture of a society whose members lead their lives with "*some* regard to what is just and right" out of their fear of God is somewhat ironic (12:16; my emphasis). When Adam is told of Nimrod's rise to power as the builder of Babel, he is "fatherly displeas'd" that his descendant should usurp the "Dominion absolute" of God, who "human left from human free" (12:63–71). But Michael reminds Adam that he should not attempt to reason from an unfallen to a fallen state:

> Justly thou abhorr'st
> That Son, who on the quiet state of men
> Such trouble brought, affecting to subdue
> Rational Liberty; yet know withal,
> Since thy original lapse, true Liberty

Is lost, which always with right Reason dwells
Twinn'd, and from her hath no dividual being;
Reason in man obscur'd, or not obey'd,
Immediately inordinate desires
And upstart Passions catch the Government
From Reason, and to servitude reduce
Man till then free. (12:79–90)

Adam's paternal anger exemplifies how passion overtakes reason; that Michael calls it just shows how some form of paternal authority among humans is unfortunately necessary in a postlapsarian world. Yet the archangel goes further, explaining that God subjects people to violent lords who constrain their outer freedom because they allow their passions to dominate the inward freedom of reason: "Tyranny must be, / Though to the Tyrant thereby no excuse" (12:95–96). Perhaps Heylyn's Mesopotamians and Assyrians can be forgiven for failing to assert their ancient liberties, for real liberty is no longer available to any of us; we are all caught up in a cycle of conquest and voluntary servitude.

Milton brings these matters closer to home by implicitly comparing Nimrod with the Stuart monarchs, just as he had explicitly paralleled the traditional founder of Babel and tyranny with Charles I in *Eikonoklastes* (p. 814). Nimrod, who is not named in Milton's text, is described as a hunter, following Genesis 10:9:

Hunting (and Men not Beasts shall be his game)
With War and hostile snare such as refuse
Subjection to his Empire tyrannous:
A mighty Hunter thence he shall be styl'd
Before the Lord, as in despite of Heav'n,
Or from Heav'n claiming second Sovranty;
And from Rebellion shall derive his name,
Though of Rebellion others he accuse. (12:30–37)

Charles, like his father, James I, was particularly associated with the royal sport of hunting, which here comes to represent the tyrant's usurping extension of man's dominion over animals to one man's dominion over other men, "before" the Lord (12:666–70). Charles' "name," as Stevie Davies has pointed out, was derived, like the title of all English rulers since 1066, from the right of conquest—for Milton a false right based on rebellion; more directly, Nimrod's name was taken by commentators to mean "rebel."[27] Charles accused his opponents of rebellion, but like Satan he occupied the bad eminence of rebellion himself. The grammatical subject of the phrase "And from Rebellion shall derive his name" is "name" and not the unnamed ruler; neither Nimrod nor Charles is in control of this complex of royal ascriptions.

Milton's anti-royalism, then, links empire to the loss of human liberty in Eden on the one hand, and to the particular loss of English liberty under Stuart tyranny on the other. The mediating term here is Babel, and it is important that it not become the vanishing mediator. For Milton's anti-imperialism has its limits. There is no excuse for tyrants, yet as we have seen, tyranny must be. The passage continues:

> Yet sometimes Nations will decline so low
> From virtue, which is reason, that no wrong,
> But Justice, and some fatal curse annext
> Deprives them of thir outward liberty,
> Thir inward lost: Witness th'irreverent Son
> Of him who built the Ark, who for the shame
> Done to his Father, heard this heavy curse,
> *Servant of Servants*, on his vicious Race. (12:97–104)

Ham, a transgressive son like Nimrod, is also justly abhorred, and his violation of paternal rule condemns his vicious African descendants to servitude. Milton is a poet against empire, but he also stigmatizes the East as the origin of empire while refusing to exclude the corrective role that dominion plays in a fallen world.

A closer look at Milton's description of the construction of Babel itself will establish the place of *Paradise Lost* within the geographical and antiquarian tradition of Asian empire. Nimrod,

> with a crew, whom like Ambition joins
> With him or under him to tyrannize,
> Marching from *Eden* towards the West, shall find
> The Plain, wherein a black bituminous gurge
> Boils out from under ground, the mouth of Hell. (12:40–42)

Having left Eden, the site of a Paradise that no longer exists, Nimrod's army finds itself at the doorstep of a terrestrial Hell. They are traversing the same landscape described by Heylyn:

> though in general the Countrey was extremely fruitful, yet in some places was it covered with a slimy matter, which the overflowing of the waters, and the nature of the soil together, did bring forth abundantly. Used by them in their buildings, instead of morter, then which more durable and binding; and therefore chosen for the cement of the Tower of *Babel*, Gen.11.3. Some also tell . . . of a like open place near a Town called *Ait*, which continually throweth out boiling pitch (named therefore *Hell-mouth* by the *Moors*) filling therewith the adjoyning fields; and that herewith the people use to pitch their boats. (p. 784)

Heylyn is probably borrowing most directly from Cartwright, who similarly tells of a place called Ait three days away from Babylon: "The Moors call it, the mouth of hell" (pp. 105–6). The Babel builders in Milton's version use the local bitumen to construct their "City and Tow'r" of brick, as Josephus had asserted and the eyewitness Cartwright had recently confirmed: "It was built of burnt bricke cimented and ioyned with bituminous mortar" (p. 100). Milton's tacit incorporation of the Moorish epithet "the mouth of Hell" places his version of the Babel story on the contemporary map of Southwest Asia as well as in a lost antiquity.

Milton was well aware that this map was dotted with ruined monuments. God's reason for ruining Babel is described in terms that at first sight seem strange, and at second seem even more strange. The Lord "Comes down to see thir City, ere the Tower / Obstruct Heav'n Tow'rs" (12:51–52). The reference to towers in Heaven being obstructed by the earthly tower is unexpected, even if it fits with the biblical deity's apparent fear that the builders will now be able to do anything that they imagine (Gen. 11:6). Heaven's buildings have been mentioned before—their leading architect was the rebel angel Mulciber:

> his hand was known
> In Heav'n by many a Tow'red structure high,
> Where Scepter'd Angels held thir residence.
>
> . . . .

> nor aught avail'd him now
> To have built in Heav'n high Tow'rs; nor did he scape
> By all his Engines, but was headlong sent
> With his industrious crew to build in hell.
> (1:732–34, 748–51)

This passage comes from the description of Pandemonium, the demonic monument that to a great extent lies behind Milton's Babel. The "crew" of builders in hell looks forward to Nimrod's crew at hell's mouth, and their palace is specifically compared to "*Babel*, and the works of *Memphian* Kings" (1:694):

> Not *Babylon*,
> Nor great *Alcairo* such magnificence
> Equall'd in all thir glories, to enshrine
> *Belus* or *Serapis* thir Gods, or seat
> Thir Kings, when *Egypt* with *Assyria* strove
> In wealth and luxury. (1:717–22)

The builders of Babel repeat Satan's defiance in constructing their own version of Pandemonium, and the later monumental works of eastern empire continue this rebellion.

For Nimrod's crew are monument builders, who seek to "get themselves a name, lest far disperst / In foreign lands thir memory be lost" (12:45–46). One wonders what the concept of "foreign" might have meant when the whole earth was of one language and one speech. It is revealed here to be the product of a metropolitan attitude that seeks to differentiate itself from others while maintaining its preeminence, rather than the result of a natural diversity of peoples. That the inevitable dispersal is brought about through the differentiation of language compounds the irony of the namelessness of Nimrod and his people in Milton's text. Babel itself is named, but only indirectly: "thus was the building left / Ridiculous, and the work Confusion nam'd" (12:61–62). Later it is equated with "that proud City, whose high Walls thou saw'st / Left in confusion, *Babylon* thence call'd" (12:342–43). Milton resists the growing cult of ruins in the seventeenth century; following Cartwright, Ralegh, and Herbert, he finds ridiculous confusion at the site of Babel, rather than the nostalgic evocation of a lost imperial past.

Milton also sees the religions of antiquity as absurd and chaotic. The comparison of Pandemonium to the temples of Belus and Serapis in Book 1 is preceded by a catalogue of other idols. The Babel pattern of traveling and then building to get a name is repeated in the devils' careers after the fall:

> of thir names in heav'nly Records now
> Be no memorial, blotted out and ras'd
> By thir Rebellion, from the Books of Life.
> Nor had they yet among the sons of *Eve*
> Got them new Names, till wand'ring o'er the Earth,
> Through God's high sufferance for the trial of man,
> By falsities and lies the greatest part
> Of Mankind they corrupted
>
> . . . .
>
> With gay Religions full of Pomp and Gold,
> And Devils to adore for Deities. (1:361–68, 372–73)

The initial razing of the devils' angelic names is recompensed by their acquisition of new titles in the fallen and diversified languages of various peoples. Yet these competing religions are part of the cycle of empire and are each subject to ruin in their turn: that Milton's catalogue of idols parallels Homer's catalogue of ships in the second book of the *Iliad* associates idol worship with empire and conquest, as the devils marshal to their fates "At thir great Emperor's call" (1:378). The first to rise from the burning lake are the future gods of Canaan, who, "Roaming to seek thir prey on earth, durst fix/Thir Seats long after next the Seat of God" (1:381–82). Again, a false fixation follows restless movement, and the Asian idols further parody the worship of God by imitating the lost topography of Eden in miniature. Moloch leads Solomon to erect

> His Temple right against the Temple of God
> On that opprobrious Hill, and made his Grove
> The pleasant Valley of *Hinnom*, *Tophet* thence
> And black *Gehenna* call'd, the Type of Hell. (1:402–5)

This Babel-like attempt to recreate the lost mountain of Paradise on the Mount of Olives ends with another Hell-mouth, and the parallel is furthered when Moloch's colleague Chemos extends his cult from Mount Nebo to "the *Asphaltic* Pool" of the Dead Sea (1:407–11). As in Diodorus Siculus and George Sandys, the Dead Sea casts forth bitumen like Babel's pit of Ait.[28]

The male and female idols of the Baalim and Ashtaroth, or Astarte, are described next—"For Spirits when they please / Can either sex assume, or both" (1:423–24). The devils' labile forms associate their worship with sexual degeneration throughout the rest of the catalogue, just as idolatry is regularly linked with fornication in the Bible. Astarte's temple was built by Solomon, "that uxorious King," on the Mount of Olives (1:443), and the love-tale of her consort Thammuz's annual death "Infected *Sion's* daughters with like heat" (1:452–53). Dagon has reason to complain of a wound in earnest, Milton goes on, for his idol was smashed when it fell before the captive Ark of the Covenant (1:456–61). Ruined monuments are a sign of the inauthenticity and failure of ancient culture. Belial almost escapes this fate, for "To him no Temple stood / Or Altar smok'd," yet he infects the true religion with his lust and violence, and ultimately finds a home in the master-monument of the city itself—"Witness the Streets of *Sodom*" (1:492–93, 503). Sexual transgression is the correlate of metropolitan decline and fall.

The twisted family romances of the Greek pantheon have the same demonic origin as the idol worship of Asia:

> Th' *Ionian* Gods, of *Javan's* Issue held
> Gods, yet confest later than Heav'n and Earth
> Thir boasted Parents; *Titan* Heav'n's first born
> With his enormous brood, and birthright seiz'd
> By younger *Saturn*, he from mightier *Jove*
> His own and *Rhea's* Son like measure found. (1:508–13)

It is significant that Milton adds the deities of Greece as a sort of afterthought. Like the wandering gods of "Fanatic *Egypt*" (1:480), they are lumped together with the Asian devils but accorded a clearly secondary position. The Ionians, after all, are descendants of Javan, the son of Japhet, one of Noah's three sons. Milton viewed classical civilization as part of a greater antiquity, and like Boemus, Stafford, and Lloyd he saw Graeco-Roman and even Egyptian culture as deriving from the culture of biblical Asia. Yet classical learning was all the more suspect for this genealogy, as we see when

Christ rejects the temptation of Athens after he has been offered Assyria in *Paradise Regained* (4:285–364).

Greek mythology represents another illegitimate attempt to regain Eden in *Paradise Lost* as well:

> So *Jove* usurping reign'd: these first in *Crete*
> And *Ida* known, thence on the Snowy top
> Of cold *Olympus* rul'd the middle Air
> Thir highest Heav'n. (1:514–17)

Olympus, like the biblical mountains and groves, is both a substitute Paradise and a false analogue of Heaven that extends only into the middle air. Satan rules this region of the fallen earth's atmosphere, which formed the apparent limit of Nimrod's tower, "where thin Air / Above the Clouds will pine his entrails gross" (12:76–77). In "On the Morning of Christ's Nativity," the young Milton had already imagined God's reclamation of the middle air at the Last Judgment (line 164); the Nativity Ode depicts the silencing of the Graeco-Roman oracles before the rout of the Asian and Egyptian gods from their temples, a sequence that *Paradise Lost* reverses (lines 174–228).

Both Nimrod and the Olympians fell short of Heaven, far short even of "the bare convex of this World's outermost Orb," as the Argument to Book 3 describes the location of another false paradise. As Satan journeys toward the newly created earth, he alights upon the outer shell of the universe, where vain projects and their authors will fly up after the Fall:

> Both all things vain, and all who in vain things
> Built thir fond hopes of Glory or lasting fame.
>
> . . . .
>
> Hither of ill-join'd Sons and Daughters born
> First from the ancient World those Giants came
> With many a vain exploit, though then renown'd:
> The builders next of *Babel* on the Plain
> Of *Sennar*, and still with vain design
> New *Babels*, had they wherewithal, would build.
> (3:448–49, 463–68)

"The Paradise of Fools," as Milton calls this place (3:496), is the windy destiny of all those who wish to make a name for themselves, including "Pilgrims . . . that stray'd so far to seek / In *Golgotha* him dead, who lives in Heav'n" (3:476–77). Travel is once more implicated in the vain exploit of trying to regain Eden, even travel in the Holy Land, whose pilgrimage lore contributed to many of the descriptions that later geographical writers, including Milton, built upon.

Satan himself, as critics have remarked, is a figure for the traveler or explorer in the early books of the epic. He undertakes the exploit of spying out the new world, and when he comes within sight of the earth a few lines after the "Paradise of Fools" passage, he is characteristically compared to a "Scout" who beholds "some foreign land / First seen, or some renown'd Metropolis / With glistering Spires and Pinnacles adorn'd" (3:548–50). We are told that Satan views the world with envy, and this accounts for the spires and pinnacles in the simile: his metropolitan and acquisitive vision immediately superposes the future cycle of empires upon the waiting globe. Similarly, our prospect of Paradise itself is soon tainted by Satan's: "*Eden* stretch'd her Line / From *Auran* Eastward to the Royal Tow'rs / Of Great *Seleucia*, built by *Grecian* Kings" (4:210–12). Old World as well as New World images are involved in the demonic voyage of exploration.

Satan's progress through Chaos has already been compared to a mercantile voyage to the Moluccas (2:636–40), and in Book 4 he savors the scent of the Garden like European traders anticipating the lucrative spices of Asia:

> As when to them who sail
> Beyond the *Cape of Hope*, and now are past
> *Mozambic*, off at Sea North-East winds blow
> *Sabean* Odors from the spicy shore
> Of *Araby* the blest. (4:160–63)

As we have seen, this trading route around the Cape of Good Hope and through the Indian Ocean bypassed the caravans of Western Asia and was responsible in Cartwright's view for the contemporary decline of Baghdad, the successor to Babylon.

Milton may be registering the shifting economic conditions that had supposedly reduced Baghdad to a town of small trade more effectively than military conquest. As David Quint argues, "Milton, in keeping with his general criticism of the earlier epic tradition, exposes as false the distinction which that tradition draws between martial heroism and mercantile activity." Satan's primordial journey parodies Vasco da Gama's voyage in Luis de Camoens' Portuguese epic *The Lusiads*, exposing the hero's classically based adventures as a trading mission.[29] It foreshadows Asia's subjection by a succession of world economies through commercial processes that are less glamorous and even more unstable than conquest and empire.

The rich odors of Paradise beckon Satan to exploit its resources; he makes use of the wide variety of forms there to disguise his infiltration of its precincts, lighting like a cormorant on the Tree of Life itself, and shape-shifting his way closer and closer to Adam and, in particular, Eve (4:194–96, 401–3, 800). Eve is brought into the complex of associations between Eden and world economics when she performs her wifely duty by preparing for a visit from Raphael in Book 5:

> Bestirs her then, and from each tender stalk
> Whatever Earth all-bearing Mother yields
> In *India* East or West, or middle shore
> In *Pontus* or the *Punic* Coast, or where
> *Alcinoüs* reign'd, fruit of all kinds, in coat,
> Rough, or smooth rin'd, or bearded husk, or shell
> She gathers, Tribute large . . . (5:337–43)

Eve's hospitality is oddly global and domestic at the same time, a primordial anticipation of world-economic exchange. In the opening pages of the "General Introduction" to his *Cosmographie*, Heylyn proffers a similar picture of the newly created earth: "God made the world, and fitted it with all things necessary for the life of man. . . . But nothing more sets forth the Power and Wisdome of Almighty God, as it relates to these particulars, than that most admirable intermixture of Want with Plenty, whereby he hath united all the parts of the World in a continual Traffique and commerce with one amother [*sic*]: some Countreys being destitute of those Commodities, with which others abound" (p. 4). Heylyn, like Satan, sees the postlapsarian world when he contemplates the globe in its first creation. The mercantile motivations of geographical research and world history during the period are rarely revealed more clearly than in this passage.

It is significant that the commodification of the world is associated with Eve. A gendered division of labor is already in place in Milton's Garden, although it does not correspond precisely to the modern system since both Eve and Adam continue to work outside the household bower even after she persuades him to "divide our labors" (9:214).[30] Differing from some feminist critics who minimize Eve's subjection, Mary Nyquist presents a more convincing feminist argument for a hierarchical relation between the first pair in Milton. How Eve thinks and feels is more important than what she does, for her experiences "are represented as taking place in a sphere that has the defining features of the 'private' in an emerging capitalist economy: a sphere that appears to be autonomous and self-sustaining even though not 'productive.'"[31] She is formed for "softness" and "sweet attractive Grace" (4:298), but these qualities are dangerously close to the luxury and vanity of the fallen order, the order that drives world economies. Eve's provision of the fruits of the world parallels Satan's merchantlike survey of it. Ultimately, her own consumption of the forbidden fruit, which "Greedily she engorg'd without restraint," secures his hold over the earth (9:791).

Satan's global dominion will eventually manifest itself in a succession of doomed empires ruled by mortals, as the catalogue of demons in Book 1 first suggested. These empires are surveyed in another catalogue when Michael takes the fallen Adam to the top of Mount Paradise to reveal the succeeding history of humankind. The list, which runs from "*Cambalu*, seat of *Cathaian Can*," through Persia, Mombaza, and Rome, to Mexico and "the yet unspoil'd / *Guiana*" (11:388–410), looks forward to the array of empires Satan offers Christ in *Paradise Regained* while reminding us of the economic motives of conquest. Like Satan's first view of the world as a renowned metropolis, it superposes the fallen landscape of the later poem upon the still empty earth. The monumental pageant that Michael shows to Adam throughout the rest of Book 11 takes us from an altar to a forge to "Cities of Men with lofty Gates and Tow'rs" (11:640) as we pass from Cain to Tubal-cain, and from them to the warring and luxurious conquerors whom Enoch and Noah rebuke. The mobile ark is a sort of anti-monument, divinely appointed to resist destruction: "all dwellings else / Flood over-whelm'd, and them with all thir pomp / Deep underwater roll'd" (11:747–49). Eden itself, as we have seen, is wiped out as well. In *Paradise Regained*, the Temple of Jerusalem similarly serves as the unexpected culmination of a series of cities and their monuments. Satan takes Christ to its top and challenges him to jump, but he is the one who falls when Christ reveals his godhead (4:541–71). Northrop Frye observes, "The destruction of the Garden of Eden at the flood showed that God 'attributes to place no sanctity,' and the later destruction of the temple, prefigured at this point, illustrates the same principle."[32] Eden and the Temple have both become obsolescent for Milton; what they represent can no longer be attained through travel or architecture.

With the Temple we have come full circle, back to the destruction of Eden in the Flood and the Tower of Babel that supposedly replaced it. Noah's ark is "Smear'd round with Pitch" (11:731) like the Tower that offsets its saving role; Milton takes this detail from Genesis 6:14, but it also recalls how the people of Ait near Babylon employ the local bitumen to seal their boats (Heylyn, p. 784). He found other elements for his description of the destruction of Paradise in the geographical material. Alan H. Gilbert noted in his *Geographical Dictionary of Milton* that seventeenth-century descriptions of Hormuz or "Ormus," an arid but prosperous island in the mouth of the Persian Gulf, suggest Milton's displaced Mount Paradise.[33] Ludovico di Varthema, translated in Richard Eden and Richard Willes' *History of Trauayle in the West and East Indies* in 1577, tells of how water and food must be brought to Hormuz from the mainland, but says that the largest pearls in the world may be found there.[34] *Purchas His Pilgrimes* contains a lengthy section entitled "Relations of Ormuz," where we read that it is "a barren and uninhabited Iland, and a Mountaine of Salt" yet also the site of a rich trading city, "for the many and great merchandize that come to it from all places of India, and from all Arabia, and from all Persia."[35] And Herbert observes that Hormuz "procreates nothing note-worthy, Salt excepted, of which the Rockes are participant, and the Siluer-shining Sand expresseth Sulpher" (*Relation*, p. 46). The contradictory image of Hormuz, silver-shining yet sulphurous, tentatively reclaimed from infertility as a mercantile outpost of empire, lends a hollow resonance to Satan's "bad eminence" in the council scene of Book 2:

High on a Throne of Royal State, which far
Outshone the wealth of *Ormus* and of *Ind*,
Or where the gorgeous East with richest hand,
Show'rs on her Kings *Barbaric* Pearl and Gold. (2:1–4)

The fortunes of Hormuz rose and fell during the seventeenth century as it passed from Portuguese to Persian hands.[36] In his later edition Herbert writes, "ORMVS is at this day a miserable forlorne city and Ile; although but a douzen yeares ago the onely brave place in all the Orient" (*Travels*, p. 113). Milton's former mountain of Paradise has become a similar "Island salt and bare." Its position in the Persian Gulf associates the increasing economic importance of the region with the temptations of a fool's paradise and their inevitable betrayal by the vicissitudes of empire.

Hormuz, like the ruined Mount Paradise, is an island in the Persian Gulf. Yet the extensive literature on the location of Paradise contains little to prepare us for Milton's sublime picture of the very mountain upon which Adam and Michael stand being swept away,

With all his verdure spoil'd, and Trees adrift
Down the great River to the op'ning Gulf,
And there take root an Island salt and bare. (11:832–34)

In his *History of the World*, however, Ralegh cites two letters that the Nestorian Christians of the region sent to the Pope in 1552:

For in them both there is mention of the *Island of Eden* in the riuer *Tigris*, or at least, *Tigris* in both these Epistles is called the Riuer of *Eden*. This *Island* as *Masius* in his *Praeface* to these Epistles saith, is commonly called *Gozoria* (as it were, *the island*, by an eminencie)[.] It hath (saith he) tenne miles in circuit, and was sometimes walled round about, which name of the *Island Eden* may (doubtlesse) remaine to this day; though in the rest of the Region so called this name be swallowed vp, with the fame of those flourishing Kingdomes of *Mesopotamia*, *Assyria*, *Babylonia*, and *Chaldea*. (p. 51)

Cartwright, as we have learned to expect, had already offered a similar description: "And howsoeuer the beautifull land of *Eden* is now forgotten in these parts, with those flourishing countries of *Mesopotamia*, *Assyria*, *Babylonia*, and *Chaldea*, being all swallowed vp into meere Barbarism, yet this Iland stil retains the name of the Ile of *Eden*" (p. 91). Eden has been swallowed by fame or mere barbarism, by the great wheel of empire, just as it was swallowed by the waters of the Flood. Cartwright concludes that "whither this Iland were the very *Eden* of *Paradise*, is not probable," although by Herbert's time the two were apparently identified by believers in the terrestrial paradise, "Many imagining the true compasse ten miles and in that Ile in *Meso-potamia*, as yet cald *Edens*" (Cartwright, p. 91; Herbert, *Relation*, p. 141).

The island in the Tigris is not the island in the Persian Gulf that Milton envisages, no more than Hormuz is. Yet it may be one source for Milton's island, and if so the learned seventeenth-century reader's temptation to identify it with the lost Paradise may be part of the way he uses it. The geographical position of the Nestorians' Eden would help to explain why Milton's garden appears to be located on the Tigris rather than the Euphrates or the meeting point of the rivers, as it is in the tradition.[37] When Satan reenters Paradise for the final temptation, we are told

> There was a place,
> Now not, though Sin, not Time, first wrought the change,
> Where *Tigris* at the foot of Paradise
> Into a Gulf shot under ground. (9:69–72)

As in the passage on the Flood, we have a "place" that no longer exists, and that has lost its sanctity through sin. It is as if Satan infiltrates Paradise about where the island called Eden now exists; latter-day travelers perpetuate the work of Satan, perhaps, in looking for Eden there, reversing its dissolution in another Gulf. Ralegh meditates on how "the name of *Eden* in those parts is not yet quite worne out, though the Region hath beene subiect to the same change, that all other kingdomes of the world haue beene, and hath by conquest, and corruption of other languages, receiued new and differing names" (p. 52). Milton himself mentions one of the names in Ralegh's survey, Telassar, where Isaiah 37:12 places the "Sons of *Eden*" (4:213–14; Ralegh, p. 47). For Milton, however, the apparent survival of a name in the face of the cycle of conquest is suspicious. The fame and barbarism that engulfed Eden do indeed correspond to the Flood; one cannot find one's way back to Paradise through human knowledge about the external world. It is a place that is now not a place, although its decreation occurred through sin, suggesting an alternative scale of change from that of the temporal or historical register. Sin, for Milton, is bound up with language, as the Babel story makes clear. The operation of difference within language and knowledge rather than within time consigns Eden to a past more profound than any that travelers or scholars are able to recover.

III

The Nestorian Eden, along with the Eden mentioned by Isaiah and the other apparent traces of the place that Ralegh cites, are false names, even if Paradise was once located where they now are. For Milton, they are all the more false for that reason, because they tempt us to search for Paradise in a fallen world. His insistence that Paradise is lost should be read as an oblique commentary on the controversy over the past location of Eden and its continued existence. Once again, Mandeville is a good place to begin when one wants to sort out the tradition. The Egerton translation describes how the deluge created the valleys and hills on the surface of the globe, but holds that the garden of Eden remained intact: "Paradise terrestrial, as men say, is the highest land of the world; and it is so high that it touches near to the circle of the moon. For it is so high that Noah's flood might not come thereto, which flood covered all the earth but it. Paradise is closed all about with a wall; but whereof the wall is made, can no man tell. It is all moss begrown and covered so with moss and with brush that man may see no stone."[38] Mandeville's description looks forward to Milton's garden with its "verdurous wall" (4:143), but also backward to a complex tradition rooted in patristic exegesis.[39]

Augustine of Hippo was among the first writers to break from an exclusively allegorical interpretation of Genesis' account of Paradise. Whatever its spiritual meaning, one must believe that this wooded spot with its four rivers exists somewhere upon the earth, even if one does not know where.[40] The image of a garden walled about with mountains goes back to pseudepigrapha such as the second book of Enoch.[41] Tertullian traced the classical concept of Elysium to the biblical Paradise; a sixth-century poem wrongly attributed to Tertullian, *De Judicio Domini*, describes the earthly Paradise as a *locus amoenus* or "pleasant place" surrounded by a wall of flame, recalling the flaming sword of Genesis 3:24.[42] About the same time, Isidore of Seville also placed a fiery wall around Paradise, which he located vaguely in the remote east. Isidore's vastly influential *Etymologiae* treated the *locus amoenus* of classical rhetoric as both a *topos* and a geographical category.[43] Writing in the thirteenth century, Thomas Aquinas reflected the more historical aims of recent Jewish scholarship on the question of Eden, but also allowed a Jewish legend about the survival of Enoch and Elijah in the earthly Paradise that derived from Genesis 5:24 and 2 Kings 2:11. Like Augustine, Thomas saw the garden of Eden as both a real place and a spiritual description open to allegory. He does not fix it on the map, venturing to state only that it is rendered inaccessible by mountains, seas, or the torrid zone that Genesis' fiery sword may well signify.[44] In Dante Alighieri's *Purgatorio*, the wall of fire reappears before the entrance to the garden, placed atop Mount Purgatory, just below another ring of fire and the circle of the moon.[45] Dante borrowed widely from the tradition in placing his Eden on an island across the seas, and like Milton he draws on the classical *locus amoenus* for its description.[46] But where Milton's fully realized mountain garden was swept away from its original location in Mesopotamia by the Flood, Dante's still exists atop Mount Purgatory on the other side of the world, at least within the allegory of the *Divina Commedia*. Milton knew Dante, and as Joseph E. Duncan remarks, the later author may have set himself against his precursor in describing a historical Paradise at once more real and more remote in time as well as space.[47] The marked dissymmetry between their accounts of the earthly Paradise, however, exceeds authorial intention; it is part of a wider shift in the European discourse of world history, in which the "historical," arrived at by a careful sifting of language and knowledge, is marked by an uneasy combination of authenticity with absolute inaccessibility.

As A. Bartlett Giamatti suggests, the figure of Matelda, an inhabitant of Dante's garden, replaces the legendary Enoch and Elijah.[48] A prophetic figure who leads Dante to Beatrice, Matelda is also a maiden picking flowers who reminds him of Proserpina, and thus of another story of a fall into seasonal or cyclical time.[49] Later in the same canto, Matelda explains how the trees of the garden give off a fertile essence in lines that portend Milton's account of how "airs, vernal airs, / Breathing the smell of field and grove, attune / The trembling leaves" (4:264–66). But Milton insists that this place was

> Not that fair field
> Of *Enna*, where Proserpin gath'ring flow'rs
> Herself a fairer Flow'r by gloomy *Dis*
> Was gather'd, which cost *Ceres* all that pain
> To seek her through the world. (4:268–72)

The catalogue of Parnassus, Nysa, and Amara follows. These places are surpassed by Paradise, "where the Fiend / Saw undelighted all delight," particularly two new creatures, Eve and Adam (4:285–86). Satan takes Dante's place as penetrator of Eden; figuratively, the first thing both see is Proserpine gathering flowers. This time, the Fall the scene signifies leads to Ceres' linear search over the surface of the world rather than the compromise of the seasonal cycle. For Milton, presumably, Dante's claim to have entered Paradise is another version of Satan's falsification of an experience that is lost and cannot be recovered through language and learning.

By the beginning of the sixteenth century, a dual consensus had emerged among scholars that Eden had been destroyed in the Flood, but that it had certainly existed upon the earth in what was then Mesopotamia, comprising Assyria, Babylonia, and Chaldea.[50] The Mesopotamian solution was largely supported by the mention of the Euphrates among the four rivers that water Paradise in Genesis 2:10 and the common assumption that the Hiddekel was the Tigris. With his "*Assyrian* mount" (4:126), Milton thus chose the historical and geographical placement of Paradise most popular among educated Europeans, particularly Protestants. Ralegh surveys the tradition on the location of Eden from the Fathers onward in *The History of The World*, and although his tone is hardly controversial, most of the improbable theories about Paradise that he disposes of were associated with pre- or counter-Reformation Catholicism. To stop truth itself from being questioned, one must disprove the ridiculous untruths that circulate around the idea of Paradise by discovering its genuine place, "(as *Melancthon* saies) *in parte terrae meliore, in the best part thereof,* that from thence, as from a Center; the Vniuersall might be filled with people, and planted; and by knowing this place, wee shall the better iudge of the beginning of Nations, and of the worlds inhabitation" (p. 40). By locating Paradise, then, one will also gain access to the original "planting" or colonizing of the fallen world, to the Fall as a continued event of diaspora, renaming, and nation building. It is in this context that Ralegh comes across the Nestorians' isle of Eden in Mesopotamia.

But what were the absurd ideas that Ralegh felt it necessary to disprove or discount? First, "That the Floud hath not utterly defaced the markes of Paradise, nor caused Hils in the Earth," for although the Flood may have rendered the garden "one common field and pasture with the Land of *Eden*, yet the place is still the same" (p. 40). Milton, as we have seen, went further than Ralegh, taking issue even with the idea that the site of Paradise still existed; for him, it "was a place, now not," and the displacement and reduction of its mountain to a bare island in the Persian Gulf, while attesting to its general location in Mesopotamia, makes nonsense of the very notion of "place." Some commentators had contended that Paradise originally comprised the entire world.[51] Like Milton, Ralegh rejected this tradition, allowing for an unfallen nature but insisting on the specificity of Eden and of the garden or Paradise proper within it. He was especially dismissive of the notion that Paradise was situated on the other side of the world, and that a gigantic Adam had once waded the ocean to reach Jerusalem (pp. 42–43). Voyages of exploration were making Dante's symbolic universe less and less tenable. In 1498, Columbus claimed to be seeking Paradise in a protuberant area of the globe near the mouth of the Orinoco; by 1596, Ralegh himself had evoked an El Dorado at its source, but his golden city was an artificial paradise, created by invasion and war, a treasure trove stripped of Edenic imagery.[52]

Ralegh reserved his greatest disdain for interpreters such as the convert Moses Bar Cephas and the schoolman Peter Comestor, who held that Paradise was situated atop an impossibly high mountain close to or within the circle of the moon or, worse yet, that it was still hanging unsupported in the air (Ralegh, pp. 39, 43–44). He maintains, as Milton implicitly does, that Genesis 7:20 indicates the inundation of all the earth's mountains without exception. The belief in an elevated and intact Paradise had become associated with the idea that the two prophets continued to abide in the garden, "But for the bodies of *Enoch* and *Elias*, God hath disposed of them according to his wisdome" (Ralegh, p. 44). Protestants often accused their counter-Reformation opponents, often incorrectly, of holding this opinion. Contemporary with Ralegh, Samuel Purchas wrote in *Purchas His Pilgrimage* that "the great Cardinall[s] *Cajetane* and *Bellarmine* place *Henoch* and *Elias* in [*sic*] Earthly Paradise, yet liuing there vntill the time of Antichrist, which wood he cannot see (beeing in the middest of it) for Trees. But the discouery of the World by Trauellers, and descriptions thereof by Geographers, will not suffer vs to follow them."[53] Purchas himself collected such discoveries and descriptions in *Purchas His Pilgrimes*, a continuation of Hakluyt's enterprise aimed in part against the false and self-confounding learning of Antichrist, the Catholic Church. In his *Pilgrimage*, a lengthy history of world religions, Purchas made use of the Tremellius-Junius Bible of 1590 with its maps and detailed notes on the location of Eden, which in turn depended on ancient geographical authorities (*Pilgrimage*, p. 16). Junius inspired a rash of Protestant tracts on the question of Paradise well into the seventeenth century, of which the Englishman John Hopkinson's *Synopsis Paradisi* (1593), cited by Ralegh against the Enoch and Elijah theory, was one of the first and most important (Ralegh, pp. 35, 44).[54] Purchas uses Junius to place Eden in Mesopotamia by invoking the four rivers, even though their names have inevitably changed and Paradise itself has been "deformed by the Flood, and by Time consumed, and become a Stage of Barbarism" (*Pilrimage*, p. 16). Both Ralegh and Purchas evince a newly acute awareness of the region's degeneration into barbaric otherness that connects the Fall with the later cycle of empires and the observations of European travelers upon it.

Purchas cites "M. Cartwright an eye-witnesse" in this context, mentioning his account of the isle of Eden, "which if it be not part of that Garden-plot mentioned by *Moses*, yet it seemes is part of that Countrey sometime called *Eden*, in the East part whereof Paradise was planted, and not farre (according to *Iunius* Map) from that happy vnhappy place" (*Pilgrimage*, p. 17).Cartwright represents the travelers' contribution to the debate on Paradise's location, and his narrative does in fact lend it a contemporary tone, and not just through the eyewitness account of the Nestorians' island. "They are farre besides the truth," Cartwright insists,

> which haue sought *Paradise*, either beyond our knowne world, or in the middle region of the aire; . . . yea some are so mad, that they doe peremptorily set downe, that the earthly *Paradise*, after *Adam* was banished thence for his sin, was by *God* lifted vp into the aire: but *this* (as *His Maiesty learnedly sheweth in his Praemonition to al Christian Monarchs, free Princes*

and states) is like one of the dreames of the Turkish Alcoran, seeing no such
miracle is mentioned in the scriptures, hauing no ground but from the curious
fancies of some boiling braines, who cannot be content sapere ad sobrietatem.
(Cartwright, p. 94; author's emphasis)

The quotation is from James I's "A Premonition to All Most Mightie
Monarchies, Kings, Free Princes, and States" of 1609, a tract in defense of
the Oath of Allegiance directed against Cardinal Robert Bellarmine, the
great counter-Reformation adversary of English Protestantism. The chain
of references from antiquarian to traveler ultimately leads back to the
monarch, whose dispute with the Catholic Church raises the pressing issue
of the location of Eden in an unexpected context.

In the "Premonition," James counters Bellarmine's accusation that he is
a heretic by reiterating his earlier claim that Rome is Babylon and the Pope
Antichrist. The cardinal had written that Enoch and Elijah, traditionally
the two witnesses of Revelation 11:3, would come down from the earthly
Paradise should Antichrist commence his reign; because they have not, the
Pope is free of suspicion. "*Bellarmine,*" James replies, "is much troubled to
finde out the place where *Paradise* is, and whether it bee in the earth, or in
the ayre. But these are all vanities. The Scriptures tell vs, that *Paradise* and
the garden of *Eden* therein, was a certaine place vpon the earth, which
GOD chose out to set *Adam* into, and hauing thereafter for his sinne ban-
ished him from the same, it is a blasphemie to thinke that any of *Adams*
posteritie came euer there againe." Milton would seem to be in complete
accord, for his garden of Eden was also a place now not, without sanctity
in itself. "And doubtlessly," James continues, "the earthly *Paradise* was defaced at the Flood, if not before: and so lost all that exquisite fertilitie and
pleasantnesse, wherein it once surpassed all the rest of the earth. And that
it should be lifted vp into the ayre, is like one of the dreames of the
Alcoran."[55] At this point, the sovereign's authority enters the travel and antiquarian literature through Cartwright's loyal citation. But what are we to
make of the odd agreement between the first Stuart monarch and John
Milton, perhaps the principal ideological opponent of his dynasty, over the
destruction of Paradise?

Southwest Asia and the continual decline and fall of its warring empires
seemingly has little to do with this question. For James, however, Rome is

like Babylon in being the "Seate of an Empire"; the "Premonition" is addressed to the Holy Roman Emperor and a host of other rulers, and defends their supremacy over the Pope, who becomes Antichrist insofar as he attempts to "Exalt himselfe aboue all that were called Gods," that is, over other worldly monarchs (James, pp. 140, 130). Bellarmine's resort to Enoch, Elijah, and the earthly Paradise is implicitly cast as a narrowly literal reading of the Bible that covers up the symbolic embodiment of Antichrist in the counter-Reformation papacy. The two witnesses of Revelation, James asserts, are to be understood as the Old and New Testaments, and ultimately as the preachers who read and expound them properly, upholding sovereign power against ecclesiastical interference (James, p. 137). The evocation of terrestrial or floating Edens is outlandish, "Turkish," and thus anti-Christian itself. Cartwright's inclusion of James' spirited refutation of Bellarmine in *The Preachers Travels* links travel and geography to a national project of rational global exploration, an English Protestant project that opposes and erases the false imaginary of the Catholic Church and its universe. Milton was one of the heirs of this project, yet he also reveals how it was split at its origins by its own satanic drive for temporal domination. James I, Charles I, Charles II, and "all that were called Gods" are equally implicated in the Pope's imposition. The Stuart monarch rightly denies an earthly Paradise, but only in order to put himself in its place; as we have seen, for Milton he is a builder of Babel, of an artificial and metropolitan Paradise, like Nimrod, or like Christopher Whitehead.

"You cannot without indignation of minde see the accursed Serpent putting the deadly Apple into our Grand mother *Eves* hand," we read in *Paradise Transplanted and Restored.* "A fraud, I say, twice so (ill and well) practised, first by the Serpent, and then by this our *Artist*, that the one can never be remedied, nor the other mended" (I. H., p. 3). Milton's depiction of Paradise and the Fall might provoke the same response as Whitehead's figures; the artist is like Satan, displaying an image of the world and its fruits to an audience of consumers. But Milton built considerable resistance to commodification into his epic. The spectacular punishment of the devils after the Fall of humankind forms an admonition to patrons of exhibitions like the Shoe Lane spectacle. Transformed to serpents, they are presented with a grove of trees that mimic the Tree of Knowledge:

                on that prospect strange
Thir earnest eyes they fix'd, imagining
For one forbidden Tree a multitude
Now ris'n, to work them furder woe or shame;
Yet parcht with scalding thirst and hunger fierce,
Though to delude them sent, could not abstain . . .
                they fondly thinking to allay
Thir appetite with gust, instead of Fruit
Chew'd bitter Ashes. (10:552–57, 564–66)

The word *prospect*, echoing the passage describing Eden as an empire in Book 4 as well as the jargon of projects like the one in Shoe Lane, takes on a hollow resonance in this remarkable critique of a culture of consumption.

The Restoration of the English monarchy provides a closer parallel to the simulacrum described in *Paradise Transplanted and Restored* than Milton's self-critical recreation of Genesis. Indeed, *Paradise Lost* indirectly places the Restoration within the cycle of Asian empires by invoking both world tyranny and the Stuart dynasty through the portrayal of Satan and his crew.[56] More presciently, it criticizes commercial ambition as well as the hunger for territory that accompanies monarchy: its old world sweep repositions the imperial prospects of colonialism within a para-colonial vista. For all this, the epic remains a para-colonial text itself. Karl Marx would ascribe the backwardness of Asia to "oriental despotism."[57] Milton, another revolutionary thinker, regarded all despotism as oriental. Even though he included the Stuarts in his indictment of abusive power, he perpetuated the association of the East with unreasoning tyranny as Marx did after him, making Southwest Asia in particular the exemplar of demonic empire over a fallen world, a pattern that English monarchs belatedly followed. *Paradise Lost* participates in the representation of Asia in European culture as the original fallen place, its modeling as exotic backdrop, museum, and chamber of horrors.

THREE

Slave-Born Muscovites

Sidney, Shakespeare, Fletcher, and the Geography of Servitude

Imbued with the geohistorical antiquities of Southwest Asia, John Milton looked toward Northern Asia when he came to write a far-flung geographical work himself. Why should this have been so? A partial answer may be found in the Author's Preface to the work *A Brief History of Moscovia* (1682), written early in Milton's career but never set completely aside. Geographers, according to Milton, have set down longitudes and latitudes with precision, but they have "miss'd their proportions" in constructing the cultural image of the world by wasting space on superstition, ceremony, and custom. It is better

> to assay something in the description of one or two Countreys, which might be as a Pattern or Example, to render others more cautious hereafter, who intended the whole work. And this perhaps induc'd *Paulus Jovius* to describe onely *Muscovy* and *Britain*. Some such thoughts, many years since, led me at a vacant time to attempt the like argument; and I began

with *Muscovy*, as being the most northern Region of Europe reputed civil; and the more northern Parts thereof, first discovered by *English* Voiages.[1]

The *Moscovia* comes near the end of a long line of early modern descriptions of Russia and is dependent on earlier authors such as the Italian collector and historian Jovius (Paolo Giovio, fl. 1525). The English in particular were fascinated with "Muscovy," and Milton draws heavily from accounts reprinted in Hakluyt and Purchas as well for his treatise. The juxtaposition of Britain and Russia in Jovius' work may have been fortuitous, but it was not an accident in Milton's experimental geohistory.[2] His depiction of Russia is not only a model for how geographers should write; it is also a model, or anti-model, for the English on the verge of empire.

Milton states that Russia is European rather than Asian, in the far north but "reputed civil." His hedging on Russia's reputation for civility is telling, and his inclusion of Russia in Europe would have seemed a novel idea in the eyes of many Western Europeans. As we shall see, Russia was traditonally divided between Europe and Northern Asia. The account of the German diplomat and antiquarian Adam Olearius, the major non-Russian description of seventeenth-century Russia, was written about the same time as Milton's *Moscovia*, and it likewise places Russia in Europe. But Olearius is openly loath to grant the inhabitants of the region their claims to European antiquity: "Their boast is that they are descended from the antient *Greeks*, but, to do them no injustice, there is no more comparison between the brutality of these *Barbarians*, and the civility of the *Greeks*, to whom all other parts of the World are oblig'd for all their literature and civilization, than there is between day and night."[3] Earlier, it is true, Olearius describes the Russians as "corpulent, fat, and strong, and of the same colour as other *Europeans*" (p. 74). As Larry Wolff has recently remarked, "Such an observation suggested how little his readers were presumed to know about Russia."[4] It also suggests how much they were expected to forget about a long-standing tradition that typed Russians as radically, even racially, different from their western neighbors. In earlier sources and some accounts contemporary with Olearius and Milton, the Russians were linked to classical legends about barbarous peoples at the northeast fringe of the Graeco-Roman world.[5] The nomadic Scythians of Herodotus' fourth book are buried at the foundation of the early modern discourse of Russia in Western

Europe. The antithesis of hypercivilized Egypt, Scythia nevertheless shared some traits with the Greeks just as Egypt did. The Scythians, youngest of all peoples in Herodotus, represent anti-antiquity, and barbarous Russia a sort of anti-Renaissance to the English traders who stumbled across it in the mid-sixteenth century. Yet early modern Russia also offered a paradigm of territorial empire and commercial control to the English.

We get a general impression of the relation between contemporary Russia and Mediterranean antiquity in Richard Eden's additions to Peter Martyr in his version of *The Decades of the newe worlde* (1555). This influential compilation deserves more attention in its own right than I have time to give it here, for it embodies the manner in which "New World" narratives were inevitably processed through knowledge about the old world within a parochial but ambitious global project.

Eden introduces Russia in a seemingly indirect way, with several pages on the wealth that flowed into Rome from the East before its fall. "It is doubtlesse a marueylous thynge," he begins, in a miracle of understatement,

> to consyder what chaunges and alterations were caused in all the Romane Empire by the commynge of the Gothes and Vandales, and other Barbarians into Italy. . . . The desolation and ignoraunce which insued hereof, continued as it were a clowde of perpetuall darkenesse amonge men for the space of four hundreth years and more, in so much that none durst aduenture to go any whyther owt of theyr owne natiue countreys.[6]

Eden goes on to provide evidence for the pivotal role Egypt played as the conduit for the riches of India and points beyond during the time of Ptolemy XII and his daughter Cleopatra. He then swerves to a long discourse by Girolamo Fracastoro on the modern conquests of Portugal in southern climes, and how the Portuguese might consolidate their holdings by establishing colonies on the Roman pattern. The Fracastoro excerpt takes Eden to Russia by suggesting that it is seemingly the realm best equiped to undertake similar conquests in the north and open the way to Cathay. The fractured logic of Eden's itinerary finally becomes a little clearer: as imperium shifts northward, so must the route to the East. The Fracastoro piece is framed by references to the Englishman Richard Chancellor's recent expedition to Russia in search of a northeast passage, which I will discuss later in this chapter. It is plain that in Eden's eyes England, not Russia, should become the true heir of Portugal, and ultimately of Rome, as the custodian of the Eastern trade (pp. 285–89).

The placement of Russia in Eden's volume—well after the New World material but between the third section, on circumnavigations, and the fifth section, comparing the West and East Indies—makes it the linchpin of a newly constructed global system pitched toward the north. But Russia, it slowly emerges from Eden's scattered accounts, is not fit to be the new Portugal of the north, and it may stand in the way of England's aspirations for the Portuguese mantle as well. The cloud of perpetual darkness that succeeded the fall of Rome seems to have settled on Muscovy, as it was called, more permanently than elsewhere. The diplomat Johan Faber (or Fabri) attests to a people who bargain without prevarication and are commendably obedient to their powerful prince, but Sebastian Munster claims that they are "exceedingly given to drunkenness" (Eden, pp. 289–90, 292). Paulus Jovius, a principal source for Milton as well as Eden, recounts how the Russian ambassador claimed that the Muscovites had taken a leading role in the sack of Rome under the Goths, that marvelous source of alteration. They use their wives like servants and keep them under constant watch; in fact all city dwellers are placed under surveillance, a counterpoint to the tsar's familiarity with his nobles at dinnertime (Eden, pp. 313, 316–17).

Eden's section on Russia culminates with the German diplomat Sigismund von Herberstein's largely critical account of Russia, presented in a greatly reduced translation. Herberstein's *Rerum Moscoviticarum Commentarii* first appeared in 1549; it became the most influential description of Russia in western Europe until the early seventeenth century. Herberstein emphasizes the absolute power of the Grand Duke or tsar and its effect upon his subjects. "In autoritie and dominion ouer his subiectes, the prince of Moscouie passeth all the monarkes of the worlde," we read in Eden's version. "He trusteth not his owne brotherne, but oppresseth all with lyke seruitude. . . . It is vncerteyne whether the crueltie and fiercenes of the nation doo requyre so tyrannous a prince, or whether by the tyranny of the prince, the nation is made so fierce and cruell" (Eden, pp. 318, 319). Muscovy itself is a small, infertile, and cold province. Eden includes much of Herberstein's extensive treatment of northern and eastern lands controlled by the tsar, and he likewise preserves the

SLAVE-BORN MUSCOVITES **105**

German's insistence on the otherness of what he saw: "if a ryght line bee drawen from the mouthes of Tanais [the river Don] to the springes of the same, Moscouia shalbe found to bee in Asia and not in Europe" (p. 325).

The sheer size of the Russian empire was to become one of its chief qualities in the minds of English observers and their readership. Herberstein's discussion of the name "Russia" and its origin associates its territory with geographical dispersal. Some say the name comes from Russus, variously a Polish prince or a town near Novgorod, and "some also thynke that it was so cauled of the browne coloure of the nation," a motif we will run across again. But the Russians themselves dispute all this,

> Affyrminge that this nation was in owld tyme cauled Rosseia as a nation dispersed, as the name it selfe dooth declare. For Rosseia in the Ruthens tounge, doothe signifie dispersed or scattered. The which thynge to be trew, dyuers other people commyxt with th[e]inhabitauntes, and dyuers prouinces lyinge here and there betwene dyuers partes of Russia doo playnely declare. But whense so euer they tooke theyr name, doubtlesse all the people that vse the Slauon tounge . . . are increased to suche a multytude that they haue eyther expulsed all the nations that lye betwene them, or drawne them to theyr maner of lyuynge, insomuche that they are nowe cauled all Rutheni by one common name. (Eden, p. 318)

An anxiety attends the expansiveness that the success of the Russian name attests to. Unsuited to a Roman- or Portuguese-style colonial project, the Russians seem to have absorbed surrounding peoples and lands all the same in an amorphous but relentless manner.

Herberstein is departing from his fellow early modern observers in Eden's collection, who draw on classical sources to tie the Russians down to a stable origin in ancient geography. "This prouince," Munster declares, "was cauled of the owlde wryters, Sarmatia Asiatica" (Eden, p. 291). According to Faber,

> Conferrynge therfore the moste ancient of the Greeke and latine monumentes with the histories of later tyme. . . . I fynde therfore that those people whom at this day wee commonly caule Moscouites, were in tyme past (as wytnesseth Plinie) cauled *Roxolani*, whom neuerthelesse by chaungynge one letter, Ptolomie in his eyght table of Europe, cauleth *Rosolanos* as dooth

also Strabo. They were also many yeares cauled *Rutheni*. . . . They were cauled Moscouites of the chiefe citie of al the prouince named Moscouia or Mosca: or (as Volaterane saith) of the riuer Mosco. (Eden, p. 289)

Jovius agrees with the Roxolani provenance, and adds, "The name of the Moscouites is nowe newe, althowgh the poete Lucane maketh mention of the Moschos confinynge with the Sarmatians" (Eden, pp. 310, 311). The very effort to affix the Russians or Muscovites to the "monuments" of Greek and Latin literature undoes itself in a flurry of names and references.[7]

Behind all these names lie the nomadic Scythians, whose unstable link with contemporary Russia is acknowledged by Faber, Jovius, and other sources (Eden, pp. 289, 310, 292). Herberstein barely mentions the Scythians, even though he places diaspora at the origin of contemporary Russianness. The Scythians remain a partially lost origin for early modern Russia in western European accounts. A marginal note in Holland's 1601 translation of the elder Pliny's *Natural History* says the Scythians are "At this day, the Moschovites, white & black Rusians." Pliny himself despaired, however, when faced with the difficulty of defining his Scythians: "surely there is not a region wherein Geographers doe varie and disagree more than in this: and as I take it, this commeth of the infinite number of those na-tions, wandering to and fro, and abiding never in one place."[8] This image of the Scythians derives, of course, from Herodotus, and a brief look at Book 4 of *The Histories* will prepare us for the afterlife of Scythia in the Russia of Eden's time.

The account of their origins that Herodotus attributes to the Scythians looks forward to much later legends about Russia's beginnings. They claim to be the youngest nation of all. A son of Zeus was the first being to inhabit the land, and among his three sons the youngest, Colaxais, assumed su-premacy by virtue of his ability to take up four golden implements that fell from the sky. "In view of the great size of Scythia," we are next told, "Colaxais split it up into three separate kingdoms for his sons."[9] Herodotus describes the Scythians at such length in his fourth book because Darius of Persia, Xerxes' predecessor as would-be conqueror, invaded their territory in retribution for the Scythians' twenty-eight-year occupation of Media and the rest of upper Asia. The Scythians are ambivalent figures in Herodotus' text, at once enemies of Greece's enemy and invaders themselves. "Round the Black Sea—the scene of Darius' campaign," he writes, "are to be found, if we except Scythia, the most uncivilized nations in the world" (*Histories*, pp. 271, 285–86). Milton's echo of such faint praise in his description of Muscovy as "the most northern Region of Europe reputed civil" is certainly unintentional, but telling (*Moscovia*, p. 475). The Scythians, like the Russians after them, are defined by size and division. They defy the classical distinction between civilization and barbarism; they are counted civil because they can be described as a society by a civilized observer, however dispersed and nomadic a society they appear to him to be. Herodotus does not like the Scythians, as he flatly states, but he does admire them for one thing: their staying power. A people without towns and without crops, living in wagons and fighting on horseback with bows and arrows—"how can such a people fail to defeat the attempt of an invader not only to subdue them, but even to make contact with them?" (*Histories*, p. 286). That the Scythians defy contact or coherent description no less than conquest is a paradoxical sign that they possess civility, or as we might now say, that they are a culture. "Like the Egyptians, the Scythians are dead-set against foreign ways," Herodotus observes, "especially Greek ways." They are nomads who discourage travel outside their own stamping grounds. A Scythian traveler who brings home a Greek thanksgiving ceremony is summarily killed by the king himself (*Histories*, p. 295).

Comparable in their xenophobia, the Scythians are nevertheless systematically opposed to the Egyptians throughout Book 4, as François Hartog has demonstrated in his influential study *The Mirror of Herodotus*. The Egyptians call themselves the most ancient of peoples, the Scythians the youngest. Occupying the south, the Egyptians are the wisest of the nations and virtually invented civilization; the Scythians dominate the north, a region that has produced no arts, and are unlearned if not entirely uncivilized. The north-south opposition may reflect Herodotus' dependence on contemporary maps that assumed an inverse symmetry between the two hemispheres and the qualities of their inhabitants. Spatial contrast figures in another way. Egypt is characterized as a sedentary society under an absolute ruler whose grid of canals enables farming and inhibits movement. Although they paradoxically possess kings, the Scythians are generally depicted as nomads wandering from place to place in their wicker wagons.[10] From the point of view of my study, Herodotus' Scythians represent, if not an anti-civilization, then an extremely unstable one, a para-civilization against which the proper civility of other old worlds was anxiously defined. In western Europe during early modern times Russia inherited this problematic position.[11]

Both Egypt and Scythia, as Hartog points out, were cast as "in-between" countries, since the Nile marked the traditional boundary between Asia and Africa, and Lake Maeotis or the Tanais river (the Don) were often said to demarcate Asia from Europe. After 1452 the Volga competed with the Don for this role, confirming Russia's status as an in-between nation.[12] Favoring an east-west division between Europe and Asia along the river Phasis, Herodotus had placed Scythia itself in Europe. But according to Hartog his Scythians are not European, nor particularly Asian: "For them, the unquestionable division between Asia and Europe does not really exist; they pass from one continent to the other without even fully realizing what they are doing."[13] Their nomadic tendencies defy the continental matrices of a later history's racial groupings.

The nomadic Scythians violate political as well as geographical divisions. They meander through an unmarked landscape apparently untouched by power, yet Herodotus often refers to their king. Again, Hartog's formulation of the problem is authoritative for the Scythians and suggestive for early modern Russia, as we shall see. He identifies the contradiction with a "double hypothesis": to the Greeks, barbarians are by definition subjects of royal or despotic power, but nomad power remains "unthinkable": "That being so, the Scythians, who are indisputably barbarians, can know of only one kind of power, royal power. . . . However, the minute the figure of a king appears among them in the narrative, they can no longer be 'nomads.'"[14] Herodotus' incoherent depiction of Scythian rule is, however, a sort of nomadism itself—nomadism on the level of discourse, or "error," in its etymological sense.

The royal paradox, I would add, is closely related to another set of interpretive problems concerning slavery. At the start of Book 4 we are told that the Scythians blind their slaves, first because of the way the Scythians make the slaves milk their mares, and then simply because the Scythians are nomadic herders (*Histories*, p. 272).[15] Neither explanation makes sense in the text as we have it, but both relate blind servitude to the Scythians' wandering economy. Later, Herodotus describes how the king's slaves are gutted and buried with him: "these servants are native Scythians, for the king has no bought slaves, but chooses people to serve him from amongst his subjects" (*Histories*, p. 294). For Greeks, particularly Athenians, a slave was someone who had been acquired through some sort of exchange. Is this passage meant to signify the radical difference between Scythians and Greeks, as Hartog suggests?[16] Or do kings alone choose their slaves while other Scythians purchase or capture theirs? Do Scythians other than kings possess slaves at all? Are all Scythians potential slaves of their king? The "Royal Scythians" who claimed descent from Colaxais, after all, "are the most warlike and numerous section of their race, and look upon the others as their slaves" (*Histories*, p. 277). Do different "sections" among the Scythians share the same customs about slavery, or royalty for that matter? Are all Scythians ruled by a single king, or are some without governance? We have returned to the antinomy of royal power in Scythia. Because the dyad "master-slave" implies that of "king-subject" in Herodotus and the Greek discourse of power in general, slavery among the Scythians is bound to raise the same questions.[17] Furthermore, the related uncertainties about Scythian rule and Scythian slaveholding look forward to key elements in the western European discourse of Russia that the remainder of this chapter will explore: Muscovy is an absolutist empire in which anarchy paradoxically reigns, and it is a country in which everybody except the emperor is in some sense a slave.

Slavery is present from the very beginning of Herodotus' Scythian narrative, in the form of an anecdote that reappears in Russified form some 1500 years after his time. The information about slave blinding and mare milking is part of a longer story. The Scythians chased the Cimmerians out of their territory and went on to conquer most of Asia. After twenty-eight years, they return to find that the slave population, having married the Scythian women, has produced a generation of young men who block their entrance. Skirmishes are fought but a stalemate is the only result, until one Scythian points out that it is foolish to kill people who are in effect their own slaves. He proposes a stratagem: "we should stop using spears and bows, and go for them each one of us with a horse-whip. When they saw us armed, they naturally felt that they were as good as we are, and were meeting us on equal terms; but when they see us coming with whips instead, they will remember they are slaves. Once they admit that, they will never try to stand up to us." The stratagem works, and the young men flee. It may be, as M. I. Finley states, that the story exemplifies a Greek attitude Aristotle was to codify much later, that slavery is a natural, good, and just institution.[18] The malleability of Herodotus' discourse about Scythian slaveholding, I would add, makes it a suitable medium for a Greek narrative that works out the transition from enslavement as the result of military conquest to slavery as a hereditary institution that guarantees property. The sons "remember" what they have never experienced, the essential slavery their fathers have bequeathed them, and run at the sight of the whip, not an equalizing weapon but a symbolic trigger.

Herodotus' tale about the Scythians and their slaves returns in Russian dress in Herberstein. It is updated and set in the northwestern city of Novgorod, Russia's former capital. I quote from a nineteenth-century translation of the German diplomat's full text:

> It is also related in their annals, that when the people of Novgorod were besieging Corsun, a city of Greece, with a grievous siege of seven years' duration, their wives becoming weary of their solitary life, and being also doubtful of the safety or return of their husbands, married their slaves. At length the city was taken, and the victorious husbands returned from the war. . . .
> The slaves endeavoured to repel by force the masters whose wives they had married. Their masters, in great indignation, at the suggestion of some one, laid down their arms, and took thongs and ropes in their hands, as the proper mode of dealing with slaves, at which the latter became terrified, and fled.[19]

The defeated escape to a place still called the "Slaves' Fortress" but are eventually conquered and punished. Another version appears in the elder Giles Fletcher's book *Of the Russe Common Wealth* (1591), the central English description of Russia during the period. Like Herberstein, Fletcher collapses the first and second generations of slave opponents. The masters come back to discover their lands and wives in the hands of their "*Cholopey* or bondslaues," a phrase Fletcher uses repeatedly in his book when describing contemporary Russian slavery. The slaves flee at the sound of the whips this time, and "the *Nouogradians* euer since haue stamped their coin . . . with the figure of a horseman shaking a whip a loft in his hand." Fletcher makes the Scythian derivation of the legend explicit and has the Novgorodians campaigning against the Tartars while absent from home.[20]

In his *Cosmographie* (1657) Peter Heylyn reinstates the two-generational plot but attributes the stratagem to a group of Sarmatians who had tagged along with the Scythians in their Median expedition. The former slaves sally forth at Novgorod with both their sons and the women to repel the returning soldiers, only to meet with their whips. Heylyn includes Fletcher's detail about the coin, and adds that "it is the custome of all *Muscovie*, that the *maids* in the time of wooing, send such a *whip*, curiously wrought by her own hands, to that *Suter*, whom she resolves on for her husband; in token of her future subjection to him."[21] Heylyn rediscovers slavery as an essential condition that spans generations; moreover, women are essentially slaves themselves through the institution of marriage. The ancestors of the Novgorodians may have become Sarmatians and thus more European from the global viewpoint of the *Cosmographie*, but as in Paulus Jovius the harsh treatment of Russian women is a sign of the country's barbarity. The story of the whip, the first story we are told about the Scythians in Herodotus, links the Russians to a barbaric past while expressing contemporary western European anxieties about the nature of slavery.

Russia was associated above all with slavery of one sort or another by its European neighbors, even before the formal enserfment of the Russian peasantry began in the early 1590s. Richard Hellie has shown that slavery existed in Russia from medieval times, and that it was a diverse institution governed by its own laws and, after 1571, a separate chancellery. Early modern Russia was unique among large slaveholding societies in that Russians regularly enslaved each other; slavery did not depend upon ethnic difference. Perhaps 10 percent of the population were enslaved, and about half of these slaves were hereditary, the other half largely given over to various forms of voluntary slavery.[22] In addition to the enslavement of Russians by each other, there was the very different matter of the Tartars' enslavement of Russians and other eastern Slavs, a trade that passed into the hands of the Ottoman Turks during the last quarter of the fifteenth century. By the first half of the seventeenth century, Russia may have lost on average some four thousand people a year to this trade, although such a figure is hard to verify.[23]

Beyond Russia's borders, slavery was at least as likely to bring Russians to mind as Africans during the sixteenth century, despite the burgeoning trans-Atlantic slave trade. According to Abraham Ortelius, "It is a wilie and deceitfull people, and is rather delighted to liue in seruitude and slauery, than at large and in liberty."[24] The corruption of the inhabitants is regularly linked with their enslavement to the absolute power of the tsar, or emperor as he is usually styled, in contemporary English travel writings on Russia. There are a number of such accounts; the Elizabethans were more concerned with Russia than America or Africa during the later sixteenth century. Protestant England turned toward orthodox Russia as a possible ally against the Catholic Church and the Holy Roman Empire, and sought to consolidate its position in northern Europe by balancing Russian interests against the divergent aims of Holland, Poland, and Denmark.[25] Russia also represented a series of commercial opportunities to English projectors. "This trade," as two merchants wrote in 1568, "will maynetene thirtie or fortie greate shippes, . . . vent the most parte of our coullarid clothes, & in shorte tyme if neade requier all the Karsayes maid within the realme, whereby her maiesties subiectes may be sette a wourke."[26] If dynastic politics provided the machinery for contacts with Russia, English travel in the region was fueled by the need to trade in staple goods like rugged kersey cloth as well as the twin dreams of northeast and southern passages to the riches of Asia.

The Muscovy Company of merchant adventurers was chartered by the Crown in 1555, two years after its founders sponsored the first English voyage to Russia.[27] An account of the 1553 expedition based largely upon the observations of Richard Chancellor, its surviving leader, appeared in Hakluyt's *Principall Navigations Voiages and Discoveries of the English Nation* (1589). As we have seen, this voyage lies behind Eden's circuitous presentation of his Russian material in *The Decades of the new worlde*. Chancellor was raised in the Sidney household, and the narrative contains a long speech attributed to Company member Henry Sidney, friend to Edward VI and father of Philip Sidney, praising Chancellor upon his election. The captain will "commit his safety to barbarous and cruel people," Sidney is supposed to have declared, a prediction partly borne out by the subsequent description of "the barbarous Russes" and their idolatrous ways.[28] Chancellor's first contact with the inhabitants comes when he boards a fishing boat in the White Sea. The fishermen prostrate themselves in terror, but the English captain gains their trust, "comforting them by signs and gestures, refusing those duties and reverences of theirs, and taking them up in all loving sort from the ground." This incident, we are told, lent the English a reputation for gentleness and courtesy among the common people, who brought them food and were willing to trade—"except they had been bound by a certain religious use and custom not to buy any foreign commodities without the knowledge and consent of the king" (p. 18). The shadow of the emperor falls across this scene of contact, threatening commerce and underlining the unexpected servility of the people. As Daryl W. Palmer has shown, the emperor of Muscovy was to become synonymous with arbitrary power in English eyes, a disturbing prospect because "the region always appeared uncomfortably similar to England."[29]

Like many later accounts of English travel into Russia, the Chancellor narrative is about an exchange of letters between sovereigns as well as commercial ties. The travelers tell their hosts that they were sent by Edward VI to deliver "certain things" to their king, and eventually they are brought to Moscow and attain an interview with the emperor himself, Ivan IV ("the Terrible"). The description of this meeting and the feast that follows illustrates the majesty and power of the emperor among his nobles at court. He ceremonially bestows a piece of bread on each of his courtiers and names them all when he leaves, but the Russians inform their visitors that this "was to the end that the emperor might keep the knowledge of his own household, and withal, that such as are under his displeasure might by this means be known" (p. 27). Later Chancellor marvels at the willing subjection of wealthy men who give up their riches to the emperor for failing to fight in his wars. As for the poor, he notes, "there are some among them that use willingly to make themselves, their wives, and children bondslaves unto rich men to have a little money at the first into their hands, . . . so little account do they make of liberty" (pp. 29–30, 34).

The preeminence of the Russian emperor in this hierarchical society contrasts with the absence of a firm center of English power during the period covered by the narrative. When the English ships left Greenwich, the current location of the court, they discharged their canon: "it was a very triumph (after a sort) in all respects to the beholders. But, alas, the good King Edward, in respect of whom principally all this was prepared, he only by reason of his sickness was absent from this show; and not long after the departure of these ships, the lamentable and most sorrowful accident of his death followed" (p. 14). The letter from the emperor that Chancellor carries back from Russia is addressed to a dead king. In his place reigns Mary I, who is saluted at the end of the narrative with a promise that her renown will spread through the newly opened lands. At the same time, it may be significant that the preceding account of Russian customs stresses, somewhat inaccurately, that women cannot inherit property unless the emperor allows them a portion; without a male heir all lands fall back into his hands (p. 29). An implicit comparison of Russian ways with English runs throughout the text, squarely it would seem to the disadvantage of the former. But the barbarity and obedience of the Russians is not uniformly denounced. They make excellent soldiers who eat little and sleep happily upon the hard ground: "How justly may this barbarous and rude Russe condemn the daintiness and niceness of our captains, who, living in a soil and air much more temperate, yet commonly use furred boots and cloaks" (p. 28). The Chancellor account reveals an undercurrent of anxiety about the power of the emperor and the resources at his command in contrast to the English Crown and its merchant adventurers.

The absolute power of the tsar and the barbarity of his people became a constant refrain in English writing about Russia. Even the diplomatic Anthony Jenkinson, who visited Russia four times in the 1550s and 1560s on behalf of the Muscovy Company, notes in his first voyage of 1557, "This emperor is of great power, for he hath conquered much as well of the Livonians, Poles, Latvians, and Swedes, as also of the Tartars, and gentiles called Samoyeds, having thereby much enlarged his dominions. He keepeth his people in great subjection; all matters pass his judgment be they never so small."[30] Jenkinson's juxtaposition of imperial expansion with domestic oppression was not accidental. The two are mutually dependent in the Elizabethan discourse of Russia. The great map of Russia and Tartary that Jenkinson produced in 1562, dedicated to Henry Sidney and included in Ortelius' atlas eight years later, similarly sets the commanding figure of the "Imperator" Ivan IV beneath his baldachin of state in the northwest corner against the exotic and legendary scenes that ring the eastern and southern borders of his domains, a dense cluster of villages and place-names in the midst.[31] We will return to Jenkinson's adventures later.

The least diplomatic report of Russian barbarity is to be found in three poems by George Turberville, verse letters in poulter's measure evidently written while their author accompanied Thomas Randolph on his difficult embassy to Russia in 1568. Randolph himself patiently recounted in bland prose the strict treatment and months-long delays his party had been subjected to by the emperor's servants.[32] In the epistle "To Dancie," his secretary Turberville was less circumspect in commenting on their hosts: "A people passing rude, to vices vile inclin'd, / Folk fit to be of Bacchus' train so quaffing is their kind."[33] He goes on to specify the vices of the Russian peasant:

> Perhaps the muzhik hath a gay and gallant wife
> To serve his beastly lust, yet he will lead a bugger's life.
> The monster more desires a boy within his bed
> Than any wench, such filthy sin ensues a drunken head.
> . . . .
> No wonder though they use such vile and beastly trade,
> Sith with the hatchet and the hand their chiefest gods be made. (p. 76)

The charge of sodomy places Russia outside Christendom and civilization, but not without implicating the wandering Englishman who observes all this as well.[34] Turberville's letter "To Spencer" concludes by invoking the informal censorship that his economic mission with Randolph entails:

> Who so shall read this verse, conjecture of the rest,
> And think by reason of our trade that I do think the best.
> But if no traffic were, then could I boldly pen
> The hardness of the soil and eke the manners of the men. (p. 80)

The "vile and beastly trade" of the Russians is partly cloaked here by "our trade" with Russia itself. Expansion and commerce bring risks to identities as well as investments. Travel casts the sturdy domestic bond among men conventionally invoked at the beginning of each verse letter in an unfamiliar light. Turberville greets his "Dancie dear" and professes his love to Spencer; he describes his sleeping arrangements with Stafford, "that was my mate in bed," while decrying the muzhik's desire to share his bed with a boy (pp. 75, 77, 80). It is clear that Turberville can recognize absolutely no similarity between himself and the monstrous people among whom he is forced to dwell. But in the very process of casting the Russians as totally other to himself, the English observer betrays the danger that travel and trade will bring out the other within the self.

The danger of sexual transgression extends to women: the peasant's spurned wife seeks other men, resorting to cosmetics, "Wherewith she decks herself and dyes her tawny skin. / She pranks and paints her smoky face, both brow, lip, cheek, and chin" (p. 77). Here we find another explanation for the dark skin often attributed to the Russians, "brown by reason of the stove and closeness of the air" (p. 81). Complaints about makeup are common in the Juvenalian mode of satire that Turberville adopts, but the excessive use of cosmetics by Russian women is also found in other travel accounts (for instance, Giles Fletcher, p. 113 recto). Painting and sodomy both represent the lawless excess that Turberville and his fellow travelers paradoxically discover beneath the surface of the emperor's absolute control. The final epistle, "To Parker," dwells on the combination of disorder and power that its author found

> In such a savage soil where laws do bear no sway,
> And all is at the king his will to save or else to slay.
>
> . . . .
>
> Conceive the rest yourself, and deem what lives they lead
> Where lust is law, and subjects live continually in dread. (p. 83)

The emperor's lust ultimately absorbs the petty transgressions of his subjects. As an incarnation of the traditional tyrant, he embodies an abusive power that has taken the place of law, natural, human, and divine: "So Tarquin ruled Rome" (p. 83).

Giles Fletcher dwells on the excessive power of the emperor and the contradictions it conceals in *Of the Russe Common Wealth*. Dispatched by Queen Elizabeth as ambassador to the tsar in 1588, he stayed for barely a year, arguing the Muscovy Company's case against competition by Dutch and rival English traders and forestalling a Russian alliance with the Hapsburgs. Fletcher provided the most comprehensive account of Russia during the period despite his short visit, supplementing his observations with reading in history and antiquities. Despite the relative success of his mission, the Muscovy Company petitioned against the publication of his book in 1591 and succeeded in having it withdrawn. The Company, fearing harm to their agents and property in Russia from an angry tsar, listed Fletcher's unflattering references to the emperor's power and person in their complaint to Lord

Burghley, unwittingly confirming the book's picture of an oppressive king-dom.[35] Turberville's earlier apprehension about censorship for the sake of trade was borne out.

Of the Russe Common Wealth begins with the antiquity of its subject, orig-inally called Sarmatia. Fletcher discounts Strabo's derivation of "Russia" from the nation of the Roxolani. Taking his cue from Herberstein, he states that the country was renamed because "it was parted into diuerse small, and yet absolute gouernments, not depending, nor being subiect the one to the other. For *Russe* in that tongue doth signifie asmuch as to parte, or diuide" (p. 1 recto). The fascination with dispersal reappears in a slightly altered form here. Four brothers in the north, and four others in the south, divided the kingdom among themselves in the ninth century. The lack of fit be-tween "diverse small" and "absolute" goes unremarked, but it sets the tone for the rest of the treatise, in which absolute power is subtended by division, weakness, and even the lawlessness that Turberville likewise glimpsed.

Fletcher denies that "Sarmatia" came from Asarmathes, the nephew of Heber, cutting Russia off from the lineage of Shem (p. 2 recto). Later, how-ever, he conjectures that Moscow, the "Metropolite citie," was named after another, quasi-biblical figure. Citing Annius of Viterbo's edition, Fletcher writes,

> *Berosus* the *Chaldean* in his 5. book telleth that *Nimrod* (whom other profane stories cal *Saturn*) sent *Assyrius, Medus, Moscus,* & *Magog* into *Asia* to plant Colonies there, and that *Moscus* planted both in *Asia* and *Europe.* Which may make some probability, that the city, or rather the riuer whereon it is built, tooke the denomination from this *Moscus:* the rather because of the climate or situation, which is in the very farthest part and list of *Europe,* bordering vpon *Asia.* (pp. 12 recto–verso)

Russia, as we have seen, is both European and Asian at once, its metropolis virtually defining the border between the continents. Fletcher traces Moscow, and Muscovy, back to a primal scene of global colonization, evok-ing absolute power and its inevitable division once again.

With the evocation of antiquity comes the evidence of degeneration and decline. Moscow, roughly the size of London, was sacked by the Tartars in 1571 and now lies partly in waste (p.13 recto). "The other townes," Fletcher informs us, "haue nothing that is greatly memorable, saue many ruines within their walles. Which sheweth the decrease of the Russe people, vnder this gouernment" (p. 14 recto). Fletcher pities "the poore people that are now oppressed with intollerable servitude" (p. 17 recto). The rule of the emperor is responsible for his kingdom's decay. "The State and forme of their gouernment," he asserts, "is plaine tyrannicall, as applying all to the behoofe of the Prince, and that after a most open and barbarous manner" (p. 20 recto). It is hard to say which is greater, the cruelty of the inhabitants or the "intemperancie" they practice, "so foule and not to bee named." Sodomy is almost certainly meant here; the whole country overflows with it, "And no marueile, as hauing no lawe to restraine whoredomes, adulteries, and like vncleannesse of life" (p. 116 verso). As in Turberville, the surface contradiction between lawlessness and imperial rule is allowed to stand. Not only the common people, but burghers and even nobles are accounted "as seruants or bond slaues that are to obey, not to make lawes" (pp. 22 verso, 46 recto). Fletcher is particularly distressed by the lack of social mobility in Russia: "This order that bindeth euery man to keepe his rancke, and seuerall degree, wherein his forefathers liued before him, is more meet to keep the subiects in a seruile subiection and so apt for this and like Common-wealths, then to aduance any vertue" (p. 49 recto). In this, he may well have reflected the secret misgivings of the very English merchants who protested his book most loudly.

For English commerce was in some sense at odds with the sovereign power under which it sheltered, at home as well as in Russia. Fletcher nervously describes the imperial expansion of the tsar's absolutism in his chapter "Of their Colonies, and mainteyning of their conquests, or purchases by force" (p. 61 verso), noting the rapid beginnings of what Fernand Braudel has called "the invention of Siberia." Russia's need for an apparently boundless tract of exploitable territory paralleled Europe's colonization of the Americas.[36] His obsession with Russian absolutism leaves Fletcher less impressed with the imperial army than Chancellor. The Russian soldier "is farre meaner of courage and execution in any warlike seruice" than the English, he claims, "Which commeth partly of his seruile condition, that will not suffer any great courage or valure to growe in him" (pp. 59 recto–verso). But more clearly than Chancellor and the other English authors I have treated, Fletcher expresses an anxiety about the relation between metropolitan oppression and imperial expansion in Russia that is related to England's own expansive enterprise in a complex way. It is the sheer size of Russia and its empire that has made the thorough despotism that Fletcher describes necessary:

> This manner of gouernment of their Prouinces and townes . . . might seeme in that kinde to bee no bad nor vnpollitique way, for the conteyning of so large a Common-wealth, of that breadth and length as is the kingdome of *Russia*. But the oppression and slauerie is so open and so great, that a man would maruell how the Nobilitie and people shoulde suffer themselues to bee brought vnder it. (pp. 33 recto–verso)

What if the English sovereign were to attain a territorial empire or even an economic sphere of influence as large as Russia's domain? What would the consequences be for the merchants who supported it and the commoners and aristocrats at home? Space itself, the sudden possibility of covering such vast distances inland as well as across the oceans, offered a dizzying prospect to English observers at the end of the sixteenth century. Such worries seem laughably premature, but they would be less so a century, or even a few decades, later. *Of the Russe Common Wealth* was republished in 1643 and again in 1657, when it was read as an indictment of monarchy in the eras of civil war, interregnum, and the consolidation of the American colonies.

Fletcher's dedicatory letter to Elizabeth, omitted from the seventeenth-century editions, insists on the graciousness and dignity that supposedly characterize her reign in England. In his work, the queen may see "A true and strange face of a *Tyrannical state*, (most vnlike to your own) without true knowledge of GOD, without written Lawe, without common iustice." Elizabeth's people may well be thankful that "you are a Prince of subiectes, not of slaues, that are kept within dutie by loue, not by feare" (A3 verso, A4 recto). Despite Fletcher's parenthetical assurance, the book is a mirror for magistrates, Elizabeth in particular. The subsequent censorship of his volume was a reminder that the English Crown itself could exercise oppression on behalf of expansionism. *Of the Russe Common Wealth*, of course, is very far from a tract against monarchy, despite its later appeal to Parliament-men. Nevertheless, it does uncover a latent unease about the subject's status within a suddenly expanding world that might require extreme methods of control and domination.[37]

Russia came to stand for this unease in Elizabeth's England. Her subjects regarded all Russians as virtual bondslaves in a far-flung, if somewhat vulnerable, empire. Philip Sidney's poet-lover in *Astrophil and Stella* at first submitted reluctantly to love's decrees, but

> even that footstep of lost liberty
> Is gone, and now like slave-born Muscovite
> I call it praise to suffer tyranny.[38]

The words *slave* and *slav* are in fact etymologically linked through the medieval Latin word *sclavus*.[39] Fletcher offers a slightly different explanation:

> For the people called *Sclaui*, are knowen to haue had their beginning out of *Sarmatia*, and to haue termed themselues of their conquest *sclauos*, (that is) famous or glorious, of the word *Sclaua*, which in the *Russe* & *Slavonian* tongue, signifieth as much as *Glory*, or *Fame*. Though afterwards being subdued and trod vpon by diuers nations, the *Italians* their neighbors haue turned the worde to a contrary signification, and terme euery seruant or peasant by the name *sclaue*, as did the *Romanes* by the *Getes* & *Syrians*, for the same reason. (pp. 48 verso–49 recto)

The word *slave*, then, supposedly contains within itself the kind of reversal of fortune the Elizabethans perversely delighted in. Astrophil, suffering "full conquest" by love, calls it praise to suffer tyranny, just as the Slavs name themselves glorious conquerors with a word that other peoples have long since made a term of abuse.

In a confusion typical of sixteenth-century western Europe, Sidney blends the subject's servitude to the tsar, chattel slavery of Russians by other Russians, and the enslavement of Russians within the Ottoman Empire in his sonnet sequence's complex geographical allusions. In *Astrophil and Stella*, sonnet 30, busy wits press the reluctant poet-lover for geopolitical intelligence:

> Whether the Turkish new moon minded be
> To fill his horns this year on Christian coast;
> How Pole's right king means, without leave of host,
> To warm with ill-made fire cold Muscovy. (lines 1–4)

Poland was at war with Russia from 1580 to 1581. The poet's father, Henry Sidney, whose deputy governorship of Ireland is mentioned in line 9, had been connected with Russian travel as well. An early member of the Company, he patronized Chancellor and his name is prominently displayed on Jenkinson's map. Philip is subtly invoking his family's long-standing involvement in administration and foreign policy in this sonnet, in eastern and northern matters as well as Irish affairs. The lines on Turkey are usually taken as a reference to an impending attack on Spain, but Turks, with the help of the Tartars, had traditionally enslaved Russians and others from eastern Europe captured in battle. The possibility that the juxtaposition of Turkey and beleaguered Muscovy may refer indirectly to the "Russian slavery" complex is strengthened by the concluding lines of the previous sonnet, with its stress on coasts and military conquest: "And I, but for because my prospect lies / Upon that coast, am giv'n up for a slave"—a slave to Stella's love, of course, but on the Muscovite model once more (29:13–14). Fellow Europeans were fully complicit in the trade in slaves during the Middle Ages, employing slaves from all regions. Christians could not be enslaved, but the slavic inhabitants of the eastern Adriatic littoral and points to the east and north were regarded as heretics and hence fair game. Although sugar cultivation in the Mediterranean seems to have depended on serfdom rather than full-fledged slavery, it provided a pattern for the economic organization of later sugar plantations—first in the Atlantic islands, where about half the laborers were enslaved Africans, and then in the Americas.[40] Both the level of freedom and the origin of the workers shifted as sugar moved west. In the east, the Ottomans took over the slave trade around the Black Sea. Russian slaves were still being traded in the market at Bukhara as late as Jenkinson's time in the late 1550s. He matter-of-factly notes that the Persians trade cloth and silk there for "redde hides with other *Russe* wares, and slaues which are of diuers Countries."[41]

Jenkinson also records his return across the Caspian Sea toward Russia "with 25. Russes, which had been slaues a long time in *Tartaria*, nore euer had before my comming, libertie, or meanes to gette home, and these slaues serued to rowe when neede was." The Hakluyt Society editors proclaim this "the first successful attempt on record of the rescue of Russian slaves in Central Asia."[42] But it might give us pause to note the necessary use to which the "rescued" slaves were put on the voyage home. Given the constant criticism of the

Russians for their servile attitude in the travel writings, it comes as a surprise (one of those unsurprising surprises) to learn that the English themselves employed slaves in the cloth factories of the Muscovy Company. A letter from the Company in London, dated April 18 1567, instructs the factors in Russia: "We wold vnderstand how many slaues be sett to that worke, whether they be apt to that arte; if nead be we will sende more men from hence, but if slaues there be docible it weare better to traine them vp (for diuars considerations) then haue many of our nation from hence except it be master of the work."[43] Management comes from the home office, while labor is kept as inexpensive as possible, a pattern repeated on a world scale in today's international division of labor.

The use of Russian slaves by the English agents of the Muscovy Company hardly compares with the concurrent enslavement of Africans in the vast system of the triangular trade.[44] As changes in the ethnicity of slavery came home to the English at the end of the sixteenth century, however, Russians were symbolically "blackened" along with Africans because of the servile nature attributed to them in western European texts. Older notions about slavery helped the transition. The ill-made fire that may warm cold Muscovy in sonnet 30 of *Astrophil and Stella*, though Polish in origin, is tied to other metaphors of burning and branding. In sonnet 47, the poet cries

What, have I thus betrayed my liberty?
Can those black beams such burning marks engrave
In my free side? or am I born a slave,
Whose neck becomes such yoke of tyranny? (lines 1–4)

Again, love-service—here submission to Stella's dark eyes—has absorbed and troped the violence of slavery. If slavery is associated with blackness in *Astrophil and Stella*, it is principally the blackness of the brand burned onto the flesh, and not the color of the flesh itself. Slavery is an artificial condition, it seems, enforced by a mark that signifies conquest in battle and the loss of honor, the "liberty" of the aristocratic warrior. This is an old, in some sense "preracial" notion of slavery. The example of the "slave-born" Muscovite, however, suggests that one can also be born a slave whose neck "becomes" the yoke of tyranny as well as suits it. *Astrophil and Stella* marks a transitional phase in the English conception of slavery, a gradual process of racialization in which branding is turned into a different, putatively essential kind of blackness. The Muscovite embodies this transition. A member of a nation that unsteadily straddles the boundary between Europe and Asia, the Muscovite is also assimilated to the racial typology of color that accompanied the massive system of African slavery in the Americas. The triangular trade, after all, was one of those methods of extreme domination that the new world of the sixteenth and seventeenth centuries ostensibly required, one practiced by, rather than upon, European subjects. Conflated with the Tartars and Turks on their borders who participated with Europeans in the earlier slave system, Russians are "othered" as subservient and "black" in a number of sixteenth-century English texts. The Muscovite nevertheless continues to represent the possibility of "white" slavery that comes to haunt the anxious proprietors of the new geography, a possibility they must exclude from its operations.

Our reading of *Astrophil and Stella* has prepared us for the surprising connections among Russia, servitude, and blackness in Shakespeare's *Love's Labour's Lost*.[45] When the lovers entered the stage disguised as Russians in early performances of the comedy, they were evidently preceded by "Blackamoors with music."[46] These figures come from nowhere; there is no indication that they are also in disguise, and they do not participate in the ensuing action, apart perhaps from providing the music for some portion of it. Twentieth-century scholarship notices them only in connection with the question of Russian disguise and its sources. The claim was made long ago that Shakespeare's blackamoors are related to the "Ne-gro-Tartars" of the Gray's Inn Revels of Christmas 1594–95. The Prince of Purpoole received an ambassador from the Emperor of Russia and two of his colleagues, suitably costumed; they thanked the prince for the services of his six Knights of the Helmet against the "Bigarian" and the curiously spelled "Ne-gro-Tartars" on behalf of the emperor. The knights themselves had entered just before, leading in three prisoners.[47] But the differences between the Gray's Inn episode and *Love's Labour's Lost* are at least as striking as the similarities. The blackamoors are musicians, servants of a sort but hardly captives. The Gray's Inn prisoners were dressed as "Monsters and Miscreants," with no mention of racial disguise; they were in fact allegorical personifications picked up on the return from Russia, named Envy, Malcontent, and Folly.[48] The name *Negro-Tartar* appears a little later in the text of the entertainment; I would suggest that it is a corruption, perhaps unknowing but probably willful and humorous, of "Nogai" or "Nagay Tartar," terms given by Elizabethan travelers in Russia to the inhabitants of the area around the lower Volga River, a warlike people who had recently made peace with the tsar. "Bigarian" may similarly be a play on Boghar or Bokhara (modern Bukhara), a city beyond the Caspian Sea that was a principal market for the Persian trade in slaves from Russia and eastern Europe.[49]

It is true, however, that a connection between Russia and blackness is evident in English texts well before the middle of the sixteenth century. Edward Hall chronicled a device of 1510 in which two lords appeared at Henry VIII's court in Muscovite costume along with two other lords and six ladies dressed as "Nigers, or blacke Mores"; the ladies' faces and arms were covered in thin black cloth. Hall's account was reprinted in the second edition of Holinshed in 1587.[50] Herberstein, in Eden's influential version, writes of "many blacke men, lackynge th[e] use of common spech" who come from Lake Kitai in Siberia to trade precious stones. Aaron is called a "swart Cimmerian" in Shakespeare's own *Titus Andronicus*, a play that also confounds north-south color lines by leaguing the Moor politically and sexually with the Goth Tamora.[51]

In *Of the Russe Common Wealth*, Giles Fletcher wrote that Russia was divided under its ancient name of Sarmatia into "White" and "Black": "*Blacke Sarmatia* was all that countrey that lieth southward, towards the *Euxin*, or *Black Sea*" (p. 2 verso). Of Tartars in general he remarks, "For person and complexion they haue broad and flatte visages, of a tanned colour into yellowe and blacke" (p. 72 recto). These references are all very different, but together they suggest that a discourse linking Russian travel and an increasingly racialized blackness was emerging around the time of *Love's Labour's Lost*.[52] This complex, I suggest, lies behind both the Russian-blackamoor pairing in Shakespeare's play and the rather different case of the Negro-Tartars of Gray's Inn, whatever the lines of local influence may or may not be. The reason for the association of Russia and blackness is bound up with the geography of slavery between the fifteenth and seventeenth centuries. Slavery hardly seems the point in the Russian disguise scene with its blackamoor musicians, and we should not be too quick to assume that it is being represented on stage. But slavery lies behind the love-play of the text, concealed in the court of Navarre's fascination with blackness, beauty, and the gentler servitude of erotic courtship. The action of the play also unites male and female aristocrats in the middle of western Europe by setting them against various social and cultural groupings on their borders, real and fantastic.

The most striking thing about erotic relations between men and women at the court of Navarre is how they are rendered in spatial, almost in carto-graphic, terms, long before the fanciful Muscovites appear in Act V. The king decrees "that no woman shall come within a mile of my court" (1.1.119–20). Don Armado accordingly informs on Costard, having wit-nessed him dallying with Jaquenetta: "But to the place where: It standeth north-north-east and by east from the west corner of thy curious-knotted garden" (1.1.238–40). The comic superposition of large-scale cartographic space on the tiny locale of the court intensifies with the arrival of the Princess of France and her ladies. She is an ambassador from her father, sent to reclaim part of Aquitane from Navarre. That this situation may refer to a 1579 mission by the historical Marguerite de Valois to her husband Henri of Navarre over a dowry that included Aquitane only confirms the link be-tween territory and courtship that the play's fictional action fulfills.[53] No map appears in the stage directions to his negotiation with the princess in Act I, but the episode nevertheless looks forward to the sober map scenes in *King Lear* and *1 Henry IV*.[54] The king says he would prefer a sum of money to Aquitaine, "so gelded as it is" (2.1.149); *geld* is a technical term signifying the reduction in value of land, but it clearly implies a sort of castration as well. Gelded Aquitane represents an obstacle between the king and the princess; a more pressing obstacle is the king's own decree against admitting women to his little academy, which in its turn is rendered spatially when the ladies are forced to encamp outside the court.

The micro-cartography of the court is cumbrously overlaid with the macro-cartography of international politics. Diplomacy, as the travel writ-ings consistently demonstrate, provided the framework for the English con-ception of Russia, the tsar's painstaking ceremonies oddly complementing the awkward barbarism attributed to his people. Russian missions to England confirmed the impressions of English travelers. Ivan IV's ambassa-dor came to England to woo Lady Mary Hastings, Elizabeth's cousin, on be-half of his alliance-seeking master in 1582. According to the contemporary manuscript account of Jerome Horsey, who served some eighteen years in

Russia himself, the emissary's unsuccessful proposal was comically abject.[55] It has long been thought that this episode lies behind the elaborate courtship of the French noblewomen by Navarre and his "Muscovites" in *Love's Labour's Lost*. The play's Russian masquerade might well have been intended to overcome the self-distancing of dynastic courtship by symbolically, and parodically, negotiating and diminishing its difficult terrain by contrast. The space between the princess's camp and the king's court, or even between France and Navarre, is seemingly eclipsed by the difference between Europe and barbarous, servile Muscovy.

Given the contemporary association between Russia and male-male sodomy, however, Muscovite disguise may not have been the best choice for a group of courtiers determined to escape a self-imposed vow to avoid women's company.[56] The ladies take the stratagem as "mockery merriment" and determine to answer it "mock for mock" by masking themselves and jumbling their identities (5.2.139–40). The scene is marked by a quibbling failure in communication:

> *King.* Say to her, we have measur'd many miles
> To tread a measure with her on this grass.
> . . . .
> *Ros.* It is not so. Ask them how many inches
> Is in one mile: if they have measur'd many,
> The measure then of one is easily told.
> (5.2.184–85, 188–90)

Courtly dancing measures are confused with measurement itself as the women refuse to play along. There is something maplike in the pedantic concern with units of measurement. In Anthony Jenkinson's map of Russia, for instance, a chart converting Russian versts into English miles and Spanish leagues occupies the bottom center of the layout. The narrative of Jenkinson's first trip to Russia displays a matching scrupulosity where distances are concerned: "the way to Moscow is as followeth: from Vologda to Commelski, twenty-seven versts; so to Olmor, twenty-five versts, so to Teloytske, twenty versts," and so on.[57] Jenkinson's precision looks back to the itinerary format of medieval travelers, but it became associated with the charting of a vast territory that was almost totally new to the English. The conceit of Russia in

Love's Labour's Lost fails to overcome the apprehension about limitless space and lawless excess, and may actually have aggravated it.

The language of economic calculation runs throughout the Muscovite scene. Like scales of measurement, the cash nexus almost counteracts the anxiety about limitlessness by offering a means of parceling out space and managing it. As Henri LeFebvre argues, however, the early modern sense of space canonized in Descartes' notion of "extension" is perfectly compatible with commodification and the money-form, since each system reduces reality to a homogeneous code or measure.[58] Terms of praise become conditions by which people are made equivalent to property. Acting as herald, Moth hails the princess and her company as "the richest beauties on the earth" and "A holy parcel of the fairest dames"; Boyet remarks that they are no "richer" than the taffeta they wear (5.2.158–60). The Russians ask them to "Price you yourselves: what buys your company?", but the women will not be bought (5.2.224–26). It is the Russians who eventually offer their "service" to each lady (5.2.276, 284). The Elizabethan conjunction of Russia with commercial ventures and an ambiguous relation to servitude also lies behind these exchanges.

It is here that the presence of the blackamoors on stage becomes important as well. Berowne asks the ladies, "Vouchsafe to show the sunshine of your face, / That we, like savages, may worship it" (5.2.201–2). These lines, like the reference to "sun-beamed eyes" at line 169, recall the burning marks of *Astrophil and Stella*. They also look back to an earlier passage, tying the Russian scene to a larger complex of racial difference in the play. "Who sees the heavenly Rosaline," Berowne asks,

> That, like a rude and savage man of Inde,
> At the first opening of the gorgeous east,
> Bows not his vassal head, and strooken blind,
> Kisses the base ground with obedient breast? (4.3.218–22)

The figure of the savage or "Indian" worshiping the sun and perhaps being darkened by it assimilates love-service to an emerging sense of racial difference; it is connected to the discourse of Russia through the idea of servility and the "gorgeous east." Berowne's praise of Rosaline in these terms is complicated by her own appearance, which is in some way "dark" as Katherine's badinage early in Act V attests (5.2.20–42). "By heaven, thy love is black as ebony," the king states in Act IV, to which Berowne replies by praising the exotic wood, a valuable commodity (4.3.244–46).

His defense of Rosaline's black beauty is offset by the king's well-known words on black as the badge of hell, the school of night, and, significantly, the hue of dungeons, linked through conquest and captivity with slavery (4.3.251–52). Dumaine's earlier praise of Katherine as so white she would make Jove swear Juno was an "Ethiop" confirms the king's opinion (4.3.115–16). But Berowne declares that his companions' mistresses use cosmetics. Women should paint themselves black like Rosaline if they want to imitate her natural beauty: "Your mistresses dare never come in rain, / For fear their colours should be washed away" (4.3.260–62, 267–68)—a glancing reminiscence of the Russian women in the travel accounts, perhaps, in a play that also stages the popular view of Muscovite men.

Chimney sweepers, colliers, and Ethiops boast a similar complexion to Rosaline, Berowne's friends retort (4.3.263–64). *Love's Labour's Lost* initially suggests a southern Europe where people are darker in complexion than the English audience (as in "tawny Spain," 1.1.172). The historical Navarre, a border area like Russia, was situated amid France, Spain, and the Mediterranean world, and Moriscos were still to be found in its vicinity during the later sixteenth century.[59] Perhaps we are to conceive of the blackamoor musicians as undisguised natives of Navarre, despite their pairing with the mock Russians.

Ultimately, however, the play subjects this hybrid world to the metaphorical difference of white and black. Even Berowne, despite his suggestive name and rhetorical efforts on behalf of black beauty, imagines Rosaline's hand as "white" (5.2.230, 411). The relation of blackness to beauty remains unstable in the play, but in general it consolidates the ideal of whiteness by offering a contrast to it.[60] The blackamoor musicians almost serve the same purpose in the Russian scene, but the ladies reject their Muscovite suitors, who remain bound up with the blackness and crudity that Russia signified in the travel material. It is left to the pedants and the clowns, with their pageant of the Nine Worthies (another geohistorical farrago), to offer the contrasting image that brings aristocratic men and women together: "'tis some policy," as Berowne remarks, "To have one show worse than the king's and his company" (5.2.508–9). Dynastic politics ultimately intervenes one final time with the French king's death, however, to suspend the consolidation of male and female aristocrats in marriage.

Economic movements may provide a provisional explanation for why the process of othering should be figured through sexuality and gender in the love discourse of Sidney and Shakespeare. Berowne's Rosaline is not so much black as a mixture of shades: "Of all complexions the cull'd sovereignty / Do meet, as at a fair, in her fair cheek" (4.3.231–32). The pun is daring: Rosaline is "fair" in that like a fair she unites contrasting principles for common profit. The slave market of Bukhara also comes to mind. But chattel slavery is subsumed in the language of courtship, in the desire to possess women on the one hand and the offer to serve them on the other. To some extent, love is one of several types of elite discourse behind which the shift in global labor and its racial character can be worked out. It is, however, more than an ideological screen. Women, aristocratic and bourgeois alike, were assigned the role of consumer in the expanding commercial consciousness of Europe, alternately glorified and scapegoated as the source of the demand for luxury goods that drove an expanding system of global trade.[61] Love discourse, with its preexisting ambivalence toward the exalted but capricious lady, dictated that elite men serve their women, providing them with exotica, including, as in *Love's Labour's Lost*, outlandish knowledges and images as well as commodities. Of course, Shakespeare's play parodies the failure of the exotic. As Berowne vows to Rosaline,

> And I will wish thee never more to dance,
> Nor never more in Russian habit wait.
>
> .   .   .   .
>
> Henceforth my wooing mind shall be express'd
> In russet yeas and honest kersey noes. (5.2.400–401, 412–13)

But both kersey cloth, associated with the Russia trade by contemporaries, and the commodities of the gorgeous east were produced within a developing system of global labor and exchange that made the desires of European women its pretext. The terms of heterosexual courtship became intimately bound to the lost labors of slavery and other forms of economic servitude.

The consolidation of "white" aristocrats like Berowne and Rosaline, then, is made possible by class and economic difference as well as a developing sense of racial difference. The constant association of all Russians, including aristocrats, with bondslaves in the travel material assimilates class to race, in fact; this may be the distinguishing feature of Russia in early modern European discourse, a feature that made the figure of the Muscovite an absorbing one for upwardly—and downwardly—mobile subjects in a widening world. Steady commercial relations and political maneuvers in northern Europe kept Russia on the English map under the Stuarts during the early seventeenth century. In 1618 John Fletcher, the nephew of Giles, wrote a play set in Moscow called *The Loyal Subject*. It was performed at court by the King's Company and revived several times thereafter. Unlike his censorious uncle, John Fletcher makes the occasionally violent intrigue of his wholly fictional Russian court a pretext for entertaining rhetorical set-pieces on masochistic obedience. *The Loyal Subject* seems to present a positive take on absolutist imperialism on the Russian model, or anti-model; even if its primary purpose is tragicomic sensationalism, Fletcher's play marks a revaluation of the English view of Russia under James I.[62] Moreover, it does so precisely through its perversely entertaining exploration of the masculine imperial subject's unstable place. Not only is *The Loyal Subject* the only play during the period set wholly in Russia, it is also one of the few plays in which a key male character is cross-dressed as a woman throughout much of the action. Fletcher flirts with the amalgamation of class and race in the Western idea of Russian servility, while subtly recalling the relation among gender, sexuality, and consumption in *Love's Labour's Lost*.

The Loyal Subject was very loosely adapted from Thomas Heywood's *The Royall King and Loyall Subject* (ca. 1600), which in turn was based on the story of Ariobarzanes in William Painter's *The Palace of Pleasure* (1575).[63] Painter's is an oriental tale, set in Persia, but Heywood locates his dramatic version at the English court during an indeterminate past while following the details of Painter's plot quite closely. Fletcher's choice of Moscow for the action of his play may allude to his uncle's expertise while reflecting James' recent interest in Russia.[64] It also represents a compromise between East and West: Russia, a way station for English travelers to Persia, remains both European and Asian. Fletcher retains some of the English coloring Heywood had imparted to the story despite moving it eastward once again, but his setting thoroughly evokes the Elizabethan and Jacobean image of Russia as well.[65] *The Loyal Subject* exploits the tension between otherness and potential similarity that English travelers had long perceived in Russia and its political order.

The Loyal Subject shares some basic ingredients with the earlier versions. In all three texts, a loyal follower comes under suspicion when he is seen as trying to excel his ruler in some way. The disgraced nobleman retires to the country, but the ruler demands that he send his two daughters to court. Painter and Heywood have the ruler marry the first daughter and then send for the other while offering the rehabilitated subject the hand of the princess. Misunderstandings over dowries get the follower in hot water once again, but his loyalty shines through and he is spared execution by a repentant ruler. Fletcher alters the plot drastically, and his changes are linked with the change in setting. The old general Archas resigns when his young rival the prince becomes Duke of Russia, but he is called back into service against the Tartars; victorious, Archas and his soldiers are nevertheless insulted by the duke and his jealous favorite Boroskie. The duke then punishes Archas for a half-imagined fault by demanding that he send both his daughters, named Honora and Viola, to court as waiting women to his sister Olympia. At this point, Fletcher veers sharply from the established story. He is not interested in the daughters except as foils for two original characters, Archas' sons. Theodor, hypermasculine and militaristic, leads Archas' troops against the duke, eventually joining with the Tartars when Archas is imprisoned on another pretext and tortured by the evil Boroskie. The other son, young Archas, has been present from the beginning of the play dressed as the woman "Alinda," one of Olympia's servants (his uncle disguised him to protect him from the new duke). The remainder of *The Loyal Subject* concerns the complications that ensue from Theodor's rebellion and young Archas' cross-dressing; the Duke falls in love with "Alinda" while Olympia is strangely drawn to her. The sons—soldier Theodor and, in a more complex way, cross-dressed Archas-Alinda—are different variations on elements in the Russian discourse that we have met above.

Since young Archas first appears already dressed as Alinda in the second scene of the play, the seventeenth-century audience may have been uncertain whether the young male actor was playing a male or female role. When Alinda is introduced to Olympia, the jealous waiting-women describe her in terms that suggest hidden masculinity while alluding to the image of the Russian woman as well. Her hands are strong enough to strangle the neck of a lute, and her "manly body" looks set to pitch the bar. We are also told that Alinda has "a black eye." "What thinke ye of her colour?" Olympia asks. "If it be her owne / 'Tis good black bloud," the gentlewoman replies, "right weather-proofe I warrant it."[66] Is Alinda wearing makeup, as Russian women reputedly, and boy actors possibly, did? The "black" blood of her complexion probably indicates a high sanguine temperament thought more suitable for a young man. Along with the blackness of her eyes, however, Alinda's "color" ties her to the wider discourse of Russian blackness that we also see in *Love's Labour's Lost*.

Honora and Viola are likewise implicated in the blackness complex. Fearing his sisters' susceptibility to seduction at court, Theodor mockingly presents them to a pair of gentlemen:

> doe you like their complexions?
> They be no Moors: what think ye of this hand gentlemen?
> Here's a white Altar for your sacrifice:
> A thousand kisses here. Nay, keep off yet gentlemen,
> Let's start first, and have fair play: what would ye give now
> To turne the globe up, and finde the riche *Moluccas*?
> To passe the straights? (3.4.9–15)

By the seventeenth century, as Olearius attests, Russians have become white, however dark their eyes or high-flown their complexions. But Theodor's fleer hints that Russian women, though no Moors, may hide the partly Moorish Moluccas beneath their appearance.[67] English travelers originally sought out Russia to reach the Far East and thus "turn the globe up"; the consuming sexuality Theodor imputes to his virtuous sisters represents another sort of dark destination. He says his sisters will wait upon a man, "Drink drunk, and take Tobacco," and bids them "keep close your ports" (3.4.42, 53). Throughout the course of the action women are exchanged like slaves, yet the stigma of foreign trade, excessive luxury, and wayward sexual desire are also attached to them. Olympia dismisses Alinda from her service when she suspects her new waiting-woman of encouraging the attentions of the love-struck duke. Later, she bemoans her mistake:

> Rashly, and madly I betrai'd her modesty,
> Put her to wander, heaven knows where: nay, more sir,
> Strucke a blacke brand upon her. (5.2.79–81)

The bond among blackness, servility, and Russia appears in an indirect and allusive form in *The Loyal Subject.*[68] It is transferred to female, or putatively female, characters. In this way, the text maintains an important tie with the established discourse of Russia while freeing its male characters to enact its main concern, the relation between masculinity and political status in an imperial context.

Nevertheless, the spectre of inadequacy and servile passivity haunts Fletcher's male subjects. At the start of the play, Theodor explains why his father Archas gave up the generalship. When the old duke was alive, he gave command of the army to his son the Prince, the present duke. The prince mustered the army in a sloppy manner and the old duke commanded Archas to correct his mistakes, saying,

> Goe *Archas* speedily,
> And chide the Boy, before the souldier finde him,
> Stand thou between his ignorance and them,
> Fashion their bodies new to thy direction;
> Then draw thou up, and shew the Prince his errours. (1.1.43–47)

Ashamed, the prince threatened Archas and the general vowed to resign when the young man came to the throne. Their antagonism arose from rivalry over the fashioning of the male body, specifically, the body of soldiers necessary for imperial control.

In the next scene, we see how young Archas' "manly body" has been fashioned by Alinda's "behaviour" and appearance (1.2.14, 16). It is Alinda who will attempt to make peace between the rivals by refashioning their relationship in gendered terms. Petitioning Archas to take up arms once more against the Tartars, Alinda entreats,

> If ever you have lov'd; for her sake, sir,
> For your owne honesty, which is a virgin,
> Look up, and pitty us. (1.5.67–69)

Archas' honesty or honor is figured as a virgin for whom he should fight. Alinda uses similar language in accusing the duke of casting off his previous mistress, "Beau-desert":

she has a plainer name: Lord *Archas* service;
Do you yet remember her? there was a Mistris
Fairer then women, far fonder to you sir,
Then Mothers to their first-borne joyes: Can you love? (3.3.60–63)

The duke's love makes Alinda a go-between of sorts between Archas' interests and his own. Alinda recommends one of Archas' daughters, Viola or the
significantly named Honora, as fitter objects for the duke's affections. The
play tends toward this solution, in which the heterosexual order will consolidate aristocratic identity under the sovereign through the recognition of
the noble subject's honor—the sovereign's marriage to aristocratic honesty.
The cross-dressed Alinda urges and seemingly embodies such an imaginary
resolution of masculine conflict. But the duke's love for Alinda blocks the
very compromise it is supposed to effect.

Male cross-dressed characters are rare on the early-modern stage;
Epicoene comes to mind, but unlike Jonson's creation the voluble Alinda
is anything but a silent woman. Added to the plot by Fletcher along with
the Russian setting, the conceit of Alinda recalls the association of Russia
with sodomy. There is no necessary relation between sodomy and cross-
dressing during the period in general, nor does cross-dressing figure in
descriptions of Russian sodomy. Fletcher effects a variation, converting
the male-male sexuality in the Russian material to male cross-dressing in
order to make male bonds a playful but acceptable vehicle for the masculine subject's loyalty to masculine absolutism. The conceit is not entirely
successful, despite Alinda's running commentary. The lesbian desire that
Alinda produces in Olympia is recognized but ultimately scanted by a text
obsessed with male relationships. Furthermore, the duke is more interested in tenors than vehicles. He kisses Alinda upon first seeing her; when
he subsequently sends her a ring it is the waiting-women who literalize
its phallic message: "No doubt you'l find too/A finger fit for you"
(1.2.101, 2.2.37–38). As Olympia eavesdrops, Alinda resists the duke's attentions but considers lying with him "for good fellowship" (3.3.93).
Ultimately, Alinda rejects him:

When you have got my Maiden-head, I take it,
'Tis not an inch of an Apes taile will restore it. (3.3.111–12)

Although Alinda's female disguise supposedly ensures that the duke skirts sodomitical desire in paying court to her, there is a strong suggestion that it is Alinda's masculine attributes, scornfully ennumerated by the waiting-women at the start of the play, that attract the all-powerful ruler. The duke is already under the sway of Boroskie, who is listed in the *dramatis personae* as a "malicious seducing Councellor." It is Boroskie's cowardly failure to lead the troops against the Tartars that compels Archas' return to action, a repetition of the prince's deficiency as a general and Archas' correction of it before the play begins. The sodomy that lurks within the early modern idea of Russia threatens to break the surface of *The Loyal Subject* by means of a new aligment of effeminacy and male-male bonds.

Slavery is the defining feature of the discourse of Russia, and like sodomy it is repressed in the play only to return at crucial moments in the action. Russian slavery is not depicted on stage; the servants who occasionally appear with a piece of news or flagon of wine are much like the servants in other plays of the period. *The Loyal Subject* is about military honor under absolutist rule rather than slavery: its title character is a general, the crisis of the play concerns his son Theodor's armed rebellion against the duke, and much space is given over to a bluff Ancient or ensign who voices the discontent of the common fighting man. Drawing on English curiosity about the Russian army that travelers like Chancellor and his uncle Giles had displayed, Fletcher seeks to replace the figure of the slave with the figure of the *soldier* as the defining instance of Russian identity. Entertaining Muscovite absolutism as the precedent for an imperial England, Fletcher replaces the subject's servility with the hardiness and devotion he also found in the observations of English commentators on Russia.

Slavery, however, begins to overtake soldiery once more when absolutist power is abused, just as sodomy does. At the start of the play, Archas divests himself of his arms, piling them up in a trophy or "ceremonius Embleme" as he recalls routing the Tartar, and thus creating a concrete on-stage symbol of Russian military identity for his men and the English audience (1.3.85). Like Walter Ralegh, recently returned from his adventure on the Orinoco only to face execution, Archas imagines one last sally but resolves to become a hermit. His "wasted body, . . . dry'd up with troubles," he says, is good only for quiet and "holy prayers" (1.3.103–6). The duke is unimpressed, even when Theodor pursues his father's metaphor to include all soldiers:

> Royal sir, I know not
> What you esteem mens lives, whose hourely labours,
> And losse of bloud, consumptions in your service,
> Whose bodies are acquainted with more miseries,
> And all to keep you safe, then Dogs or slaves are. (1.3.123–27)

The masculine body is enslaved rather than glorified when military service goes unrecognized. Literal punishment is inflicted upon Archas' body upon his capture later on: "Your valiant old man's whipt; whipt Gentlemen, / Whipt like a slave" (5.4.4–5). Despite his earlier defense of his soldiers as "men of free-born minds," Archas condemns them for trying to save him from the whip, the ultimate sign of slave status within the Russian discourse (2.1.182).

The body of the soldier, wasted by battle and rent by torture, is reduced and penetrated by tyranny: soldiery almost gives way to slavery and sodomy despite the play's attempt to rewrite the traditional view of Russia. *The Loyal Subject* nevertheless achieves a tragicomic, or unsuccessful, resolution. Archas retains his heroic status because of his masochistic allegiance to the duke, not in spite of it. "Let downe your anger," he tells the soldiers,

> Is this not our Sovereigne,
> The head of mercie, and of Lawe? who dares then,
> But Rebels scorning Law, appear thus violent?
>
> . . . .
>
> Are we not all his Subjects? (4.6.67–69, 73)

The guilty ruler exclaims, "Thou stocke of virtue, how am I bound to love thee" (4.6.106), and finally rejoicing in Archas' honest obedience he takes the general's daughter Honora to wife. Faced with the "strange metamorphosis" of Alinda into young Archas, the duke likewise gives the boy to his sister in marriage ("Here take him"), despite both parties' evident bashfulness (5.6.81–90). Heterosexual closure becomes a symbol for the subject's loyalty at the end of the drama. That it is a hastily improvised and manifestly insufficient symbol is part of the play's humor, which may owe more to the burlesque of Shakespeare's sham Muscovites than at first appears.

Fletcher seemingly resolves the conflict between abject slave and rebellious soldier in his play by entitling it *The Loyal Subject*. Both a subject and loyal,

Archas represents an uneasy compromise between the independence and servility that split the individual under early modern sovereignty, and that English
travelers projected in extreme form onto Russia. The appeal of this compromise
to the Stuart monarchy was confirmed when Fletcher's play was promptly revived with the reopening of the theaters at the Restoration of Charles II in
1660; it was performed again in 1661.[69] Contemporaries might have found a
counterstatement to Fletcher's theatrical refashioning of male sexuality as political loyalty in the English translation of Olearius, published in 1662 and dedicated to the Muscovy Company. According to Olearius, sodomy and theatri-
cality are indeed closely linked in Russia: "Those who lead Bears about, Juglers
and Puppet-players, who erect a Stage in a moment, by the means of a coverlet, which, being ty'd about their wast, is brought over their heads, and within
it show their Puppets, representing their brutalities and sodomies, make sport
to the Children, who are thereby induc'd to quit all sentiments of shame and
honesty" (p. 81). The skirtlike coverlet, raised to hide the arms of the puppeteer
while revealing his nether parts, suggests both cross-dressing and sodomitical
reversal. "But handsomely and well?", Theodor mimics the faint praise his soldiers receive from the Duke's minion, "what, are we juglers?" (2.1.113).

John Milton would certainly have questioned John Fletcher's theater of
loyal subjectivity in Russian dress. His *Moscovia* was in fact largely dependent on the playwright's anti-absolutist kinsman for its tone as well as its information: "Dr. *Giles Fletcher* went Ambassador from the queen to *Pheodor*
then Emperour; whose Relations being judicious and exact, are best red entirely by themselves" (p. 534). Milton may be directing his readers to the
"entire" freestanding edition of Giles Fletcher's book published in 1643
under the title *The History of Russia, or, The Government of the Emperor of
Muscovia*. The version in Hakluyt that Milton himself had at his elbow cen-
sored most of the elder Fletcher's disapproving comments about the tsar. As
noted earlier in the chapter, the 1643 edition, reissued in 1657, was read
throughout the Civil War and Commonwealth period as a coded critique of
absolutism at large and of absolutist tendencies in England.

The tsar severely cut down the Muscovy Company's trading privileges
when Charles I was beheaded in 1649, precipitating three unsuccessful English
embassies to Russia; as Secretary for Foreign Tongues, Milton helped prepare
the final envoy in 1657 and may have been involved in the earlier projects.
Charles II corresponded with the tsar during his exile, and in 1664–65 Milton's

flexible friend Andrew Marvell accompanied Lord Carlisle on his mission from Charles.[70] The revivals of both Fletchers during these decades can be seen as opposing moves in a cultural duel between monarchical and antimonarchical sides who looked to the Elizabethan and Jacobean past for their differing understandings of Russia and of empire in general. Although an early text, the *Moscovia* may have been affected by later debates and Milton's participation in them. It certainly registers the Elizabethan astonishment at the tsar's power: "He bore the Majesty of a mighty Emperour; his Crown and Sceptre of pure gold, a Collar of Pearls about his Neck, his Garment of crimson Velvet embroider'd with precious stone and gold" (p. 536). Milton's implicit tributes to the modest industry of English explorers throughout the *Moscovia* contrasts with the emperor's almost satanic majesty.

The English, however, have also come to resemble Satan in the empty materialism of their quest for wealth in a land of slavery. The magnificent depreciation of the English voyagers in Milton's quiet rhetoric is worth quoting in full at this point in my study:

> The discovery of *Russia* by the northern Ocean, made first, of any Nation that we know, by *English* men, might have seem'd an enterprise almost heroick; if any higher end than the excessive love of Gain and Traffick, had animated the design. Nevertheless that in regard that many things not unprofitable to the knowledge of Nature, and other Observations are hereby come to light, as good events ofttimes arise from evil occasions, it will not be the worst labour to relate briefly the beginning, and proscecution of this adventurous Voiage; untill it became at last a familiar Passage. (p. 524)

A barely fortunate fall, the discovery of Russia matches Satan's venture through Chaos and the well-traveled bridge it established between Hell and Earth in *Paradise Lost*.[71] Only knowledge and observation survive Milton's critique, yet they are valuable booty in themselves, for together they animate the cautionary "design" or model of empire and its consequences for political subjectivity and racial identity. The line from Giles Fletcher to John Milton traces the genealogy of English responses to such a model and the troubling place of Russia within it.

FOUR

The Performance of India and Dryden's *Aureng-Zebe*

Our survey of early modern Russia has already brought us to a distant prospect of India. The treatise on "The vyage to Cathay and East India by the north sea" in Eden's *Decades of the newe worlde* (1555) links India with Muscovy, for the overland route to the riches of the East would wend through Muscovy. India and Russia were both external to the European world economy during the sixteenth and seventeenth centuries, but they represented different degrees of otherness.[1] If Russia was a sort of anticivilization in western European eyes, India appeared to be an incoherent and dynamic mixture of civilizations and time periods. Eden provides a plethora of economic and geographical detail from classical texts to demonstrate the key role India and its readily accessible wealth played in the Roman Empire. Just as Egypt had served Rome as the economic gateway to India in the south during antiquity, Eden's circuitous argument implies, so Russia should serve England in the north.

The parallel assumes, however, that the India of classical authors was the same India that lay beyond Russia, the same India that the Portuguese had attained by sea, a proposition by no means self-evident in the sixteenth century. Eden turns to cultural evidence to cap his economic argument:

> The places of Arabie and India named of Strabo and Plinie, are the selfe same where the Portugales practise theyr trade at this daye, as the maners and customes of the Indians doo yet declare. For euen at this presente theyr women vse to burne theym selues alyue with the deade bodies of theyr husbandes. Which thynge (as wryteth Strabo in his. xv. booke) they dyd in owlde tyme by a lawe, for this consideration that sumtyme being in loue with other they forsooke or poysoned theyr husbandes. And forasmuch as accordynge to this custome, the owlde poete Propertius . . . hath in his boke made mention of the contention that was amonge the Indian women which of them shuld bee burned aliue with theyr husbandes, I haue thought good to subscribe his verses.[2]

Eden makes the practice of widow sacrifice into a sign of cultural continuity, a bridge between the India recorded in the texts of classical European antiquity and the commercially promising India of his day.[3] His turn toward culture is part of a European preoccupation with religion in general and Hindu practices in particular in travel material from before the mid-seventeenth century.

Much current work on India is concerned with the Mughal court and with European views of its political, economic, and military organization.[4] This chapter tells a different story, a story intended to supplement without replacing the familiar narrative of diplomatic and commercial contact between Europe and the Mughals. One reason for my concern with non-Mughal materials, and thus with mostly Hindu, religious, and cultural representations, is the sheer number of sixteenth- and seventeenth-century printed sources from Europe that do not deal primarily with the Mughal empire. This wing of the archive has been partially lost to sight. Despite the archive's biases, of course, Hindu and other religious groups in India possessed their own political and economic organizations, and should not be aligned exclusively with "culture" any more than the Mughals, with their vibrant interest in the visual arts and alternation of Islamic and syncretic tendencies, should be seen in strictly statist terms.

In Richard Eden, women become the representatives of culture over time as well as space, and of a fundamental uniformity that supposedly lies behind the apparent diversity and instability of India as well. The link between woman and India in early-modern English eyes reached an apogee of sorts 120 years after Eden in John Dryden's heroic play *Aureng-Zebe* (1675), with which the following discussion concludes. To the male European gaze, the burning woman was the ultimate sign both of disintegration and continuity in India and by extension the other old worlds, a spectacular consolidation of monumentality and performance in which body becomes statue and is consumed in the very act of commemoration.

The verses from Propertius (ca. 23 B.C.) that Eden cites vividly show how female bodies in motion paradoxically stabilize the notion of "Indianness." The passage constitutes one of the earliest European depictions of widow burning or *sati*, as the practice has been called in English since the nineteenth century. I quote text and translation from a twentieth-century scholarly edition:

> felix Eois lex funeris una maritis,
> quos Aurora suis rubra colorat equis!
> namque ubi mortifero iacta est fax ultima lecto,
> uxorum fusis stat pia turba comis,
> et certamen habent leti, quae viva sequatur
> coniugium: pudor est non licuisse mori.
> ardent victrices et flammae pectora praebent,
> imponuntque suis ora perusta viris.

"Blest is that peerless law for the burial of Eastern husbands, whom the crimson dawn colours with her steeds! For when the last torch is set to the dead man's bier his wives stand round, a pious company with streaming hair, and struggle for death one with another, who living shall follow her dead lord; 'tis shame to be debarred from death. The victors burn and offer their breasts to the flame and lay charred faces on their husband's body."[5]

Some consideration of the term *sati* itself will bring us back to Propertius' poem and the work it performs. English usage of the word arose in the context of attempts to regulate and finally abolish widow sacrifice in British India during the mid-eighteenth to early nineteenth centuries. As Gayatri Chakravorty Spivak puts it, "*sati* or *suttee* as the proper name of the rite of widow self-immolation commemorates a grammatical error on the part of the British." In Sanskrit, *sati* is the feminine form of *sat* ("to be," "being," "true," "good") and means "good wife." It refers to a person, not an action.[6] The assimilation of persons, bodies, and things to actions or movements, as we shall see, was a chief characteristic of the European discourse on India since Propertius' time, although the redefinition of *sati* was a very late and perhaps accidental addition to the formation. Like the early modern texts he influenced, the Roman poet does not, of course, use the word or any other term for widow burning. But his verses take their dynamism from the pious yet disordered group of wives (*pia turba*) with their streaming hair; they struggle for the right to burn with the body, and the victors lay their scorched or perhaps already burnt (*perusta*) faces on their somehow still-present husband amid the flames. It is above all female bodies that are sublimated by movement and performance in the discourse on India.

Although the presentation of *sati* in the Propertius passage is wholly affirmative, it contains several elements that also figure in the pathbreaking attempts by Lata Mani and Spivak to reevaluate the abolition of *sati* by the British authorities in 1829. These elements appear in the intervening discourse of early modern European times as well. "Blest is that peerless law for the burial of Eastern husbands," Propertius writes. The notion that *sati* was mandated by some monolithic "law" would remain a constant in European descriptions for almost two thousand years. From the late eighteenth to early nineteenth centuries, as Lata Mani has charted, the British consulted learned Brahmans about the status of *sati* in Hindu sacred writings. Despite the often provisional nature of these pundits' replies and wide regional variation in the practice of *sati*, the result was an inaccurately uniform and text-based notion of both *sati* and Hindu personal law. Ultimately, this law was said properly to forbid *sati*, which had supposedly emerged from a tainted version of the law. The protection of Indian women was the putative goal, yet the documents show that it was the "feasibility" of banning a religious rite with a popular following in Bengal, not the moral imperative of stopping widow burning, that motivated the British investigation. Far from modernizing India, the resultant legislation produced traditional authority in abolishing *sati*; in the process women were reduced to will-less victims or passive heroines.[7] Spivak shows how *sati* was turned from a ritual into a crime, a violation of the law itself, the law of British India: "the protection of woman (today the 'third-world woman') becomes the signifier for the establishment of a *good* society which must, at such in-augurative moments, transgress mere legality."[8] In codifying Hindu law, the British inevitably overturned their image of it, as well as their own code of noninterference.

In Mani's view, women were doubly erased by the inauguration around 1829 of two related yet somewhat conflicting versions of Hindu "tradition" in colonial discourse. One version, to which she devotes the most space, equated tradition with archaic religious scriptures and made the figure of the Indian woman the site of disagreements over their import. In the other, "Tradition . . . is posited as a timeless and structuring principle of Indian so-ciety enacted in the everyday lives of indigenous people. . . . It is thus that officials can speak of returning to natives the truth of traditions that had been interrupted by the 'Islamic interlude.'"[9] Both versions make woman the emblem or sign of tradition while erasing women's will, subjecthood, or agency. Nevertheless, there is a tension between the two versions of tradi-tion in Mani's account: one should probably conclude that by the 1820s tra-dition as timeless popular principle was thought to be recoverable from the scriptural tradition of pundits and British administrators. The colonial scene abetted the identification of Hindu tradition with India itself, exclud-ing Islam, for instance, along with other religious and secular ways of un-derstanding the Indian past.[10] Mughal attempts to discourage *sati* were re-cast as an inadequate policy of compromise with a corrupt tradition the Mughals' presence had somehow helped create. In the legislation of 1829 the British perpetuation of Mughal tactics since the seventeenth century was effectively elided.[11]

Early modern European accounts of *sati* differ in many ways from the Enlightenment discourse upon which most recent theoretical considera-tions of the practice are based. The Propertian notion of law provides a common thread, but from the fourteenth through seventeenth centuries there are no scriptures, no pundits, and little reference to monuments or the visual arts as sources of legal tradition. To the European observer, "tradi-tion" was already present in Mani's somewhat secondary sense: "a transhis-torical and ubiquitous force *acted out* by people" (my emphasis). As Mani herself notes, this notion of tradition was akin to the "manners and cus-toms" material in Enlightenment travel writing, a descriptive genre that de-rived, I would add, from early modern travel writing.[12] The essence of a people was discoverable in their customs, habits, and daily behavior. It was performative, and thus open to the observer's eye and scholar's wit—or so European observers and scholars assumed, with no systematic recourse to the writings, monuments, or learned members of the Indian communities they surveyed until well into the seventeenth century.[13] Action, performance, and thus the body mark the pre-Enlightenment discourse of India, and the Indian body was largely, but not exclusively, a female body.

The concluding lines of the passage from Propertius, omitted in Eden, read,

> hoc genus infidum nuptarum, hic nulla puella
> nec fida Euadne nec pia Penelope.

"But here the race of brides is faithless; here doth no woman show Evadne's faith or Penelope's loyalty" (3.13.23-24). For the Romans, India was above all the land of somatic contrast. "What barbarous country more rude and wild than India?" Cicero asks in *Tusculan Disputations*:

> Yet amongst its people those, to begin with, who are reckoned sages [*sapientes*] pass their lives unclad and endure without show of pain the snows of the Hindu Kush and the rigour of winter, and when they throw themselves voluntarily into the flames they let themselves be burnt without a moan; whilst the women in India, when the husband of any of them dies, compete with one another to decide whom the husband loved best . . . and she who is victorious, accompanied by her relatives, goes joyfully to join her husband on the funeral pyre.[14]

Propertius and Cicero make women the emblems or representatives of their people, and use the example of *sati* to admonish their luxurious contemporaries.

For Cicero in particular, however, the woman's body is an extension of the man's, and civilization itself is at base masculine. The composite figure of the Indian woman as the sign of India returns again and again in European representations of the subcontinent, but there is a foundational concern with the male body throughout the material as well. Cicero, after all, begins his passage with the Indian sages, who suffer snow and fire alike without the protection of clothes. He clearly has the Greek tradition of the gymnosophists or "naked philosophers" in mind. Diogenes Laertius refers to the *gymnosophistas* when citing the lost history of Clitarchus (ca. 310 B.C.), but the word was probably a later coinage; Strabo (64 B.C.–A.D. 21) apparently presumes that the readers of his Greek geography will be familiar with it.[15] Clitarchus wrote a lost history of Alexander the Great, and it was after Alexander's Indian campaign near the end of the fourth century B.C. that the Indian sages entered the imagination of European antiquity. The contemporary name for them, accurately enough, was *Brachmanes*, from Brahmans, and it probably appeared first in another historian of Alexander, Aristobulus, whom Strabo cites.[16]

The earliest Greek work devoted to India was Ctesias' *Indica*, from the late fifth century B.C., which is preserved only though citation in other works. Ctesias evidently did not mention the Indian sages, but he emphasized that all Indians were exceptionally just and professed a contempt of death.[17] His work was mostly given over to descriptions of legendary flora and fauna, such as the gryphon and the scorpion-tailed manticore (pp. 11, 44). He seems to have reserved special attention for strange bodily types among the inhabitants: it is here that we find the Pygmies and the Cynocephali, or dog-headed people (pp. 15, 21–25). The next Greek author whose work substantially survives was the Seleucid diplomat Megasthenes, who wrote at the end of the fourth century B.C. An abstract of his book in Diodorus Siculus shows that his interests were entirely different from Ctesias'. Instead of wonders, we have a rudimentary description of society. India is bounded on the north by Scythia, and its people, unlike their northern neighbors, are "apt for any art or possession" because of the healthy land they dwell in.[18] The Indians never colonized others, nor were they ever colonized; but Megasthenes goes on to discuss the invasions of Dionysus and Herakles, culture-heroes and precursors of Alexander (pp. 96–97). The Indians are divided into seven "tribes," of which the Philosophers are foremost. The Philosophers conduct sacrifices, tend to the dead, and predict bad weather and other disasters (p. 97). According to Strabo, "Megasthenes makes another division in his discussion of the philosophers, asserting that there are two kinds of them, one kind called Brachmanes and the other Garmanes." Among the Garmanes— *Sramanas*, or extreme ascetics—are a smaller group of forest dwellers or Hybolii, who eat leaves and wear nothing except for tree bark.[19]

Pomponius Mela, the pioneering Roman geographer from the first century A.D., helped focus the tradition in *De Chorographia*. The Indians are defined by bodily practices. Some will eat no living thing; others honor their dead by consuming their organs. "The wiser sort of them, which are trained up in the profession and studie of wisdome, linger not for death, but hasten it by throwing themselues into the fyre, which is counted a glorie."[20] Pomponius' contemporary Pliny the Elder writes that "among the Indians be certaine Philosophers, whom they call Gymnosophists, who from the Sunne rising to the setting thereof are able to endure all the day long, looking full against the Sunne, without winking or once moving their eies: & from morning to night can abide to stand sometimes upon one leg, and sometimes upon the other in the sand, as scalding hot as it is."[21] In Pliny, the funeral pyre has been replaced by sun and hot sand. A little later, in a description of India modeled on Megasthenes, Arrian described the seven tribes or castes and especially the Sophists, who go naked all year long, sheltering from the sun in the shade of huge trees during the summertime.[22] Arrian also records that "the Indians do not rear monuments to the dead, but consider the virtues which men have displayed in life, and the songs in which their praises are celebrated, sufficient to preserve their memory after death" (p. 204). In his better-known *Anabasis of Alexander*, Arrian cites Megasthenes and the lost work of Nearchus in describing the Indian sage Calanus, who sought Alexander's patronage but ended by throwing himself into the pyre when he fell ill.[23]

An enduring pattern is established in these early texts: monuments are replaced by bodies, bodies that assume the rigid postures of statues themselves, are consumed by flames, and are commemorated in death by rituals and performances. Nakedness and a strict or peculiar diet also mark the Indian body. The somewhat contradictory fundamentals of the discourse were in fact already present in crude form in Herodotus. One tribe of Indians, he writes, kill their friends when they become sick despite their protests; another will take no life of any kind, have no houses, and are vegetarians.[24] The image of India and its "Brachmans" was fixed in the fourth century A.D. in the influential *Alexander Romance*. After conquering India, Alexander visits the Brachmans or gymnosophists, who tell him that they possess nothing he can take away from them. He asks them a series of questions whose quizzical answers point toward the vanity of earthly power.

Alexander's first question, "Do you not have graves?" is a significant one. "This place we live in is my grave," the gymnosophist replies. "I shall lie here in the earth and bury myself in the sleep of those who dwell under the earth."[25] Much of the classical discourse on India had been lost—burial of the dead runs against the tradition—but the question and its answer carried the antimonumental pattern into the Middle Ages.

By the early fourteenth century European travelers had reached India and their observations augmented the gradual recovery of classical knowledge.[26] The presence of monumental architecture and statuary was often noted by the moderns, but its significance in the travel tradition remained ambiguous. Friar Jordanus framed his travels in India as a succession of wonders almost in the manner of Ctesias. "Here there be many and boundless marvels," he tells the reader in *Mirabilia Descripta*, "and in this first India beginneth, as it were, another world; for the men and women be all black, and they have for covering nothing but a strip of cotton tied round the loins."[27] Jordanus is struck by the Indians' consumption of rice and neglect of bread despite their cultivation of wheat. Later he tells us, "The people of this India are very clean in their feeding; true in speech, and eminent in justice, maintaining carefully the privileges of every man according to his degree, as they have down from old times" (p. 22). India is another world from Europe not because of its geographical situation at the imagined antipodes, but because of the different bodily demeanors and practices of its inhabitants. What goes in at their mouths is balanced by the truth of what comes out of them; the community that regulates this symmetry, though homogeneous in Jordanus' view, is differentiated within according to degree. Caste is typically reduced by Jordanus to a simplified social grid for European observers, yet it is still through some notion of caste as a social relation that he ties the Indians to antiquity or "old times," rather than through their knowledge of the gods or monumental buildings.

Jordanus does note the importance of buildings to Hindu worship:

In this India the greater part of the people worship idols, although a great share of the sovereignty is in the hands of the Turkish Saracens, who came forth from Multan, and conquered and usurped dominion to themselves not long since, and destroyed an infinity of idol temples, and likewise many churches, of which they made mosques for Mahomet, taking possession of their endowments and property. 'Tis grief to hear, and woe to see! (p. 23)

There are several elements in this passage that later Europeans would repeat time and again. Indian antiquities seem perpetually to have been destroyed, or under threat of destruction, or neglected and in decay. Islam— Jordanus' "Turkish Saracens" or, properly, the Mughal sultanate of subsequent accounts—has acted as a great eraser, almost wiping clean any monuments that might link India with a European classical past. In Jordanus' lament, it is unclear whether it is the destruction of the Christian churches only that is such a woe to see, or whether the pagan temples are included in his regret over a past lost to the Islamic invader. If Hinduism is made out to be ontologically as well as historically prior to Islam in Jordanus' exemplary evocation of a marvelous Indianness, it is because this priority serves a European insistence that the India of medieval and early modern times is the same as the India of Graeco-Roman antiquity.[28]

The link with European antiquity is stressed by the Venetian Niccolo Conti, who traveled all the way to Taprobane or Ceylon (Sri Lanka).[29] His observations, gathered in the second quarter of the fifteenth century, sustain the note of ambivalent admiration in Jordanus. Conti warns of man-eaters in Taprobane who use heads as currency, but he maintains that the governing Brahmans are wise astrologers who cultivate a civilized way of life (pp. 8–9). Dividing India into three parts, he claims that the third and furthest region, the great Hindu kingdom of Vijayanagar in the south, "excels the others in riches, politeness, and magnificence, and is equal to our own country in the style of life and in civilization. For the inhabitants have most sumptuous buildings, and handsome furniture; they lead a more refined life, removed from all barbarity and coarseness. The men are extremely humane, and the merchants very rich" (p. 21). The mixture of difference and "equality" with Italian manners extends to religion in the subcontinent as a whole: "Gods are worshipped throughout all India, for whom they erect temples very similar to our own, the interior being painted with figures of different kinds. On solemn days these temples are adorned with flowers. Within them they place their idols" (p. 27). The presence of Islam and other Indian religions is hardly recognized. Conti seems at pains to indicate a potential compatibility between Hindu and Christian belief. "All worship idols," he remarks at the outset, "nevertheless when they rise in the morning from their beds they turn towards the east, and with their hands joined together say, 'God in Trinity and His law defend us'" (p. 13). Conti is probably referring to the linkage of Brahma with the principal gods Vishnu and Shiva in some forms of Hindu worship. Recollections of Alexander and classical antiquity are capped by parallels between a supposedly trinitarian Hinduism and Christianity.

The eastern voyages of another Italian adventurer, Ludovico di Varthema, were published in 1510 and went through many editions. According to Varthema, the inhabitants of the northwestern kingdom of Gujarat "are a certain race which eats nothing that has blood, and never kills any living thing. And these same people are neither Moors nor heathens. It is my opinion that if they were baptised, they would all be saved by virtue of their works, for they never do to others what they would not that others should do to them."[30] Varthema is apparently recalling either Hindu ascetics or followers of Jainism in what was a Muslim kingdom. His most influential piece of garbled syncretism, however, helped to demonize Indian religion in European eyes for centuries to come. Writing of the southwestern coastal city of Calicut, Varthema claimed to have seen the chief idol in the king's private sanctum. Called Deumo, the idol represents the Devil, worshiped in preference to God by the king: "The said devil has a crown made like that of the papal kingdom, with three crowns; it has also four horns and four teeth with a very large mouth, nose, and most terrible eyes. The hands are made like those of a flesh-hook and the feet like those of a cock." Deumo is flanked by two figures of "Sathanas," each devouring a damned soul (p. 137). The entire passage has been examined in detail by Partha Mitter in his masterful book *Much Maligned Monsters*: Varthema's tableau corresponds to nothing in Hindu iconography and clearly derives instead from medieval European images of "Sathanas" enthroned in Hell. Medieval travelers had already associated India with devil worship, and an element of antipapal satire has crept into the picture with the triple mitre as well.[31] I would note that the three crowns turn the tables on the trinitarian claims made for Hinduism, revealed here as a parody of Christian belief that somehow parallels papal abuses. As Mitter demonstrates, Varthema's invention became the dominant image of Hindu idolatry in Europe. Not only was his book translated through numerous editions, but its description of Deumo was also copied by later travelers who inserted it into their own eyewitness accounts. Deumo proved particularly popular in England, making his first appearance in Richard Eden's translation of Sebastian Munster's rendering in 1553, and then under Varthema's name in Eden's 1577 volume.[32]

Varthema's demonization of Calicut and its ruler occurred just as the Portuguese were poised finally to take over the city. Vasco da Gama's trading mission to the city in 1497 had been the culmination of seventy years of Portuguese interest in the East and its spice trade. With the vanquishing of local Muslim sultanates and the violent wresting of sea-lanes from Arab traders, the Portuguese rapidly established colonial outposts at Bombay, Goa, and Calicut itself. One of the earliest and most important Portuguese travelers was Duarte Barbosa, who wrote his description of India around 1518. Unlike Varthema, Barbosa stresses the Muslim character of Gujarat and its port city Cambay to the north, but he also notes the continued importance of the Hindu traders or Banians who once ruled it, and its Brahman priests. He is among the first to acknowledge the architectural splendor of the Hindu temples he had seen, while mentioning the presumed link between Hinduism and Christianity:

> In these houses are great numbers of wooden idols, and others of stone and copper, and in these houses or monasteries they celebrate great ceremonies in honour of these idols, entertaining them with great store of candles and oil-lamps, and with bells after our fashion.
>
> These *Bramenes* and Heathen have in their creed many resemblances to the Holy Trinity, and hold in great honour the relation of the Triune Three, and always make their prayers to God, whom they confess and adore as the true God, Creator and maker of all things, who is three persons and one God, and they say that there are many other gods who are rulers under him in whom they also believe.[33]

Like Conti, Barbosa seems to be thinking of the three-headed image of Vishnu, Brahma, and Shiva, a relatively recent development in Hindu iconography. When they enter a Christian church, he adds, the Brahmans honor it and the images it contains and ask for "Santa Maria," claiming there is little difference between themselves and the Christians (p. 116).

Barbosa dryly records these matters without commentary; his stress on the "idol worship" of the Brahmans in their temples rests uneasily alongside the comparison with Christian practices, however, reminding us of the triple-crowned Deumo. The groundwork for religious assimilation proves treacherous, as trinitarian parallels lead to Brahman claims on the Blessed Virgin and intimations of Christian idolatry. The overwhelming impression of Hindu India Barbosa conveys elsewhere is one of extreme and even violent disparity, disparity within itself and certainly disparity from Christianity. He frequently remarks the fineness and permanence of temples, houses, and streets in the major cities he visits (pp. 140, 175, 202). Against these settings, however, he casts an array of distorted bodies and bizarre customs. It is to Barbosa's chapter on Vijayanagar or Bisnagua that we will turn in a few pages for perhaps the earliest sixteenth-century European description of *sati*, for instance. In this chapter he also describes another event that would become a staple of subsequent travel narratives:

> If any young maiden would marry a youth on whom she would set her fancy she makes a vow to her god that if he will arrange for her marriage she will do him a great service before giving herself to her husband. . . . Then, appointing a certain day for the ceremony, they take a great ox-cart and set up therein a tall water-lift like those used in Castille for drawing water from wells, at the end of which hang two very sharp iron hooks. She goes forth on the appointed day in the company of her relations and friends, men and women, with much music played and sung, also dancers and tumblers. She is naked from the waist up, and wears cotton garments below. When she arrives at the gate where the cart stands ready, they let down (the long arm of) the lift and push the hooks into her loins, through skin and flesh. . . . She remains hanging from the lift with the blood running down her legs, but shows no sign of pain, nay, she waves her dagger most joyfully, throwing limes at her husband. In this manner they conduct her to the temple wherein is the idol to whom she has vowed such a sacrifice. (pp. 220–22)

The flesh-hooks of Varthema's devil come to mind. In later depictions of "hook-swinging" the practice is rarely attributed to female devotees. Barbosa goes on to claim that certain women in Vijayanagar sacrificed their

daughters' virginity to crude phallic idols in elaborate temple ceremonies
(pp. 222–23).

Against Barbosa's juxtaposition of temples and the violent manipulation
of women's bodies must be set the contemporary account of Vijayanagar by
another Portuguese traveler, Domingos Paes. Composed in the early 1520s,
Paes' narrative links monumental architecture and the female body in a less
troubling manner. Its dominant image is the company of temple dancers,
who first appear to honor Ganesh in a city he calls "Darcha":

> They feed the idol every day, for they say that he eats; and when he eats
> women dance before him who belong to that pagoda, and they give him
> food and all that is necessary, and all girls born of these women belong to
> the temple. These women are of loose character, and live in the best streets
> that there are in the city; . . . They are very much esteemed and are classed
> amongst those honoured ones who are the mistresses of the captains.[34]

Paes' account of Hindu architecture is markedly dynamic: the idol is said
to perform an activity, to eat, and the women dance before it in the temple
and are then placed in the best houses in the city. The disjuncture between
the dancers' "loose character" and their "much esteemed" status is jarring.[35]
Perhaps unknowingly, Paes is recurring to what Partha Mitter has identified
as one of the founding medieval images of India, Marco Polo's description
of maidens dancing before the idol to which they have been dedicated. A
manuscript illumination in the fourteenth-century *Livre des merveilles* represents the scene as one of "Indian nuns dancing before a nun-like idol."[36]
In Paes' version all traces of syncretism are absent, but the traveler repeatedly bears witness to the importance of women and dance to Hindu worship, calling them *baylhadeiras* or bayaderes (pp. 253, 258, 264).[37]

The opening description of the temple or "pagoda" at Darcha itself is
worth dwelling on:

> You must know that it is a round temple made of a single stone, the gate-
> way all in the manner of joiners' work, with every art of perspective. There
> are many figures of the said work, standing out as much as a cubit from the
> stone, so that you see on every side of them, so well carved that they could
> not be better done—the faces as well as all the rest; and each one in its

place stands as if embowered in the Romanesque style. . . . Besides this, it has a sort of lesser porch upon pillars, all of stone, and the pillars with their pedestals so well executed that they appear as if made in Italy. (p. 233)

The reference to perspective is remarkable, given the later insistence among European observers that perspective was invented in the classical West and perfected in Italy. Whatever the accuracy of Paes' viewpoint may be, he finds a form of perspective again and again, in the reliefs of the capital's chief temple, and in the dancing hall of its palace, where "on the pillars are other images, smaller, with other images yet more subordinate . . . in such a way that I saw this work gradually diminishing in size." The dancing images carved on the pillars also have a purpose, for they serve to teach and remind the women of the final positions in various dances (p. 251, 276–77). Paes' evocation of perspective is thus linked with the dynamism of the buildings he sees: the architecture and its designs in some fashion imply movement through space, and the dancers' performances within them are an extension of the architecture itself.

The curious word *pagoda* or, as it is more often spelled, *pagode* inscribes the movement from monumentality to performance in the early modern discourse of India. The word found its way into Renaissance English texts from Portuguese and Dutch sources as *pagod*. It is used in three principal ways in European texts, to refer to a temple, an idol, or a type of coin. The best account of its origins is still to be found in *Hobson-Jobson*, Colonel Henry Yule's glossary of hybrid English and Asian vocabulary that is itself a remarkable artifact of Victorian imperialism and its antecedents in India. Like the English soldiers' slang expression for Indian festivity from which the dictionary takes its title, *pagode* represents a confluence of European and Indian languages.[38] It may have originated in the mis-hearing of some indigenous word or expression, but at bottom it remains a Portuguese word with no stable cognate in any "native" tongue. It seems related to *pagão*, Portuguese for "a pagan"; other sources may include the Sinhalese and Persian words for temples. Suggested Chinese origins came along after the word was introduced to China by Europeans, where it took up permanent residence as the familiar "pagoda." The closest non-European cognates are Sanskrit *bhagavat*, "holy" or "divine," and *Bhagavati*, an epithet applied to female divinities. Like the word *fetish*, which has a comparable early history, *pagode* remains a non-European European word that eventually compressed vastly different religious beliefs and geographical regions.[39] It was, perhaps, the first "Orientalist" word.

Pagode also binds together different meanings, modulating from the architectural through the anthropomorphic to the idea of exchange and circulation itself in the money form, depending on the text in which it appears. Along the way, it accumulates other associations through metonymy and paronomasia. The primary referent seems to be temple, or idol-temple, a religious structure organized around worship of a particular deity. According to Paes, "These pagodas are buildings in which they pray and have their idols; the idols are of many sorts, namely, figures of men and women, of bulls, and apes, while others have nothing but a round stone which they worship" (p. 234). The translation of Fernão Lopez de Castanheda's *First Booke of the Historie of the Discouerie and Conquest of the East Indias*, which appeared in 1582, introduced the word into English at a relatively early date. In his second book Castanheda employs *pagode* to denote both temples and idols; in the translated portion it refers primarily to buildings: "all the kynges [of Calicut] doe dye in one *Pagode*, which is the house of praiers to their Idolls." Castanheda also uses it for Hindu deities themselves, however. When the nobles rebuke their king, "The Divell is oftentimes in them, but they say it is one of their Gods or *Pagodes*, for so they call him."[40] The possessed body mediates between sacred buildings and idols that assume a range of forms.

The influential account of Jan Huyghen Van Linschoten, whose detailed observations were published in Holland in 1596, notes the coins: "They are Indian and Heathenish money with the picture of a Diuell vpon them, and therefore are called *Pagodes*."[41] The 1674 edition of Thomas Blount's *Glossographia* contains the entry: "*Pagod* (quasi Pagan-God), an Idol or false god among the Indians; also a kind of gold coin among them equivalent to our Angel."[42] The coins bore an image of either a temple or a deity; "devils" rather than Angels, their implicit similarity to the English coins bearing a religious image is not explored. A stamped coin is a kind of miniature idol in circulation. It suggests a somewhat disturbing link between commerce and religion, not so much among the Indians as the Portuguese and eventually English authorities who took over the minting of pagods as part of their economic strategy. The English translation of the Italian traveler Pietro della Valle, published in 1664, speaks of a minor Indian ruler "who

in all hath not abouve 2000 Paygods of yearly Revenew."⁴³ The pun buried
in "paygods," like the partially false etymology from "Pagan-God" in the
dictionary definition, shows how the word in English lent itself to the ac-
cretion of secondary but telling meanings. The word *pagode* marks a cultural, economic, and ultimately imperial contest among the Portuguese,
Dutch, and English as much as a set of Indian artifacts or places.

In 1598 Linschoten's travels appeared in English translation, complete
with pagod in the sense of idol or statue as well as coin. He arrived in Goa as
a client of the Portuguese archbishop, well schooled in antiquities, as he tells
us at the outset: "Beeing young, and living idlelye in my native Countrie,
sometimes applying my selfe to the reading of Histories, and straunge adventures, wherein I tooke no small delight, I found my minde . . . much addicted
to see and travaile into strange Countries, thereby to seeke some adventure."⁴⁴ Like Varthema and Barbosa before him, the Dutchman begins his adventures in Gujarat, with its mixture of Islamic and Banian or "Pythagorean"
culture, by which he means Hindu and Jain beliefs (p. 60). After an opening
survey of remarkable places and practices, Linschoten returns to the city of
Cambay in Gujarat and its Banians. They believe in reincarnation and will not
eat meat. "But," he adds, "they have Idoles and Images, which they call
Pagodes, cut and formed most ugly, [and like monstrous Devils] to whom
daily they offer. The Devill often times answereth them out of those Images."
The reference to devils was added in translation. In a variation on Barbosa,
Linschoten claims that pagods are used to deflower new brides (p. 223). Much
later, he throws in a recollection of Varthema's Deumo, citing a temple painting of a toothsome pagod with a triple-crowned mitre on its head, like a monster from the Apocalypse (p. 296). Linschoten notes the cleanliness of the
Hindus he saw and records the bathing tanks for washing and altars for burnt
offerings that accompany Hindu temples: "They have on every hill, cliffe,
hole, or denne their Pagodes and Idols in the most divilish and deformed
shapes, cut and hewed out of the stones and rockes, with their furnices hard
by them, and a cesterne not farre" (pp. 226–27). Demonic forms dominate the
Indian landscape.

Gradually, the pagod comes to represent India and the East in general to
Linschoten. "The Pagodes and Images are many and innumerable throughout the Oriental countries," he asserts in introducing the famous cave temple
complexes on the neighboring islands of Salsette and Elephanta or Gharapuri,

near Bombay. The English translation calls the skillful temple excavations "holes," which, at Salsette, "are al full of carved Pagodes, of so fearfull, horrible and develish formes and shapes that is an abomination to see" (p. 289). At Elephanta

> standeth an high hill, and on the top thereof there is a hole, that goeth down into the hill, digged and carved out of the hard rock or stones as big as a great cloyster: . . . and round about the wals are cut and formed, the shapes of Elephants, Lions, tigers, and a thousand other such like wilde and cruel beasts: also some Amazones and many other deformed thinges of divers sorts, which are so well and workmanlike cut, that it is strange to behold. (p. 292)

The admixture of admiration with horror in these passages leads Linschoten to blame the Portuguese for partly destroying the sanctuaries. He ends by attributing Elephanta to the superior skill of Chinese colonists rather than local inhabitants, the beginning perhaps of the pagoda's trek farther and farther east in the European imagination.

Ralph Fitch may have been the first English writer to use the word in an original work based on firsthand experience rather than a translation; his narrative of captivity, escape, and travel in India and Malacca from 1583 to 1591 appeared in the second edition of Hakluyt's *Principal Navigations* (1598–1600). Fitch's pagods, like Linschoten's, are idols rather than buildings. The people of Bijapor are great idolaters, "And they have their idols standing in the woods, which they call Pagodes. Some bee like a cowe, some like a monkie, some like buffles [buffaloes], some like peacockes, and some like the devill."[45] There is a similar catalogue of animals culminating in the devil when we come to the pagods of Benares. Fitch portrays the ceremonies performed by pilgrims to the holy city:

> by breake of day and before, there are men and women which come out of the towne and wash themselves in Ganges. And there are divers old men which . . . give the people three or foure strawes, which they take and hold them betweene their fingers when they wash themselves; and some sit to marke them in the foreheads, and they have in a cloth a little rice, barlie, or money, which, when they have washed themselves, they give to the old men which sit there praying. Afterwards they go to divers

of their images, and give them of their sacrifices. . . . They never pray but in the water, and they wash themselves overhead, and lade up water with both their handes, and turne themselves about, and then they drinke a litle of the water three times, and so goe to their gods which stand in those houses. (Foster, pp. 20–21)

In this early English account, Hindu worship is characterized by obsessive attention to the body and its rituals on one hand, and repeated sacrifice to the pagods on the other.

The English became particularly fond of the malleable term *pagod* as their influence spread in India during the seventeenth century. A contrast is offered by two later figures who both used the word to mean "temple." Edward Terry, chaplain to Sir Thomas Roe on his embassy to the Mughal emperor Jahangir in 1616–19, praised the great mosques he saw at Agra in the Muslim north but described Hindu temples as "little churches which they call Pagodes, built round, in which are images for worship made in monstrous shapes."[46] William Methwold, an important official of the East India Company, echoed Terry's diminutive in describing the "little religion" of the Hindus of the east-central sultanate of Golconda in 1625, who "doe hold the same principles which their learned clergie, the Bramenes, have from great antiquitie."[47] Methwold provides a not unsympathetic, if urbanely condescending, account of diverse Hindu beliefs:

But all these thus distinguished are in religion one body, and have their pagodes or idoll temples common to all, but not of all equally affected, some inclining in their devotions to one saint, some to another; of which pagodes I have seene many some of them for the materials and structure worth the gazing upon, and may well bee (as they report) the ancient works of great kings. . . . [T]he tutelar saint of the place being seated in most eminencie, unto which the heathens themselves performe very little adoration, wel knowing their substances, and wanting those distinctions, which some Christians find out to coozen themselves withall. (p. 20)

Hook-swinging, Methwold later writes, is no less meritorious, if no better grounded, than Christian self-flagellation (p. 24). He remarks upon "Another saint they have, or rather devill, for in their opinion it is a maligne spirit, and brings upon them such deseases as befall them, especially the small poxe" (p. 22). Despite its many-armed form, the idol represents a devil because that is how Methwold thinks the local people perceive it, not because it is an image of Satan.

For Methwold, as for earlier observers, Hindu worship appeared particularly kinetic, but his interest in the way bodies interact with sacred spaces complements the ironic suspension of Christianized moral judgment that infuses his text. The narrative opens with a fine evocation of the ritual cleansing of bodies in the Ganges (p. 1). Later he writes of an idol in the form of a man to which every grain of thrown rice is supposed to stick, and of another that would only accept half of any liquid poured into its aperture, "an excellent sociable quality, and well becomming an ale-house kanne" (p. 22). Such sarcasm is characteristic of Methwold, but he does not dampen his admiration for Golconda's idol processions: "About midnight the saint is drawne forth in procession, handsomely carted and well clothed, with much clamour of drummes, trumpets, hoboyes and such like, that country musicke, and very artificiall fireworkes" (p. 21). The procession dynamically links sacred places, images, and bodies, dancing or marching, boldly delineating the exotic while recalling the processions of Catholic "saints"—or the rural progresses of Protestant monarchs.

Methwold's benign idol procession cuts against a tradition in European depictions of Hindu ceremony. A few hundred miles north of Golconda, at Puri, the annual dragging forth of the image *Jagannatha* on its cart by crowds of devotees had long since given rise to the legend of the "Juggernaut" who crushes the deluded faithful. The Juggernaut *topos* became a principal feature of the English discourse on India; through it, bodies and idols were fused yet again, in a grotesque and violent fashion that bears careful examination. Friar Odoric, a contemporary of Jordanus, seems to have instituted the Juggernaut myth in the fourteenth century, without visiting Puri or attempting to name the idol: "the whole body of the people, join together and draw it forth from the church with loud singing of songs and all kinds of music; and many maidens go before it by two and two chaunting in a marvelous manner. And many pilgrims who have come to this feast cast themselves under the chariot, so that its wheels may go over them, saying that they desire to die for their God."[48]

In Mandeville's *Travels* we read of an elaborate ceremony on the Coromandel Coast in which devotees cut off pieces of their bodies and then throw themselves before the carriage.[49] Conti places the procession in Vijayanagar; and an Italian traveler of the late sixteenth century, Gasparo Balbi, first called the idol a "pagod," connecting it with the ambiguous superposition of human and architectural form that term already implied.[50]

It was Linschoten's nameless idol-cart that transmitted the tradition to the seventeenth century:

> At this Carte hang likewise many Cables or Ropes, whereat also all the country people, both men and women of pure devotion doe pull and hale. In the upper part of this Carte standeth a Tabernacle . . . wherein sitteth the Idoll, and under it sit the Kings wives, which after their manner play on all instruments, making a most sweete melodie, and in that sort is the Carte drawne forth, with great devotions and processions: there are some of them, that of great zeale and pure devotion doe cut peeces of flesh out of their bodies, and throwe them downe before the Pagode: others laye themselves under the wheeles of the Carte, and let the Carte runne over them, whereby they are all crushed to peeces. (pp. 294–95)

As in Odoric, the musical participation of women looks back to the tradition of temple dancers. Here the temple itself is on the move, rolling over and incorporating the bodies that dance before it, or provoking their spectacular self-mutilation, a detail also found in the medieval account (Odoric, p. 145).

In 1633 the East India Company sent its chief merchant, Ralph Cartwright, to the Mughal governor of Orissa in a bid for trading privileges in the northeast. William Bruton accompanied Cartwright and wrote a pamphlet describing "that mighty *Pagodo* or *Pagod*, the Mirrour of all wickedness and Idolatry," which he named "Jagarnat." Many elements in Bruton's putatively eyewitness report, however, are suspiciously biblical in inspiration: "This Idoll is in shape like a great serpent, with seven Heads, and on the cheekes of each Head it hath the forme of a Wing upon each cheeke, which wings doe open and shut, and flappe, as it is carried in a stately Chariot, and the Idoll in the midds't of it: and one of the *Moguls* sitting behinde it in the Chariot upon a convenient place with a Canopy, to keepe the Sunne from injuring of it."[51] The description crests when the worshipers throw themselves before the chariot. The frontispiece depicts their bodies beneath the surprisingly small wheels of a long pageant wagon, with the seven-headed dragon and umbrella-wielding "mogul" above. Bruton generally seems aware of the differences between Mughal rulers and Brahman priests, but he collapses them at the sensational moment of ultimate religious transgression.

Transgression, not otherness: Christianity is part of the syncretic scene and the Bible its distant backdrop. Bruton specifically cites the dragon of Revelation 13:1, and says he was also reminded of the beast in verses 16 and 17, which I quote from the King James version: "he causes all . . . to receive a mark in their right hand, or in their foreheads: [17] And that no man might buy or sell, save he that had the mark, or the name of the beast, or the number of his name." Similarly, "the *Brammines* are all marked in the fore-head," Bruton explicates, "but those that doe buy and sell, are all marked in the left shoulder; and all such . . . (not being marked) are most severely and grievously punished" (p. 30).

Although it dimly recalls Varthema's papal mitre, the seven-headed serpent that Bruton drags in from Revelation is unprecedented in earlier Juggernaut variants. The mark of the beast offers us a clue to the dragon's presence, which may have more to do with the commercial context of Bruton's narrative than with anything Bruton may have seen or heard about in Orissa. The East India Company, chartered in its first form by Queen Elizabeth in 1600, had successfully defied the Portuguese and the Dutch, and by the 1630s it was making precarious inroads on the east coast of the subcontinent. Cartwright's mission to Orissa entailed ceremonial compromises with the Mughal governor, who "presented his Foot to our Merchant to kisse, which hee twice did refuse to do, but at the last hee was faine to doe it" (p. 14). The visit to Jagarnat is immediately followed by a list of the commodities of the region and unexpected praise for the honest dealing of its inhabitants. Beneath Bruton's indignation at the Brahmans' idolatry one can discern the apprehension that his English companions are likewise succumbing to a kind of Mammon.

Juggernaut is made the central ritual of Hinduism by Thomas Bowrey, a sea captain who kept a journal and sketchbook throughout his sojourn in Bengal during the 1670s. By this time, the company had been rechartered and strengthened under Charles II, who gave it total authority over English residents in its holdings and the right to declare war on non-European rulers in India. Bowrey is mostly unconcerned with East India Company business in his animadversions; he was a private trader of some means, in many ways one of the first English tourists as well as a businessman. He depicts the Hindus as harmless idolaters, pacified under the spell of their Brahmans and hence subdued by the warlike but tolerant Moors.[52] They worship many sorts of idols in temples curiously worked to depict music and dancing. "Of all the false Gods these idolatrous people Worship (save John Gernaet), a Cow is held in greatest reverence," he remarks, "beinge kepte within their Pagods" (p. 8). Later Bowrey reveals his belief that "They are indeed the Ancient Gentiles, and, as I imagine, of the seed of those who revolted from Moses, forgettinge God to Worship a Molten Calfe" (p. 25). Like Bruton, Bowrey assimilates Hindu worship to a biblical pattern of backsliding and transgression, rendering it all too familiar rather than totally alien. But who is John Gernaet?

The Hindus, Bowrey explains, are precise in their idolatrous ways, and if a man is judged to have broken the law he loses caste. "The Party soe misdemeaninge him selfe, whether he be rich or poore . . . must take his travaile to the great Pagod Jn°. Gernaet, the remotest part of the Golcondah Kingdome"; here he gives presents to the Brahmans and feasts with them, and so regains his sanctity (pp. 12–13). John Gernaet, of course, is our Juggernaut, or what Bowrey hears, or professes to hear, when the name *Jagannatha* is spoken. It is a perfect example of Hobson-Jobson—but let us examine Bowrey's account before considering its lexicology. He begins with the women who sing and dance in the temple, "very delicate to hear and behold were it acted in a better Sence, and not onely soe in theire Cathedral Pagod" (p. 14). The desire to isolate Indian performance, to sequester it from its troubling religious context on an enlightened stage of good sense, looks forward to Dryden's *Aureng-Zebe*. The temple dancers seldom marry, Bowrey writes, and if they do a jealous husband and *sati* await them, as he promises to relate. John Gernaet is thus tied to yet another commonplace of Indian discourse. "But first," Bowrey goes on, "I will describe Some of theire activities of body, danceinge before the front of the Pagod as I my Selfe have often Seene with admiration much rarer then Ever I beheld amongst us Europians, or indeed any Other people in Asia" (p. 14). Here

Hindu worship is typically distinguished as particularly bound up with "activities of body," and Bowrey provides a lively sketch of the dancers at this point.

His verbal picture of the idol they honor stresses its weight and size: "In that great and Sumptuous Diaballicall Pagod, there Standeth theire greatest God Jnᵒ. Gernaet, whence the Pagod received that name alsoe. The Imadge is of massy Gold very richly wrought, and in the full Stature of a man" (pp. 15–16). The slippage among temple, idol, and perhaps coinage underlies Bowrey's description. The idol and its cart easily incorporate images of more dancers:

> This Chariot is of Exceedinge great weight, beinge made of Very Solid wood, very rich, with much iron worke thereon and finely Engraven, with the Shapes of men and women dancinge, as alsoe many hideous Shapes of Satyrs, bulls, bears, Tigers. . . . [I]t is so Ponderous, that although it be fitted . . . with good wheels on each Side, yet [it] requireth more then an hundred Stronge men to draw it alonge Upon hard and Smooth ground (and this they accompt the Arke of God). (p. 17)

Celebrants come from miles around to cast themselves under the wheels of the cart, "which is accompted by all of this Sect a most Noble, Heroick, and Zealous death" (p. 28). Some at least of the pilgrims who lost caste and sought out the idol to regain it end by gaining a still higher form of nobility. John Gernaet changes from theater to backdrop to chief actor in a drama that gradually consumes bodies and finally produces an effect of heroic admiration among a community of believers.

Is the name "John Gernaet" simply, in the Victorian phrasing of Henry Yule, another "typical and delightful example of that class of Anglo-Indian *argot* which consists of Oriental words highly assimilated, perhaps by vulgar lips, to the English vernacular"?[53] Bowrey's "Garnaet" echoes Bruton's "-garnat," converting these syllables into a sort of surname. A garnet is a semiprecious stone, reddish in shade and so named after the pomegranate, whose associations with the classical underworld the sailor Bowrey gives no hint of knowing.[54] Yet stoniness, and that of a gem stone in particular, seems an appropriate association for a massive idol whose eyes, Bowrey maintains, are diamonds (p. 16). Granite, a word that seems to have entered English about the middle of the seventeenth century, may also lurk within Garnaet; it was derived from the Italian *granire*, to grind or granulate, and denotes a particularly hard and heavy stone. But from the fifteenth century on a garnet was also a nautical term for a kind of tackling used in hoisting. Since it derives from Dutch *garnaat*, this sense glances at the linguistic consolidations and competitions of seafaring and empire as they were particularly played out in India.[55] *Jagannatha* itself is Sanskrit for "Lord of the World," a title of Krishna, an avatar of the leading deity Vishnu. The assimilation of the Orient to the English and other vernaculars by vulgar lips suggests the Juggernaut's own Moloch-like progress.

The idol-cart, gaudy and massive, ultimately grinds down the worshipers who draw it along on ropes, garnets perhaps, tackling that also suggest its similarity to a ship. In Bowrey the vehicle is made of wood and iron; he calls it an "ark," and although the immediate implication is a demonic parody of King David dancing before the Ark of the Covenant, Noah's Ark may also be suggested, given the engravings of bulls and other animals on the chariot's metal-work. The Hindus believe in Adam and Eve and Cain and Abel, but not, Bowrey maintains, the great Flood (p. 26). He begins his account of the procession by asserting that "Their irreligious Religion is wholy Composed of nothinge Save Idolatry, intermixed neither with Judaisme nor Mahometisme, but quite averse from them both, . . . more Especially from Christianitie" (pp. 14–15). As in Bruton, however, it is not alterity but transgressive recombination that shapes Bowrey's understanding of what he witnessed and heard at second-hand.

The nautical implications of John Gernaet go beyond yet another possible assimilation of the profane to the sacred. Bowrey has a sailor's eye and he may be drawing on a sailor's vocabulary; innocently or with sly humor, he personalizes the exotic object of fear with a homely (if uncanny) nickname. John Gernaet is his Moby Dick. The East India Company itself was to be rechristened by its servants, British and Indian, as "John Company." The origins of the name are obscure, although it may have been developed on an analogy with *Jan Compagnie*, the sobriquet of the VOC, its Dutch East Indian rival.[56]

Are John Company and John Gernaet mirror images of each other? There is a danger in projecting a late-nineteenth-century imperial context backward in time to the commercial strivings of the East India Company amidst its European rivals and Indian partners in the seventeenth century.[57] K. N. Chaudhuri—an economic historian who eschews overestimations of European imperialism—shows that "armed trading" nevertheless "remained an integral part of the commercial presence in Asia," because fortresses and geographical possessions were necessary for accumulating goods, avoiding customs duties, and generating income from safe-conduct passes.[58] By 1687 the Court of Directors went further, proposing to "establish such a Politie of civill and military power, and create and secure such a large Revenue as may bee the foundation of a large, well-grounded, sure English Dominion in India for all time to come."[59] The directors followed the lead of Sir Josia Child, who was a principal figure in the Company's hierarchy when Bowrey wandered India. As governor in the 1580s, Child pursued a policy of military aggression against the Mughals after the takeover of Madras and Bombay; he failed and the Company reverted to peaceable trade, but the period of Child's dominance from the 1670s until 1690 constituted a proto-imperial experiment.[60] As an independent trader, Bowrey himself felt the Company's wrath on several occasions. Although they came to buy and sell, in Bruton's biblical phrase, some members of the East India Company already aspired to roll over everything and everyone in their path by means of its military and political machinery. And just as pilgrims throughout India came to John Gernaet for a chance to regain status, perhaps through the supreme sacrifice of life and limb, so John Company would lure a range of British exiles, adventurers, and patricians to the subcontinent. Eventually, Bruton's Jagarnat would assume the familiar form Juggernaut: the false suffix -*naut* strengthens the adventitious link to navigation, and the interpolated "r" sound recalls "Argonaut" as well. The Greek hero Jason's venture for the golden fleece seems a bizarre association until the idol's landlocked reflection of Europe's own brutal progress toward the riches of the east is recognized.

The Elizabethans found a figure for their own misgivings about geographical expansion and the power it entailed in the Russian tsar; perhaps Juggernaut can be allowed to stand for something like this in my reading of the seventeenth-century discourse of India in England. It may not be coincidental that François Bernier, reporting in 1671 on recent power struggles at the Mughal court, should produce a French rendering of the legend: the *Compagnie des Indes Orientales* was founded in 1664. Bernier was in turn translated almost immediately into English and served as the stimulus for the intrigues of Dryden's *Aureng-Zebe*. According to the French observer, the cart of "Jagannat" is drawn on "a stately engin of wood . . . which Engin is put upon fourteen or sixteen wheels, such as the carriages of Canons may be."[61] The gun-carriage comparison, like the implicit resemblance to a ship, suggests the idol may be taken as a metonym for European power as much as oriental cruelty. As in Bowrey, fanatic celebrants throw themselves beneath the wheels, "perswaded, that there is no action so heroick nor so meritorious as that" (p. 111). That both texts should place an emphasis on the heroic, or on heroism as a kind of delusion born of extremity, is remarkable. If anything, Bernier's account is more ugly than the English versions because of its incidentals. "The *Brachmans*," he states, "for their particular advantage and interest . . . do entertain the People in these errors and superstitions, and they proceed even to such infamous cheats and Villanies, that I could never have believed them, if I had not fully informed my self of it" (pp. 111-12). He offers a variation on the link of idols with rape, claiming that the Brahmans entice a maiden to stay behind as the bride of Jagannat: "one of these lustful Priests enters at night by a little back-door unto the Temple, deflowreth this young Maid, and maketh her believe any thing he pleaseth" (p. 112). The breaking of bodies under the wheel of the idol-cart culminates in the priestly violation of a single female body.

Custodians of an absolute patriarchy European men abhor and perhaps secretly covet, the fictive Brachmans or Brahmans mediate between monumental and performative elements in the travelers' evolving picture of India. They play a prominent role, as we have seen, in most contributions to the Juggernaut legend, and they reappear in the *sati* material as well. Before turning to *sati*, it will be useful to examine the image of the Brahman and other male figures of Indian religious devotion in European texts. Brahmans are associated with bodily discipline as well as idols and monumental public space. Barbosa introduces them as priests "who manage and rule their houses of prayer and idol-worship" (p. 115). They are one of three classes and are notable because of their behavior: "These eat nothing subject to death, they marry only one wife, and if she dies, do not marry again. As a mark of their dignity they wear over their shoulders three linen threads" (p. 217). Linschoten's chapter "Of the Indians called Bramanes, which are the ministers of the Pagodes, and Indian Idoles, and of their manner of life"

mixes praise for their honesty as royal advisors with suspicion of their learning: "They are very subtil in writing and casting accounts, whereby they
make other simple Indians beleeve what they will." The Brahmans do not
eat animals and pray all day to whatever creature they first see in the morning (pp. 247–48). Fitch mentions their dietary constraints but devotes a lot
of space to other bodily rituals: "They pray in the water naked, and dresse
their meat and eate it naked, and for their penance they lie flat upon the
earth, and rise up and turne themselves about 30 or 40 times, and use to
heave up their hands to the sunne, and to kisse the earth, with their armes
and legs stretched along out, and their right leg alwayes before the left"
(Foster, p. 19). As with Boemus, their nakedness links the Brahmans to the
gymnosophists of the classical tradition.

Pierre d'Avity unearths a more complex connection in *The Estates,
Empires, & Principalities of the World*, translated in 1615. The "naked philosophers" lived in desert places and were so patient they would stand barefoot
in the sun all day:

> Among these Sages, were also the Brachmanes, who desired nothing but
> what nature required, and did liue of that which the earth did willingly
> bring forth. They hold that these men were descended from the children of
> *Abrahams* concubines, who sent them into the East, as we read in the holie
> writ, where it is said that they carried certaine gifts from him. These gifts
> of *Abraham*, besides gold and clothes are the arts and sciences, especially
> Astrologie, and natural Magicke.[62]

The reference is to Genesis 25:6. Henry Lord, in one of the first European
studies of Hinduism, makes the derivation of "Brahman" from "Abraham"
explicit and traces the gloss to Origen.[63] But English geographical texts during the seventeenth century generally give an increasingly negative account
of the Brahmans and their bodily behavior. Peter Heylyn goes so far as to
distinguish them from the "Brachmans" of Greek antiquity: "To these
Gymnosophists, or *Brachmans*, the *Bramines* do now succeed, both in place
and authority; but differ from them most extreamly in point of learning, and
the civilities of their lives; these *Bramaines* being the most impure, libidi-
nous, and sensual beasts in all the Countrey."[64] Orthographical variation becomes an insurmountable divide between past and present, in a manner

reminiscent of the divide between wise Egyptians and counterfeit gypsies in English discourse.

Pietro della Valle, however, preserved the connection with the past precisely by evoking the Hermetic tradition associated with Egypt. The Brahmans, he claims, equate their god Brahma with Pythagoras; the stories they tell of their animalistic gods must be allegories after the Egyptian and Greek manner, and their division into castes and white clothes link them to the Egyptians as well (pp. 73–78). But Pietro shifts the emphasis from Brahmans to other Indian ascetics, the yogis or "jogis" who adopt more extreme bodily practices. Near Surat he saw a great banyan tree worshiped as an idol, "Before whom, upon a little hillock, stands continually one of their Gioghi, who among the Indians are a sort of Hermits; and sometimes I have seen a Woman too standing there." They gesture to the tree by lowering and raising their arms in supplication, then "some make their prayers only standing, others prostrate themselves with their whole body, groveling upon the earth, and then rise again, others touch the ground with the head and forehead" (pp. 37–38). Pietro describes their naked bodies, smeared with earth and pigment, and the fasting and breathing exercises that produce spiritual states that he says mask communion with the Devil and sexual excess (pp. 105–8). Yet he asserts, "There is no doubt that these are the ancient Gymnosophists so famous in the world, and, in short, those very Sophists who then went naked and exercis'd great patience in sufferings, to whom *Alexander* the Great sent *Onesecritus* to consult with them, as *Strabo* reports" (p. 99).

A horrified fascination with India's religious mendicants was a commonplace of European descriptions of India, from Marco Polo onward. Unlike the Brahmans, who are associated with secret knowledge and hidden temple spaces, yogis and other holy figures are almost a feature of the landscape; their remarkable bodies dot the countryside and crowd the marketplace. At the start of the sixteenth century, Barbosa casts their way of life as a response to Mughal rule. In Delhi, he says, many Hindus of noble birth adopt poor clothes and sojourn throughout the region. The bodies of these "Jogues" are distorted by painful brass girdles and heavy chains. "They go about in bands, like Egyptians with us," refusing to stay in one place under the Moors. Ashes cover their limbs and their hair hangs in matted locks. "I have often asked them wherefore they went about thus," Barbosa writes, "to which they replied that they always carried these iron chains as a penance for the great sin they had committed, in that they were unwilling to endure taking arms for the defence of their honour, and had allowed themselves to be overcome by a wicked people like the Moors; and that they went naked as a token of their great loss of honour" (pp. 130–31). Nakedness here is an indirect sign of political resistance rather than a philosophical practice.

By Bernier's time, however, yogis were often conflated in European accounts with fakirs, the holy wanderers of Islam whose bodily discipline assumed similar forms. The French traveler groups fakirs, "Jauguis," and dervishes together as "Religious Heathens." He prefers the former name, however, giving fakirs the heavy chains and describing how they freeze their bodies in contorted postures for days on end.[65] Bowrey follows his John Gernaet episode with a similar description: "I have likewise Seen Severall Fackeers, who, in their infancie, have been hunge Up by the Arms with their fists grippen fast, (in imitation of a continual liftinge Up of hands to God Almightie) but by hanginge up Some few years in this Posture, theire nerves have soe hardened that . . . they can never pull downe their arms one inch" (p. 22). Like the pagod and Juggernaut, the corporal deformation of figures such as these blends bodies with monuments through performance, here converting the male body into a kind of statue. The association of India with somatic performance, originally a sign of antiquity, increasingly betokens the loss of the past in early modern texts. The tendency to merge Hindu and Muslim elements, such as yogis and fakirs, is part of this erasure of history. Not a blank but a smudged and indistinct slate is all that is left for European interpreters to reinscribe. The emphasis was placed more and more on practice and activity and less on the temples, mosques, and visual reminders of antique glory that earlier travelers acknowledged, and that remained central to European accounts of other old world civilizations. Ironically, many monumental sites remained in use during the period; despite complaints of recent Mughal or Portuguese depredations, India was not dominated by immemorial ruins the way Egypt or Southwest Asia was. Perhaps it was because of this, as well as their extreme strangeness and illegibility to Western eyes, that Indian monuments were rendered invisible by European observers, ephemeral stage-sets for a hideous human drama.

As a genre, the *sati* account is perhaps the prime example of how Europeans saw India as a place where monuments were replaced by bodies in motion, and grotesque, tortuous, and finally self-destructive motion at that. Instead of a tomb, the corpse of the husband is typically consumed along with an elaborate pyre beside a flowing river, complete with a platform or tower from which the living widow joins her spouse. The immolation of widows further complicates the ambivalent notion of heroic sacrifice in the Indian scene, displacing it onto the body of the woman. Despite its abiding appeal to European readers, Bernier introduces the topic with a world-weary shrug after his Juggernaut episode:

> there are so many Writers of voyages relating the custom of the *Indian* Women, burning themselves with their Husbands, that I think something will at last be believed of it. For my part, I am going to take my turn also, and to write to you of it like others; yet in the mean time observing withal, that 'tis not all true what is said of it, and that now they do not burn themselves in so great a number as formerly, because the Mahumetans, that bear sway at present in *Indostan*, are enemies to that barbarous custome; not opposing it absolutely, because they are willing to leave their idolatrous people, who are far more numerous than themselves, in the free exercise of their Religion, for fear of some revolt. (pp. 113–14)

The paragraph is full of twists and turns. Bernier twice refers reflexively to Indian women burning "themselves" but calls this a "custom" and a "barbarous custom." Are the women responsible for their actions or is their behavior dictated by social and religious usage? *Sati* is less frequent than formerly because the Islamic rulers oppose the custom, not the will of the women. The intentions of the wives are lost in a general conflict between conquerors and conquered. Furthermore, a time signature is subtly added: *sati* was common in an idolatrous past, and the latecomers who "bear sway at present" uneasily restrict without banning it to avoid a revolt that would return the country to its primary state. Bernier manufactures authority for his rendition of *sati* by divulging that the earlier stories were only partly true: here is a French eyewitness, writing for a French audience about the manners of a people the French have now to contend with. Yet the example of selective Mughal opposition to *sati* as a form of self-interested imperial control would already have been familiar to the English readers who rapidly absorbed Bernier in translation.

As he recognizes, Bernier comes in the midst of a long series of formulaic European *sati* accounts, leading back to Propertius and other classical authors. The medieval to early modern cycle began with Friars Jordanus and Odoric, who neatly reflect the split between coercion and intention in the figure of the widow that Bernier's self-consciously belated version encodes less directly. The idolaters of Malabar have a detestable custom, Odoric records: "For when any man dies, they burn him, and if he leave a wife they burn her alive with him, saying that she ought to go and keep her husband company in the other world. But if the woman have sons by her husband she may abide with them, an she will" (p. 139). Here "they" burn the widow, although an element of volition creeps in should she have sons and choose to die anyway. Jordanus tells a different tale: "In this India, on the death of a noble, or of any people of substance, their bodies are burned: and eke their wives follow them alive into the fire, and, for the sake of worldly glory, and for the love of their husbands, and for eternal life, burn along with them, with as much joy as if they were going to be wedded; and those who do this have the higher repute for virtue and perfection among the rest. Wonderful!" Jordanus typically regards widow burning as another "marvel" of the East, adding that he has seen five living women accompany one dead husband in the fire (p. 20). His widows burn themselves voluntarily, and there is a hint of admiration for such wifely constancy in his tone.

In the fourteenth century, *sati* was one of the first things Niccolo Conti mentioned upon recounting his entry into India. The opening description, however, contrasts with the fuller account he provides elsewhere in his narrative. It is the custom in Cambay, Conti remarks, for wives to burn themselves with their husband to add to the pomp of his funeral; the dearest spouse "places herself by his side with her arm round his neck, and burns herself with him" (p. 6). Later he gives a different impression:

> In central India the dead are burned, and the living wives, for the most part, are consumed in the same funeral pyre with their husband, one or more, according to the agreement at the time the marriage was contracted. The first wife is compelled by law to be burnt, even though she should be the only wife. But others are married under the express agreement that they should add to the splendour of the funeral ceremony by their death, and this is considered a great honour for them. The deceased husband is

laid on a couch, dressed in his best garments. A vast funeral pyre is erected over him in the form of a pyramid, constructed of odiferous woods. The pile being ignited, the wife, habited in her richest garments, walks gaily around it, singing, accompanied by a great concourse of people, and amid the sounds of trumpets, flutes, and songs. In the meantime one of the priests, called Bachali, standing on some elevated spot, exhorts her to a contempt of life and death, promising her all kinds of enjoyment with her husband, much wealth, and abundance of ornaments. When she has walked round the fire several times, she stands near the elevation on which is the priest, and taking off her dress puts on a white linen garment, her body having first been washed according to custom. In obedience to the exhortation of the priest she then springs into the fire. If some show more timidity (for it frequently happens that they become stupefied by terror at the sight of the struggles of the others, or of their sufferings in the fire), they are thrown into the fire by the bystanders, whether consenting or not. Their ashes are afterwards collected and placed in urns, which form an ornament for the sepulchres. (p. 24)

Conti includes both Jordanus' intentionalist and Odoric's coercive explanations for *sati* in his travels. The further Europeans penetrate the subcontinent, perhaps, the less agency they perceive in Hindu women.

Conti's description contains a number of significant details. The first wife is legally compelled to burn herself, while the others have entered into a private prenuptial understanding to do so, expressly to add to the funeral's dignity. The Propertian mythology of uniform Hindu "law" is clearly reflected in this passage. Law, however, is subordinate to ceremony and performance, as is funereal monumentality. In central India the deceased's pyramid is consumed with him, not left as a reminder for future generations. The wives, like temple dancers, walk around the pyre with musicians, singing as the priests exhort them; bathed and clothed in white, each leaps into the flames in compliance with the priestly words. Those who balk are forcibly thrown in. A sort of residue of the monumental survives in the urns that adorn the sepulchre of the dead man, otherwise undescribed. The emphasis, however, is on spectacular but ephemeral ritual, an activity that nevertheless dissolves the agency of its principal participants.

Two important sixteenth-century accounts, by Barbosa and Cesare Federici, return a measure of agency to the wife. Barbosa says the women of

Vijayanagar "are bound by very ancient custom, when their husbands die, to burn themselves alive with their corpses" (p. 213). If poor, the wife simply throws herself into the flames "of her own free will." If wealthy, she holds a feast and follows an elaborate public ritual, mounting a horse so that she may be seen by the people, riding to the pyre, and ascending a wooden scaffold from which she distributes her jewels and addresses the men and women in the crowd. She reminds the men of their obligation to the women who are willing to sacrifice themselves, "being free to act," and the women of their responsibility to sacrifice themselves. The avowals about free will and the remarkable picture of a woman speaking forcefully in public are thus somewhat compromised by exhortations to duty. The widow turns about three times, "worshipping towards the direction of the sunrise"—the solar worship of the simple Indian would become another commonplace, particularly in English discourse, and here its link to the fiery death of the "good wife" is made plain. She is given a pitcher of oil to throw in the pyre, and then throws herself in after it, her kin stoking the flames with oil and wood. An element of coercion again enters the scene, for we are told that those who refuse to immolate themselves are dishonored, and some are made prostitutes and temple dancers. Barbosa subsumes any trace of the monumental in ritual performance. In contrast to Conti, he states, "The ashes that remain after these ceremonies are thrown into running streams" (pp. 214–16). In fact, in many parts of India small monuments or shrines, sometimes in the form of simple carved stones or cairns, were set up near river banks to commemorate burned widows, as the English traveler John Fryer noticed much later.[66]

Cesare Federici's narrative of his eastern travels was published in Venice in 1587 and appeared in English translation the following year. Set once more in Vijayanagar, Federici's story echoes Barbosa's in many ways, but this time the widow waits a month or so to burn herself in a separate pyre. The river setting is prominent in this account; the woman gives away her jewels before washing herself in the river and only then ascends the platform by the pyre. Federici stresses her control over the ceremony: she sets the day, feasts as long as she wishes, then commands that her fire be kindled. He compares the woman to a bride in a wedding procession, yet the absence of the husband's body places her center stage: carrying a mirror in one hand and an arrow in the other, she sings and speaks to the assembled crowd (pp. 9 verso–10 recto). But Federici's widow does not remind husbands and wives of their duties; instead, "she talketh and reasoneth with the people, recommending unto them hir children and kindred." The moment of immolation is elided in his account, however: "When this sillye woman hath reasoned with the people a good while to hir content, there is another woman that taketh a pot with oyle and sprinkleth it ouer her head, . . . and afterwards throweth the pot into the fornace, and both the woman and the pot goeth together into the fire" (p. 10 recto).

Federici concludes by offering an explanation for *sati* that is at odds with the image of female will and control he has presented. When he asked why widows burn themselves, he was told that in ancient times wives used to poison their husbands and take lovers. Widow sacrifice was decreed as a solution to this problem; "now by reason of this law they are more faithfull to their husbands, and count their liues as deare as their owne, because that after his death, hir owne followeth presentlye" (p. 10 recto). Linschoten, who appeared in English translation ten years later, echoes Federici in his testimony about the mood of the doomed woman: "she taketh al her Jewels, and parteth them among her frends, & so with a cheerfull countenance, she leapeth into the fire" (pp. 70–71). The Dutch traveler also offers the same reason for *sati*:

> The first cause and occasion why the women are burnt with their husbandes, was, (as the Indians themselues do say) that in time past, the women (as they are very leacherous and inconstant both by nature and complexion) did poyson many of their husbands, when they thought good, (as they are likewise very expert therein:) thereby to haue the better means to fulfill their lusts. Which the king perceiuing, & that thereby his principal Lords, Captains, and Souldiers, which uphelde his estate and kingdome, were so consumed and brought unto their endes, by the wicked practices of women, sought as much as he might to hinder the same: and thereupon he made a law, and ordayned, that when the dead bodies of men were buried, they shold also burne their wiues with them, thereby to put them in feare, and to make them abstain from poysoning of their husbands. . . . So that in the ende it became a custome among them, and so continueth. (p. 71)

A law, here established by the king, has somehow become custom, and custom has become cheerful compliance, as the natural lechery of women is converted to virtue. How can a threatened punishment for poisoning the husband become the ground of spontaneous wifely fidelity? The divide between female will in the present and ancient coercion remains sharp.

Perhaps this is why Strabo, recording the explanation, remarked that "the law is not stated in a plausible manner, nor the cause of it either."[67] The poisoning story, in fact, comes from European antiquity, despite the travelers' claim to have heard it from the Hindus themselves. According to Strabo's contemporary Diodorus Siculus, it was an "ancient custom" for the Indians to marry for love, but this led to mistaken choices, wifely infidelity, poison, and the law that widows must burn with their husbands' bodies or lose all religious privileges. Less skeptical than Strabo, Diodorus writes that female disorder was soon converted into its opposite, and that wives now strive with each other to burn with the corpse. In an account that may have inspired Propertius, he tells of two wives who competed to die in the pyre of Ceteus, an Indian general in Alexander's army during the fourth century B.C.[68] The description he gives of the winner's suicide is startlingly close to the early modern accounts I have been examining: he includes the bridelike procession, the singing, the distribution of jewels, the "heroic" death. Whatever the source of the poisoning tale or the enumeration of ritual stages in later *sati* accounts, it is clear that the genre reflects a long-standing European fascination with India as much or more than firsthand reporting of actual practices. As early as Diodorus and Strabo, at least, Graeco-Roman authors placed Indian culture somewhere between permanence and performance, force and volition, through the body of "the Indian woman."

According to Diodorus, some Greek witnesses of the fourth-century *sati* were provoked to extravagant praise, others to condemnation of a barbarous custom.[69] Nicholas Withington, who furnished one of the first eyewitness English accounts in 1616, registers similar reactions among East India Company servants. The wife "indures the fyer with such patience that it is to bee admired," but "at the sight whereof our Agente was soe greeved and amazed at the undaunted resolution of the younge woman that hee said hee would never see more burnte in that fashion while hee lived."[70] This mixture of amazement, repulsion, and prudential avoidance would characterize the Company's response to *sati* until its attempt to abolish it through legislation in 1829. Writing about the same time as Withington, Roe's chaplain Edward Terry falls into the amatory discourse his readership understands to explain the widow's resolution: "many yong women are ambitious to die with honor (as they esteem it), when their fiery love brings them to the flames (as they thinke) of martyrdome most willingly; following their dead husbands unto the fire, and there imbracing are burnt with them; but this they doe voluntary, not compelled." But Petrarchan intimations of love's flames are undone by the debunking style. The music of other accounts becomes shouting in Terry's, as the spectators try to drown out the screams of the "tortured creature," like the Ammonites when they gave their children to Moloch.[71]

It is in a continental European observer that we find a favorable depiction of the widow as a conventionally lovelorn heroine. Pietro della Valle published his travels of the 1620s in epistolary form, and they appeared in an English translation in 1664. Pietro, who was a great proponent of Egyptian origins, mentions Diodorus' story of the two wives early in his letters from India, and it is clear that both Diodorus and Federici influenced his lengthy eyewitness description later on (p. 77). At Ikkeri he says he came across the procession of a widow who was resolved to burn herself, "as 'tis the custom with many Indian Women." She rode on horseback with a lemon in one hand a mirror in the other, in which she beheld herself while singing a lament (p. 266). Pietro thinks the proceedings "a Custom, indeed, cruel and barbarous, but, withall, of great generosity and virtue in such Women and therefore worthy of no small praise" (p. 267). He visits the woman, who is decked as a bride and surrounded by her attendants in her courtyard, telling her "that I was a Person of a very remote Country, where we had heard by Fame that some Women in India love their husbands so vehemently as when they dye to resolve to dye with them." Pietro, who attempts to dissuade her, is surprised to discover that her husband was a mere drummer, since "Heroical Actions" such as hers are rare in people of few means. He describes her pleasing appearance to the reader and writes, "I promis'd her that, so far as my weak pen could contribute, her Name should remain immortal in the World. . . . My Muse could not forbear from chanting her in a Sonnet which I made upon her death, and reserve among my Poetical Papers" (pp. 276–77). Mention of the poem, which is lost, adds to the odd tone of the entire episode. Pietro's interview with the widow, whom he names "Giaccama," echoes the wooing of his wife Maani Gioerida, a Persian Christian he married at Baghdad in 1616. It also recalls her sickness and eventual death near Hormuz in 1622, upon which he wrote a sonnet cycle, also lost. The language of love and female heroism renders the immolation of widows legible to the European male gaze, finally revealing the erotic impulse that helped to structure the gaze. A circumstance remains hidden throughout the exchange, however: Pietro carried his own wife's embalmed body with him throughout his Indian travels, burying it only upon his return to Rome in 1626.[72] Love discourse almost exposes an asymmetrical but telling affinity between European and Indian funeral practices where beloved spouses are concerned: the bonds forged between death and love seem irreducibly strange despite their specific embodiments and differing degrees of violence throughout a range of cultures and times. As Michel de Montaigne remarked in another context, "habit had led me not to perceive the strangeness of this action, which nevertheless we find so hideous when it is told us about another country."[73]

Seventeenth-century English accounts struggle to convert the disavowal or relativism of earlier narratives into an emotive turbine of East India Company ideology. Peter Mundy, a factor for the Company in the early 1630s, provides a detailed if formulaic account of a *sati* he witnessed at Surat, complete with illustration. He offers no moral commentary, only noting that "The Mogull haveinge Conquered their Countrie hath almost abolished that Custome, soe that it may not bee done without speciall lycense from the kinge or Governour of the place where they dwell."[74] The English increasingly came to view the Mughal empire as a model for political as well as economic power on the subcontinent. Heylyn's *Cosmographie*, which supplies an ideological overview of mid-century travel lore, reimagines the vast ruins of Chitor in central India, "either demolished by the wars, or suffered to decay by the *great Moguls*, who would not willingly have any thing in the *Indies* of more Antiquity, than themselves; and therefore are rather inclined to build new Cities, than uphold the old" (p. 886). Heylyn is at once criticizing the Mughals and conveying an important lesson of empire. The English would eventually both decry the loss of an essential India and create their own India, preserving the past, as Bernard S. Cohn shows, by relegating it to the museums of their Indian and metropolitan cities.[75]

Unlike Mundy, Heylyn expresses unsparing religious and moral horror at *sati*. Some heathenish customs are unique to India,

Amongst which I reckon for the most savage, the forcing of poor women to burn themselves with their husbands bodies. . . . And because they will be sure not to have that infamy stick upon them, they have ordered that the woman who shall so refuse, must shave her head, and break her Jewels, and not be suffered to eat, drink or sleep, or company with any body till her death. A life more miserable than the Flames which they seek to shun. This makes them leap into the fire with joy and greediness, and to contend which shall be foremost.

Ostracism and starvation now explain the widow's behavior. Heylyn quotes Propertius and adds a translation:

A shame 'tis not to dy: they therefore strive
Who may be fam'd to follow him alive.
The Victor burns, yields to the flame her brest;
And her burnt face doth on her husband rest. (p. 900)

The classical authority here serves to memorialize a "savage" custom, bound up with a chromatic racial difference that parodically subsumes the poetic conceit of burning love in the burnt face of the woman.

The well-traveled Bowrey independently confirms on the ground, as it were, what Heylyn postulates amid the papers and lexica of his study. Bowrey, as we have seen, links *sati* to temple dancing and hence to Juggernaut (p. 14). In his eyewitness account he empties the widow of any trace of will whatsoever. Like the other victims, she submits to the zealous discourse of "the Hellish Brachmans, who discourse with them very Zealously or at least wise pretendinge it, highly commendinge the fidelitie of those vertuous women" (p. 36). Although the widow is "Seemingly Extraordinarily cheareful," Bowrey has an explanation: "the Satyrical Priests give them something to intoxicate them, by which they are Exited to this Valour and Eagernesse of working theire owne destruction" (pp. 37–38). Rhetoric and drugs wholly negate the woman's volition. Solely from the viewpoint of analyzing what this moment in a European text means to Bowrey and his hypothetical readers, it would be as mistaken to join him in denouncing the widow's powerlessness as to condemn him for obliterating some originary volition that she may have been exercising.

For Bowrey's description is part of a preexisting discourse that is largely shaped by his own culture, its expectations, and its recent ambitions. He is among the first to gratify his audience with a tale of rescue.[76] "I have knowne One," Bowrey writes,

> who was rescued from the hands of those Heathenish Devils, (at the Very instant she was to be consumed by fire); it was done by a parcell of English Seamen. . . . She was a younge fresh complexioned Girle not exceedinge tenne years of age. Some few hours after her conveyance to an English house, she began to be much in her sences, but admired how she came thither, and, upon information of the whole Story, She was very penitent and Sorry that she shold condescend to such Evil councel of her Friends and the Brachmans, and, in a few days, beinge better instructed, She was Baptized, and lived with the English in our Factory of Metchlipatam. (p. 40)

The widow, young and "fresh complexioned," emerges as if from a dream to both Christendom and life in Company territory. She is sorry to have heeded the Brahmans' counsel, but gives herself over to better instruction with equal compliance. Bowrey's moral outrage resolves itself into a fantasy of conversion and control.

As may be the case with the name John Gernaet, however, there are signs of anxiety over the similarity between English desires and Indian practices in Bowrey's text. He calls widow burning a "cruell Tragedy," yet strains on horseback "to get the better Spectacle of this barbarous action" (pp. 35, 37). On the one side, there is the troubling fascination with an outrage he repeatedly terms devilish and infernal; on the other, there is the precedent of Mughal opposition to the crime. Bowrey insists that the imperial authority is worthless and corrupt: "they dare not rescue any by force and Violence, by reason the Idolaters doe annually purchase theire freedome of theire heathenish laws, and Diabolicall customes, with noe Small Summs of moneys" (p. 39). A parcel of English seamen is free to do more. The real spectacle from the European perspective consisted in a struggle among men, from which the English in particular felt increasingly excluded, and it was necessary to demean the effectiveness of Mughal intervention. Easy as this was to accomplish, however, it brought fears that English ambitions for economic gain and political power would similarly generate corruption and compromise.

The translation of Bernier with which I began my survey of *sati* accounts might well have increased such anxieties in English readers. Bernier explains how the Mughals try "indirectly" to avert widow burning:

> they oblige the Women, ready to burn themselves, to go and ask permis-
> sion of the respective Governors, who send for them, make converse with
> their own Women, remonstrate things to them with annexed promises, and
> never give them this permission, but after they have tryed all these gentle
> ways, and till they find them fixt in their sottish resolution. Which yet hin-
> ders not but that many burn themselves, especially of those that live upon
> the Lands of the *Rajas*, where no Mahumetan Governors are. (pp. 114–15)

Gentle ways, including the assistance of one's own women, do not always work; territorial jurisdiction remains the key. Bernier next tells us that he himself was asked by the parents of a widow, "as sent from my *Agah*," to discourage her from committing herself to the flames.[77] He finds her beat-ing the feet of her dead husband with loosened hair, surrounded by four or five "brain-sick *Brahmans*" and a group of old women (pp. 116–17). Exasperated, Bernier threatens to have the children's pensions stopped should their mother kill herself: "Then take thy Children," he tells her, "thou unhappy Creature, and cut their Throats, and burn them with thee; for they will be starved, I being now ready to return to *Danechmend-kan*, and to annull their Pension." His words, spoken "with the loudest and most menacing tone" he could muster, break the woman's spirit and dis-pel the old women and Brahmans (p. 118). In the role of an agent of Mughal power, Bernier finds economic intimidation and violent language to be the best means of prevention. He has become part of the oriental scene, rather than remaining a spectator of it.

Bernier comes near the end of an early modern tradition of widow burn-ing narratives, a European tradition that paved the way for the fetishizing of *sati* in the moral and legal discourse of imperialism during the later eigh-teenth and nineteenth centuries.[78] He rounds up some familiar explanations for the practice:

> Many persons, whom I then consulted about this custom of Women burn-
> ing themselves with the Bodies of their Husbands, would perswade me, that

what they did was from an excess of affection they had for them: But I understood afterwards, that it was only an effect of Opinion, prepossession
and custome; and that the Mothers, from their youth besotted with this superstition, as of a most vertuous and most laudable action, such as was un-
avoidable to a Woman of honour, did also infatuate the spirit of their
Daughters from their very infancy: Although, at the bottome, it was nothing else but an Art of the Men, the more to enslave their Wives, thereby to
make them have the more care of their health, and to prevent poisoning of
them. (pp. 122–23)

Bernier organizes the explanations into a structure where the women's firsthand attribution of their actions to their own affection is nevertheless the
most superficial and least authoritative explanation. Later he finds their behavior to proceed from opinion or custom, fostered by their mothers, but
"at the bottome," he concludes, even the mothers are stand-ins for the men,
who artfully instituted the custom to prevent their murders. Tacit recourse
to the Graeco-Roman discourse of India for the last word sets the stage for
masculine struggle over the bodies of women; similarly, the widow in
Bernier's tableau gives way to her elderly female attendants and the brain-
sick Brahmans, who finally slink away.

At this point, we are ready to turn to Dryden's *Aureng-Zebe*, a play that
marks the end of one stage in England's particular obsession with Indian
performance and heralds the start of another. Dryden wrote his final heroic
tragedy in verse in the wake of Bernier's epistolary chronicle of recent
events in India.[79] The French traveler's first two volumes were translated
under the title *The History of the Late Revolution of the Empire of the Great
Mogul* and published in 1671. Dryden's play appeared in quarto in 1675,
which is also the year of its earliest recorded performance at the Theatre
Royal in Drury Lane. Departing drastically from Bernier, Dryden introduces *sati* to provide a dual climax to the plot of dynastic struggle:
Melesinda, wife of Aureng-Zebe's brother and rival Morat, announces that
she will burn on his pyre and exits with a procession of priests and slaves to
accomplish her resolution, while Nourmahal, the evil wife of the still-living
emperor and Aureng-Zebe's stepmother, vividly imagines herself burning
with her hated husband's corpse as she expires in the striking mad-scene that
concludes the drama. This is deeply strange, of course, because the Mughals

were Muslim, and as we have seen they opposed widow burning among their Hindu subjects. The difference between Muslim and Hindu ways is clear in both the first installment of Bernier's letters, from which the plot of *Aureng-Zebe* is very loosely adapted, and the *Continuation*, in which the accounts of Juggernaut, *sati*, and other customs are found. Earlier in the play, Dryden himself is at pains to suggest the Mughal court's Islamic character: there are mentions of a mosque and "our Prophet's" commands.[80]

Dryden's apparent confusion of Hindu and Mughal practices is related to another puzzle: why the first imaginative work in English to depict Indians in India should deal exclusively with Muslim characters at all, when, as we have seen, the travel and antiquarian traditions are largely taken up with the Hindus. It is true that sections devoted to Mughal architecture and administration can be found in most lengthy treatments of India, and that the writings of Sir Thomas Roe on his embassy to Jahangir early in the seventeenth century limn a detailed portrait of a sophisticated ruler and the exacting procedures of his court. Currently, most historical and cultural studies work concentrates on the Mughals during the period.[81] Early modern European travel writing, however, largely concerns Hindu India and grants it temporal and ontological priority. Like Heylyn after him, even Roe remarks that the Mughals have ruined the ancient buildings of the Hindus, "I know not out of what reason, unless they would have nothing remembered of greatness beyond theyr beginnings, as if theyr famely and the world were coevalls."[82] It is precisely because an essential Indianness was attributed to the Hindus that they were not represented directly on the English stage. The differences between the geohistorical archive and Renaissance drama are stronger in the Indian case than the Egyptian or Russian. European travelers were obsessed with Hindu culture as a series of increasingly pure performances, but a playwright requires plot as well as performance. The Mughals were cast as latecomers, yet it was by virtue of their belatedness that they possessed the thing that Dryden needed to make India legible to his English audience—"history." History, revolution, empire, greatness: the principal terms of Bernier's title already suggest a master plot, and the plots of the intriguing princes and their followers rendered the Mughals adaptable to late-seventeenth-century court drama in England. The Hindus, although wrongly relegated to the status of a people without history, retained their priority for European observers in a manner that Dryden's heroic tragedy also uncovers. The Indianness they were thought to embody always threatened to erupt within the historical continuum superposed upon the landscape, a lesson not only for the Mughals but for any imperial power that might dream of succeeding them.

Aureng-Zebe purports to be inspired by conflicts at the Mughal court in the old capital of Agra during 1658 (Dryden set it in 1660, as if to signal his symmetrical refashioning of recent events). Shah Jahan, Dryden's emperor, fell ill after sending three of his sons to distant provinces, his eldest, Darah, commanding the fort at Agra. When rumors of his death reached them, the younger brothers advanced on Agra. Aureng-Zebe and Morat defeated Darah, who is mentioned but not depicted in Dryden's version. The victorious brothers confined their father to the fort, but it was not long before Aureng-Zebe had Morat executed for murder. He went on to kill Darah and drive out the remaining exiled brother. Dryden opens his play with Aureng-Zebe's unaided recapture of Agra from Darah. Aureng-Zebe lets his father remain at liberty and remains loyal to him throughout. Morat is admitted to the citadel with his army by the emperor, who has fallen in love with Aureng-Zebe's beloved, Indamora, and wants to dispose of his son and rival. Aureng-Zebe is apprehended, but his stepmother Nourmahal falls in love with him; spurned, she attempts to poison him but is prevented by Morat, who has also fallen in love with Indamora and wishes to please her by giving his brother Aureng-Zebe a one-day reprieve. Indamora, like Nourmahal and Morat's rejected wife Melesinda, is Dryden's invention; she is "the captive queen of Cassimere" or Kashmir. Morat claims both Indamora and the reins of power from the emperor, who reconciles with Aureng-Zebe and sends him first against Morat and then against Nourmahal, who has her own army. Morat dies of his wounds while attempting to rescue Indamora from the jealous Nourmahal's dagger. Aureng-Zebe reconquers the fort and accepts Indamora and an apology from his father amid the twinned fates of the widowed Melesinda and the maddened Nourmahal, who has poisoned herself.[83]

The reasons Dryden's Mughal women end like the Hindu wives of the travel material can best be understood through an examination of the way references to *sati* gradually accrue throughout *Aureng-Zebe*, long before Act V. Under an injunction not to reveal the emperor's advances to her, Indamora decries the origin of love, calling it "an aery good" made by

"Opinion" (1.1.372). Opinion, a word laden with more significance for Dryden than for us, is the enemy of reason and self-government. There may be an echo here of the "Opinion, prepossession and custome" to which Bernier attributes widow burning, the barbaric and spectacular act of putative love that defies European and Mughal notions of right reason and proper religiosity. Reconciled to his beloved as she breaks her vow of silence on his father's conduct, Aureng-Zebe suddenly asserts that he will share her punishment:

> In Death's dark Bow'rs our Bridals we will keep:
> And his cold hand
> Shall draw the Curtain when we go to sleep. (1.1.427–29)

The wedding that is also a funeral recalls *sati*, but the darkness, the cold, and the man's offer to join the woman in death reverse the terms of the tradition and render the similarity seemingly far-fetched.

Dryden not only makes Aureng-Zebe into a loyal and heroic figure with such noble sentiments, he creates a new type of dramatic hero in the process. His protagonist usually eschews the rants of earlier heroic plays in favor of reasoned debate and modest, if often ardent and moving, protestation. Aureng-Zebe may be neither the first full-fledged sentimental hero nor an advance scout for the Enlightenment, but Dryden makes the Mughal prince an early site for new modes of masculine European self-fashioning.[84] At the start of the play, a courtier contrasts him with Morat:

> But *Aureng-Zebe*, by no strong passions sway'd,
> Except his Love, more temp'rate is, and weigh'ed:
> This *Atlas* must our sinking State uphold;
> In Council cool, but in Performance bold. (1.1.102–5)

The tension between council and performance is never fully resolved in Aureng-Zebe's character. He fights for "A Parent's Blessing, and a Mistris Love" (1.1.111), but it is his love for his mistress Indamora that divides him from his father.

Although Indamora seems wholly a force for good, elsewhere in the play it is women who introduce unreason and discord into empire. The brothers formed factions, "When each, by curs'd Cabals of Women, stove, / To draw th'indulgent King to partial Love" (1.1.19–20). Women "Emasculate" power, Morat tells Nourmahal; in serving men's pleasure they also consume the rewards of conquest, "And murmuring Crouds, who see 'em shine with Gold, / That pomp, as their own ravish'd Spoils behold" (4.1.200–202). Love and empire, though counterpoised in *Aureng-Zebe*, are often rendered mutually convertible as well. "Beauty a Monarch is," Indamora tells her jailer Arimant in chastely accepting his devotion, "Which Kingly power magnificently proves / By crouds of Slaves, and peopled Empire loves" (2.1.74–76).[85] Aureng-Zebe himself attacks Indamora when he thinks she gained his reprieve from Morat through love. "Ah Sex, invented first to damn Mankind!" he exclaims, "Hence, by no judgment you your loves direct; / Talk much, ne'er think, and still the wrong affect" (4.2.101, 104–5). A few words from Indamora, however, have him professing a more extravagant love for her than ever:

> Love mounts, and rowls about my stormy mind,
> Like Fire, that's born by a tempestuous Wind.
> Oh, I could stifle you, with eager haste!
> Devour your kisses with my hungry taste!
> Rush on you! eat you! wander o'er each part,
> Raving with pleasure, snatch you to my heart!
> Then hold you off, and gaze! then, with new rage,
> Invade you, till my conscious Limbs presage
> Torrents of joy, which all their banks o'rflow! (4.2.144–52)

Now it is masculine desire that consumes what it invades: the interweaving of fiery love, penetrating conquest, and scopophilia suggests that empire is complicit with opinion or irrational passion, perhaps with the passion that *sati* aptly symbolized to the European gaze.

The combination of love, violence, and fire is so traditional that the link with *sati* appears unnecessary. And so it may be, but with Bernier in the background and the specific patterns of the play before us a different picture emerges. "My first flames can ne'r decay," the emperor assures his suspicious wife (2.1.221). "What's Love to you?" Nourmahal demands. "You importune it with a false desire: / Which sparkles out, and makes no solid fire" (2.1.296,

299–300). She recalls these lines, as we shall see, in her imagined *sati* later on. A puzzling epithet thrown Aureng-Zebe's way by Morat also looks forward to the end of the play. "Seize him, and take the preaching *Brachman* hence," Morat exclaims, after a typically stoic pronouncement by his captive brother (3.1.216). In Bernier, Aureng-Zebe "was reserved, crafty, and exceedingly versed in dissembling, insomuch that for a long while, he made profession to be *Fakire*, . . . renouncing the World, and faining not to pretend at all to the Crown." He affects to be a fakir when Morat comes to power.[86] Muslim fakirs are not the same as Hindu Brahmans, but we have traced the way fakirs and yogis were confused within the discourse of bodily discipline in which the Brahman served as master signifier. Moreover, the emperor accuses Aureng-Zebe of hypocrisy, "And preaching in the Self-denying Cant" (3.1.241). Aureng-Zebe then tells Morat he may become a bear or lion in his next life, "if Transmigration be" (3.1.308–9). "Hence with that dreaming Priest," Morat retorts. Self-sacrifice and promises of rebirth were the burdens of the Brahmans' exhortations in the *sati* stories, and the dreaming Aureng-Zebe does foreshadow the "Priests" who accompany Melesinda in procession as she makes her funeral vow.[87]

The Brahman taunt also recalls the often careless syncretism of some travel accounts, and it is certainly characteristic of a play written to amuse an audience whose knowledge of Indian religions was negligible. Carelessness, however, was also the tool of an emergent para-colonial gaze that increasingly blurred the multiple alterity of India into a monotonous sameness in metropolitan popular culture. As the drama progresses, the Mughal and Hindu worlds Dryden vaguely evokes gradually come closer and closer together. This is accomplished largely through the female characters of the play. Women are associated with passion, and passion with the irrationality of Hindu ritual and belief; the figure of the *sati* widow represents the conjunction of women and an imagined Hinduism, and more generally she serves as the play's emblem for the fragility of religious and national identity in the imperial scene.[88]

Mughal power is steadily corrupted from within throughout the play. Women both point this process out to the men and increasingly come to embody it. A series of exchanges between Indamora and Morat from the middle of the action illustrates this contradictory situation. When the triumphant Morat determines to kill Aureng-Zebe, she entreats,

> Piety is no more, she sees her place
> Usurp'd by Monsters, and a savage Race.
> From her soft Eastern Climes you drive her forth,
> To the cold Mansions of the utmost North.
> How can our Prophet suffer you to Reign,
> When he looks down, and sees your Brother slain? (3.1.461–66)

The "Monsters" summon the maligned monsters of Hindu temple decoration, and the opposition between them and "our Prophet" underlines the implied distinction. It is Piety who has been usurped, but her displacement counters the partial conquest of India by the Muslims and especially the Mughals. A "savage Race" has returned, at a time when the word "race" was assuming its basic modern denotation. Yet it is the Mughals who have themselves, in the person of Morat, become what they subjected. The passage thus performs a number of operations. Hindu believers are rendered a homogeneous race, Muslims are both more advanced and precariously belated, and the monstrosity of the Hindus threatens Muslim reign somehow from within. Piety, which here betokens a communal identity bound up with familial integrity, has fled from the civilized East to the cold North, perhaps as far as Drury Lane.

Morat and Indamora meet again after he captures the citadel for the second time. She reads her would-be lover a lesson on the nature of imperial power: "'Tis base to seize on all, because you may;/That's Empire, that which I can give away" (5.1.106–7). Amidst a flurry of nautical metaphors, Morat says he will give up the crown, but adds, "I, in this venture, double gains pursue,/And laid out all my Stock to purchase you" (5.1.128–29). Between the lines, one finds the suggestion that maritime commerce, exchange, and an economic sphere of influence avert the corruptions of territorial empire. Morat, of course, does not quite get it; he has invested in Indamora's love and expects a return. When the erroneous news of Aureng-Zebe's death arrives, Indamora despairs and Morat is further moved: "Love softens me; and blows up fires, which pass/Through my tough heart, and melt the stubborn Mass" (5.1.151–52). However idealized the imagery of burning and softening may be here, the language of commercial empire remains bound up with passion and the threat of dissolution it brings.

Later, as Morat lies bleeding after saving Indamora from Nourmahal, she mourns the supposed loss of Aureng-Zebe by asking him to take her with him because there is nothing worth living for on earth. Morat, content to die by her side, says,

> I leave you not; for my expanded mind
> Grows up to Heav'n, while it to you is joyn'd;
> Not quitting, but enlarg'd! A blazing Fire,
> Fed from the Brand. (5.1.434–37)

Unfortunately for Indamora, Aureng-Zebe overhears these declarations, and their final lovers' quarrel ensues when he reveals he has survived the battle. Even if Morat was not her lover, why did she value life after she thought Aureng-Zebe dead? "Not that I valu'd life; but fear'd to die," she explains, "Think that my weakness, not inconstancy" (5.1.518–19). Aureng-Zebe at first rebuffs a love mixed with fear: "she ne'r lov'd who durst not venture all" (5.1.530). Through Aureng-Zebe's argument with Indamora Dryden glorifies the ideal of the suicidal woman in the afterglow of the symbolic fire fed from the brand of Morat's sacrificial death. Yet Indamora gets the final word; she is right, it seems, to fear death, and Aureng-Zebe surrenders when she threatens to part from him forever.[89]

At this point, however, there enters "a Procession of Priests, Slaves following, and last Melesinda in white" (5.1.610, SD). Finally, a woman rather than a man will cast herself into real flames, correcting and literalizing the play's central trope. When Indamora, unfamiliar with the custom, asks what it means, Aureng-Zebe explains,

> 'Tis the Procession of a Funeral Vow,
> Which cruel Laws to *Indian* Wives allow
> When fatally their Virtue they approve;
> Chearful in flames, and Martyrs of their Love. (5.1.612–15)

Dryden's presentation of *sati* is stylized and spare compared with the travel accounts, yet he preserves a few subtle elements from the tradition and all of its ambiguities. Aureng-Zebe now finds dying after one's lover cruel, perhaps because it has become a matter of law; yet the law is cruel insofar as it allows Indian wives willfully to "approve" or prove their virtue. There is something "fatal," however, in this act of will. Nevertheless, like the widows in Linschoten and Bowrey, the widow is "cheerful" when she enters the fire.

The phrase "Indian wives," like the "Indian women" of Pietro della Valle and Bernier, blurs the distinction between Hindu and Muslim women—not to mention women of other religions, or the substantial distinctions among Hindu women to begin with. Indamora is evidently unfamiliar with the *sati* ritual, yet Melesinda earlier told her that she craved a "Funeral Marriage" after Morat's death; and she adopts the procedure, complete with priests, almost intuitively, even though Aureng-Zebe had ordered Morat entombed (5.1.363, 445).[90] "This is the Triumph of my Nuptial day," Melesinda states, and now she need never be jealous again:

> My love was such, it needed no return;
> But could, though he suppli'd no fuel, burn:
> Rich in it self, like Elemental fire,
> Whose pureness does no Aliment require.
> In vain you would bereave me of my Lord;
> For I will die: die is too base a word;
> I'll seek his breast, and kindling by his side,
> Adorn'd with flames, I'll mount a glorious Bride. (5.1.619, 628–35)

All the foregoing imagery of love's flames, masculine fuel, and burning embraces is retrospectively tied to *sati* by this speech. The emperor's response to the situation is notably weak: "Let no false show of Fame your reason blind" (5.1.623). Although he invokes the "reason" that European modernity would lay proper claim to, the emperor's single line stages the travelers' contention that Mughal response to *sati* was inadequate. The confusion of Hindu and Muslim practice at the climax of the play serves a similar purpose. A supposedly essential Indianness bursts through the body of a woman within the Mughal court, exposing the Mughals as poor custodians of imperial rationality.

An air of noble self-sacrifice, however, still adheres to Melesinda. Dryden wishes to have it both ways: *sati* serves a heroic ideal, as it did for Pietro, as long as it remains in a vanquished, "savage" past, or is indirectly represented on the tragic stage as an aesthetic novelty. Melesinda's *sati* corresponds to the "good" half of the tradition, exemplifying wifely love, the marriage bond, and female volition. Significantly, it takes place off-stage; in Melesinda's place before the public we have Nourmahal, who embodies the "bad" side of the split in the European conception of widow burning. Nourmahal has poisoned herself, and when she enters on Melesinda's exiting heels she has been driven mad by the draught and imagines herself burning alive. Her alternate attempts to poison or commit adultery with Aureng-Zebe early on recall the classical explanation for *sati*. Here poisoning is collapsed with widow burning itself, in a manner that annuls or at any rate distorts female volition:

> I burn, I more than burn; I am all fire:
> See how my mouth and nostrils flame expire.
> I'll not come near my self—
> Now I'm a burning Lake, it rowls and flows;
> I'll rush, and pour it all upon my Foes. (5.1.641–45)

The hallucinating Nourmahal performs Melesinda's unseen heroic act in ridiculous but horrifying pantomime. Dryden is concerned with achieving a spectacular effect in language, not with declaiming against widow burning or Mughal policy. Yet Nourmahal's vivid description of a burning body unavoidably serves as a reminder of why *sati* is barbaric after all, of why virtuous women should be saved from actual flames.

The empress has already exemplified the incremental heathenization of the court throughout the play: in addition to her fondness for poison, earlier in Act 5 she blames "the Gods" for her fate, "Which cannot guard their Images below" (5.1.284, 346). Her dying rant renews the parodic intimation of *sati* she tossed at the emperor before:

> Pull, pull that reverend piece of Timber near;
> Throw't on—'tis dry—'twill burn—
> Ha, ha! how my old Husband crackles there!
> Keep him down, keep him down, turn him about;
> I know him; he'll but whiz, and strait go out. (5.1.646–50)

The lines are an indictment of her husband's general lack of effectiveness, which we have just witnessed in his feeble admonition to Melesinda.

"Quench me: pour on whole Rivers," she cries, in another nod to the *sati* tradition—but her own fires cannot be doused, and threaten to consume all around her (5.1.653). Of course, Nourmahal's is an imaginary terror, and it is taken as a confession of guilt for kindling the conflicts in the royal household (5.1.668). It is a mere performance, the ultimate performance of the Indian woman on Dryden's Restoration stage.

The reduction of India to spectacle, of course, was already well under way in the travel material. Bernier refers several times to particular burnings as "tragedies," as Bowrey had before him. He can hardly express, he writes, "with what courage and resolution these poor Women atchieved such a direful Tragedy; for there is nothing but the Eye it self that can exhibite a right *idea* thereof."[91] Dryden's problem is similar to the traveler's, for he has to suggest the tragedy without directly presenting it through the visual medium of the theater. He succeeds, but paradoxically undermines the tragic moment as well. In the double climax of the play, "history" and dramatic plot are overtaken by pure performance, just as the masculine conflicts of the Mughal court give way to the timeless essence of the "Indian" woman. Through Nourmahal, the audience is left with an India that is both feminine and grotesque, ominous but finally insubstantial.

Most of the material that I have presented above would itself be regarded as insubstantial from the perspective of the accepted political historiography of modern India since the eighteenth century. C. A. Bayly's statement in the opening chapter to his recent book *Empire and Information* might be taken as a sort of rebuttal in advance to this chapter and, by extension, my entire book:

> The British understanding of Indian society—as opposed to its trades—
> may have been extraordinarily defective, but this was more the result of a
> lack of reliable informants than the consequence of orientalist stereotypes.
> Ideas of Oriental Despotism purveyed by Manucci, Bernier, by Jesuit com-
> mentators and by English travellers such as Fitch and Hawkins do not seem
> greatly to have informed their thinking. These works were not at this time
> regarded as manuals of political theory for Europeans in India. Rather they
> were attempts to make room in European mentalities for the great king-
> doms of the east. At this period 'orientalism' was largely devoid of signifi-
> cance for the exercising of power within India.[92]

It is difficult to argue with Bayly where the details of administration and policy in the mid-eighteenth century are concerned; he goes on, it must be noted, to speak of the relative importance of official orientalism later in the century. Yet cultural history, although it embraces politics in the statist sense, is not reducible to policy. Though indebted to the political historians of colonial regimes, historians of material culture should resist the dual constraint upon which political history is perhaps necessarily based: the disqualification of cultural representations, and the virtual omission of Europe's early modern past from the scene of "negotiation," "social communication," or whatever the preferred term may be.

Theories of representation have themselves neglected earlier periods, of course, rendering them vulnerable to skeptical appraisals such as Bayly's. The opening chapter or the stray paragraph are the favored genres for discussing what I have termed the para-colonial throughout the field.[93] Cohn's treatment of Roe's embassy is something of an exception to this tendency.[94] More work needs to be done outside of the Mughal court, however, and outside of the commercial circuit of the East India Company as well. A discourse wider than diplomacy and trade preceded the investigative modalities Cohn identifies. As he remarks, "India was seen by Europeans not only as exotic and bizarre but as a kind of living museum of the European past."[95] The emphasis should be placed on "living" rather than "museum" during the earlier era. Cohn presents us with part of the picture: "The literature on India of the seventeenth and early eighteenth centuries varies in its content but it established an enduring structural relationship between India and the West: Europe was progressive and changing, India static. Here could be found a kind of living fossil bed of the European past."[96] As I have shown, India was in some sense unchanging in the eyes of the European Renaissance, but it was hardly static. It was chaotic and kinetic, timeless only in its unmanageable variety, which was often figured through images of women's bodies. Thus, investigating early modern representations of India might disrupt later codifications of the subcontinent as inert and passive in colonial discourse. On the other hand, it would be wrong to idealize performativity or "the body" as an already available undoing of the monumental.[97] Bodily performance was an earlier, alternative form of modeling, a dynamic form that was for some reason typical of European representations of India from Graeco-Roman times on. Traces of a tension between the monumental and the performative can also be found throughout the old worlds I have discussed, particularly in the construction of Egypt with which I began. It was through this tension's lines of force that race was sculpted, despite its deceptively monolithic display.

Notes

INTRODUCTION

1. Christopher Columbus, *The Four Voyages of Columbus*, 2 vols., ed. Cecil Jane (London, 1930, 1933; reprint with corrections, New York: Dover, 1988), 2: 8; Vespucci, *The Letters of Amerigo Vespucci*, trans. Clements R. Markham (London: Hakluyt Society, 1894), p. 42.

2. Rudolph Hirsch, "Printed Reports on the Early Discoveries and Their Reception," in *First Images of America: The Impact of the New World on the Old*, ed. Fredi Chiappelli (Berkeley: University of California Press, 1976), pp. 537–50.

3. Myron P. Gilmore, "The New World in French and English Historians of the Sixteenth Century," in *First Images of America: The Impact of the New World on the Old*, ed. Fredi Chiappelli (Berkeley: University of California Press, 1976), pp. 519–27.

4. Donald F. Lach, *Asia in the Making of Europe*, vol. 1, *The Century of Discovery* (Chicago: The University of Chicago Press, 1965), p. 227.

5. John Gillies, *Shakespeare and the Geography of Difference* (Cambridge: Cambridge University Press, 1994).

6. Fernand Braudel, *The Mediterranean and the Mediterranean World in the Age of Philip II*, trans. Siân Reynolds (New York: Harper & Row, 1976), p. 627.

7. Edward W. Said, *Orientalism* (New York: Vintage, 1979), pp. 71–73.

8. Fernand Braudel, *The Mediterranean*, p. 612.

9. Thomas Hahn, "Indians East and West: Primitivism and Savagery in English Discovery Narratives of the Sixteenth Century," *The Journal of Medieval and Renaissance Studies* 8 (1978), 113. I owe this reference to Ania Loomba.

10. José Rabasa, *Inventing America: Spanish Historiography and the Formation of Eurocentrism* (Norman: University of Oklahoma Press, 1993), pp. 199–202; Gillies, *Shakespeare*, pp. 61, 163–64.

11. Rabasa, *Inventing America*, pp. 50–51.

12. Immanuel Wallerstein, *The Modern World-System*, vol. 1, *Capitalist Agriculture and the Origins of the European World-Economy in the Sixteenth Century* (San Diego: Academic Press, 1974), pp. 347–48, hereafter cited by volume and page

numbers; Wallerstein, *Historical Capitalism* (London: Verso, 1983), pp. 29–30. See also Braudel, *Civilization and Capitalism, 15th-18th Century*, vol. 2, *The Perspective of the World*, trans. Siân Reynolds (New York: Harper & Row, 1984), pp. 25–26.

13. Samir Amin, *Eurocentrism*, trans. Russell Moore (New York: Monthly Review Press, 1989), p. 10, and "The Ancient World Systems versus the Modern Capitalist World System," *Review: Fernand Braudel Center* 14:3 (1991), 349–85; Janet L. Abu-Lughod, *Before European Hegemony: The World System A.D. 1250–1350* (New York: Oxford University Press, 1989), p. 12.

14. Wallerstein, *World-System* 1:77; Karl Marx, *Capital*, vol. 1 (New York: International Publishers, 1967), p. 146.

15. K. N. Chaudhuri, *Trade and Civilization in the Indian Ocean: An Economic History of the Rise of Islam to 1750* (Cambridge: Cambridge University Press, 1985). See also K. N. Chaudhuri, *Asia before Europe: Economy and Civilization of the Indian Ocean from the Rise of Islam to 1750* (Cambridge: Cambridge University Press, 1990), for a magisterial overview of the environmental and social conditions of the Asian world economies during the period. On the early medieval period, see also Ronald Inden, *Imagining India* (Oxford: Basil Blackwell, 1990), pp. 213–62; Inden prefers "imperial formation" to "world system" (p. 36). A vigorous, if somewhat sweeping, account of the economic similarities among pre-Columbian Africa, Asia, and Europe is offered by J. M. Blaut, *The Colonizer's Model of the World: Geographical Diffusionism and Eurocentric History* (New York: Guilford Press, 1993), pp. 152–73; see also p. 57, where he cites Abu-Lughod and Amin.

16. Wallerstein has recently criticized the "rise and fall" model, but in doing so he retains the notion of cyclic change: *Geopolitics and Geoculture: Essays on the Changing World System* (Cambridge: Cambridge University Press, 1991), pp. 235–36.

17. Said, *Orientalism*, pp. 187–88; Patricia Parker, *Literary Fat Ladies: Rhetoric, Gender, Property* (New York: Methuen, 1987), pp. 140–41.

18. Wallerstein, *World-System*, 1:302; Braudel, *Mediterranean*, p. 551.

19. Maria Mies, *Patriarchy and Accumulation on a World Scale: Women in the International Division of Labour* (London: Zed Books, 1986), pp. 100–103.

20. Laura Brown, *Ends of Empire: Women and Ideology in Early Eighteenth-Century English Literature* (Ithaca: Cornell University Press, 1993), pp. 44–45.

21. Wallerstein, *Historical Capitalism*, p. 25.

22. Mies, *Patriarchy*, p. 95.

23. Kim F. Hall, "'I Rather Would Wish to Be a Black-Moor': Beauty, Race, and Rank in Lady Mary Wroth's *Urania*," in *Women, "Race," and Writing in the Early Modern Period*, eds. Margo Hendricks and Patricia Parker (London: Routledge, 1994), p. 180.

24. Immanuel Wallerstein, "The Construction of Peoplehood," in Etienne Balibar and Immanuel Wallerstein, *Race, Nation, Class: Ambiguous Identities* (London: Verso, 1991), pp. 79–82.

25. Michel Foucault, *The History of Sexuality*, vol. 1, *An Introduction*, trans. Robert Hurley (New York: Vintage, 1980), p. 149; author's emphasis.

26. Jeffrey Knapp, *An Empire Nowhere: England, America, and Literature from Utopia to The Tempest* (Berkeley: University of California Press, 1992).

27. Arjun Appadurai, *Modernity at Large: Cultural Dimensions of Globalization* (Minneapolis: University of Minnesota Press, 1996), p. 27. He cites Abu-Lughod, Braudel, and Wallerstein in this passage, among others.

28. Paul Smith, *Millennial Dreams: Contemporary Culture and Capital in the North* (London: Verso, 1997), pp. 10–13.

29. Samir Amin, *Capitalism in the Age of Globalization: The Management of Contemporary Society* (London: Zed Books, 1997), pp. 2, 33.

30. Smith, *Millennial Dreams*, p. 14; and see p. 20. On "primitive accumulation" as a theoretical fiction with partial roots in sixteenth- and seventeenth-century English fictions, see Richard Halpern, *The Poetics of Primitive Accumulation: English Renaissance Culture and the Genealogy of Capital* (Ithaca, N.Y.: Cornell University Press, 1991).

31. Gayatri Chakravorty Spivak, *A Critique of Postcolonial Reason: Toward a History of the Vanishing Present* (Cambridge, Mass.: Harvard University Press, 1999), p. 220.

32. Rabasa, *Inventing America*, pp. 192–209.

33. Smith, *Millennial Dreams*, p. 49.

34. Ernst Robert Curtius, *European Literature and the Latin Middle Ages*, trans. Willard R. Trask (Princeton, N.J.: Princeton University Press, 1953), p. 144.

35. Said, *Orientalism*, p. 63.

36. Edward W. Said, *Culture and Imperialism* (New York: Knopf, 1993), pp. 33–45, 111–32.

37. Said, *Orientalism*, p. 61.

38. Martin Prösler, "Museums and Globalization," in *Theorizing Museums: Representing Identity and Diversity in a Changing World*, eds. Sharon Macdonald and Gordon Frye (Oxford: Blackwell, 1996), p. 27.

39. For elements of this view, see the still useful discussion by Steven Mullaney, *The Place of the Stage: License, Play, and Power in Renaissance England* (Chicago: University of Chicago Press, 1988), pp. 60–69. See also James Clifford, *The Predicament of Culture: Twentieth-Century Ethnography, Literature, and Art* (Cambridge: Harvard University Press, 1988), p. 222. On "wonder," see Stephen Greenblatt, *Marvelous Possessions: The Wonder of the New World* (Chicago: University of Chicago Press, 1991), esp. pp. 12, 119–22. Jody Greene has criticized Mullaney's presuppositions in an article whose focus is on his account of the display of Brazilian Indians in a model village at Rouen during Henri II's royal entry in 1550. In distinguishing this spectacle from the cabinets, Greene preserves the sense that *wunderkammern* were passive collections of decontextualized objects. Greene argues that "negotiation" over the harvesting of brazil-wood was really on display in Rouen, not the erasure of a culture. I think the evidence suggests that exploitation as well as negotiation was the subject of the royal entry and that it is the relation between exploitation and negotiation, rather than physical objects, that the *wunderkammern* offered to the view as well: Greene,

"New Historicism and Its New World Discoveries," *Yale Journal of Criticism* 4:2 (1991), 163–98.

40. Donald F. Lach, *Asia in the Making of Europe*, vol. 2, *A Century of Wonder*, Book 1: *The Visual Arts* (Chicago: University of Chicago Press, 1970), pp. 44, 45.

41. Johannes Fabian, *Time and the Other: How Anthropology Makes its Object* (New York: Columbia University Press, 1983), p. 113; on political cosmology, see p. 87.

42. Justin Stagl, *A History of Curiosity: The Theory of Travel, 1550–1800* (Chur, Switzerland: Harwood Academic Publishers, 1995), pp. 56–153.

43. Timothy Mitchell, *Colonising Egypt* (Berkeley: University of California Press, 1991), pp. 6, 13.

44. Bernard S. Cohn, *Colonialism and Its Forms of Knowledge: The British in India* (Princeton, N.J.: Princeton University Press, 1996), p. 19. See also Cohn, "Representing Authority in Victorian India," in *An Anthropologist among the Historians and Other Essays* (Delhi: Oxford University Press, 1990).

45. Cohn, "Introduction," in *Colonialism*, p. 5; see also Inden, *Imagining India*.

46. Roger Chartier, *The Order of Books: Readers, Authors, and Libraries in Europe between the Fourteenth and Eighteenth Centuries*, trans. Lydia G. Cochrane (Stanford Calif.: Stanford University Press, 1994), p. 64.

47. Lach, *Visual Arts*, p. 30.

48. Chaudhuri, *Trade and Civilization*, p. 88.

49. Walter Benjamin, "Theses on the Philosophy of History," in *Illuminations*, trans. Harry Zohn (New York: Schocken Books, 1969), p. 255.

50. Walter Benjamin, "Eduard Fuchs: Collector and Historian," in *The Essential Frankfurt School Reader*, eds. Andrew Arato and Eike Gebhardt (New York: Continuum, 1987), p. 233. Compare "Theses," p. 256.

51. Walter Benjamin, [*Passagen-Werk*] "N," trans. Leigh Hafrey and Richard Sieburth, *The Philosophical Forum* 15:1–2 (1983–84), p. 38.

52. Martin Bernal, "Black Athena Denied: The Tyranny of Germany over Greece," *Comparative Criticism* 8 (1986), 3–69; V. Y. Mudimbe, *The Idea of Africa* (Bloomington: Indiana University Press, 1994), pp. 93–98. Bernal acknowledges the inadequacy of models (p. 3).

53. Said, *Culture and Imperialism*, p. 126; Said's emphasis. For other doubts about systems, see Fabian, pp. 154 and 182, note 14.

54. David S. Katz, *Philo-Semitism and the Readmission of the Jews to England, 1603–1655* (Oxford: Clarendon, 1982); Avraham Oz, *The Yoke of Love: Prophetic Riddles in The Merchant of Venice* (Newark: University of Delaware Press, 1995), chapter 2; and James Shapiro, *Shakespeare and the Jews* (New York: Columbia University Press, 1996), are quite different in their methodologies and scope. On the Turks: Nabil Matar, *Islam in Britain, 1558–1685* (Cambridge: Cambridge University Press, 1998) and *Turks, Moors, and Englishmen in the Age of Discovery* (New York: Columbia University Press, 1999); Daniel J. Vitkus, "Turning Turk in *Othello*: The

Conversion and Damnation of the Moor," *Shakespeare Quarterly* 48 (1997), 145–76, and "Introduction," in *Three Turk Plays from Early Modern England: Selimus, A Christian Turned Turk, and the Renegado*, ed. Vitkus (New York: Columbia University Press, 2000).

Islam, the Ottomans, and the figure of the Moor have in some sense constituted the dominant entry points for scholarship on early modern England and "the East." Among a number of earlier books, see Samuel C. Chew, *The Cresent and the Rose: Islam and England During the Renaissance* (New York, 1937; rpt. New York: Octagon Press, 1974); and Eldred Jones, *Othello's Countrymen: Africans in English Renaissance Drama* (Oxford: Oxford University Press, 1965). Additional recent studies include Jack D'Amico, *The Moor in English Renaissance Drama* (Tampa: University of South Florida Press, 1991); and Virginia Mason Vaughan, *Othello: A Contextual History* (Cambridge: Cambridge University Press, 1994). See also Constance C. Relihan, "Erasing the East from *Twelfth Night*," and Alan Rosen, "The Rhetoric of Exclusion: Jew, Moor, and the Boundaries of Discourse in *The Merchant of Venice*," both in *Race, Ethnicity, and Power in the Renaissance*, ed. Joyce Green MacDonald (Madison, N.J.: Farleigh Dickenson University Press, 1997). For a look at Turkish sources, see Bernadette Andrea, "Columbus in Istanbul: Ottoman Mappings of the 'New World,'" *Genre* 30 (1997), 135–36. On France and Islam during the period, see Alain Grosrichard, *The Sultan's Court: European Fantasies of the East*, trans. Liz Heron (London: Verso, 1998), originally published in French in 1978.

55. John Milton, *Paradise Lost* 11:836–37, in *The Complete Poems and Major Prose*, ed. Merritt Y. Hughes (Indianapolis: Odyssey, 1957).

CHAPTER 1

1. Martin Bernal, *Black Athena: The Afroasiatic Roots of Classical Civilization*, vol. 1, *The Fabrication of Ancient Greece 1785–1985* (New Brunswick, N.J.: Rutgers University Press, 1987), pp. 151–64. Cited by volume and page number.

2. For a probing but not unsympathetic critique of Bernal, see V. Y. Mudimbe, *The Idea of Africa* (Bloomington: Indiana University Press, 1994), pp. 93–104. On Bernal and missed opportunities concerning gender and sexuality, see the comments by Margaret Washington and Madeline C. Zilfi in Cheryl Johnson-Odim et al., "Comment: The Debate over Black Athena," *Journal of Women's History* 4 (1993), 106, 116–17, and Bernal's replies, pp. 130, 133. Kim F. Hall brought this exchange to my attention.

3. John F. Danby, *Poets on Fortune's Hill: Studies in Sidney, Shakespeare, Beaumont and Fletcher* (London: Faber and Faber, 1952), p. 140.

4. Ania Loomba, *Gender, Race, Renaissance Drama* (Manchester: Manchester University Press, 1989), p. 78.

5. Judith Butler, *Gender Trouble: Feminism and the Subversion of Identity* (New York: Routledge, 1990), pp. 25–30; *Bodies That Matter: On the Discursive Limits of "Sex"* (New York: Routledge, 1993), p. 12.

6. Herodotus, *The Famous Hystory of Herodotus*, trans. B. R. (London: Thomas Marshe, 1584), p. 70 verso.

7. See Herodotus, *The Histories*, trans. A. R. Burn and Aubrey de Sélincourt (London: Penguin, 1972), pp. 134–35.

8. These are the Dioscuri, Hestia, Themis, the Graces, and the Nereids: see Herodotus, *The Histories*, p. 150. The 1584 translation prefers Latin names and substitutes Venus for Hesta, a mistake perhaps for Vesta.

9. See Apollodorus, *The Library*, trans. J. G. Frazer (London: Loeb Classical Library–Heinemann, 1921), 2.1.3, 3.1.1; Ruth B. Edwards, *Kadmos the Phoenician: A Study in Greek Legends and the Mycenaean Age* (Amsterdam: Adolph M. Hakkert, 1979), pp. 27–28; Bernal, *Black Athena*, 1:88–98, which discusses Aeschylus' *The Suppliants*.

10. Although an English translation of Diodorus, Books I–V did not appear in print until 1653, his first four books were translated into Latin by Poggio Bracciolini in 1472, and were published in a Greek and Latin edition again in 1604 by Stephanus. John Skelton's early Tudor rendering of Bracciolini's Latin version of Diodorus was one of the first translations of a classical text during the English Renaissance, although it remained in manuscript until modern times and may not have been widely available.

11. Diodorus Siculus, *The History of the Diodorus Siculus. Containing all that is Most Memorable and of greatest Antiquity in the first Ages of the World until the Fall of Troy*, trans. H[enry]. C[ogan]. (London: John Macock for Giles Calvert, 1653), pp. 3, 47–48.

12. In the 1653 translation of Diodorus, Book IV roughly corresponds to Book III in the original.

13. Homer, *The Iliad*, trans. Richmond Lattimore (Chicago: University of Chicago Press, 1951), p. 70.

14. Homer, *Odyssey* 1:23–24, in *The Odyssey*, trans. Richmond Lattimore (New York: HarperCollins, 1975), p. 27.

15. Bernal notes the split tradition from Homer onward, and uncovers an association between Ethiopia and Colchis in Herodotus (see Herodotus, *Famous Hystory*, p. 96 recto) as well: *Black Athena: The Afroasiatic Roots of Classical Civilization*, vol. 2, *The Archaeological and Documentary Evidence* (New Brunswick: Rutgers University Press, 1991), p. 254. See also Mudimbe, *Idea of Africa*, pp. 71–80.

16. Herodotus, *Famous Hystory*, p. 77 recto; compare Herodotus, *The Histories*, p. 140.

17. Herodotus, *The Histories*, pp. 211–13, 332.

18. Shakespeare refers to Chariclea's false death in the *Ethiopica* with Orsino's threat: "Why should I not . . . / Like to th' Egyptian thief at point of death, / Kill What I love?" *Twelfth Night*, ed. J. M. Lothian and T. W. Craik (London: Arden–Routledge, 1975), 5.1.115–17.

19. Heliodorus, *An Aethiopian History*, trans. Thomas Underdowne (London: David Nutt, 1895), pp. 111, 251. I have also consulted Heliodorus, *An Ethiopian*

Romance, trans. Moses Hadas (Ann Arbor: University of Michigan Press, 1957), throughout.

20. *The Oxford Classical Dictionary*, 3rd ed., eds. Simon Hornblower and Antony Spawforth (Oxford: Oxford University Press, 1996), s.v. "Andromeda." Chemmis, the site of the Egyptian festival of Perseus in Herodotus, figures in the *Ethiopica* as a rendezvous point where much of the story is told in flashback.

21. Mudimbe, *Idea of Africa*, pp. 79–80.

22. Philemon Holland, in Plutarch, *The Philosophie, commonlie called, The Morals written by the learned Philosopher Plutarch of Chaeronea*, trans. Holland (London: Arnold Hatfield, 1603), p. 1286.

23. Johannes Boemus, *The Manners, Lawes, and Customes of All Nations, Collected out of the Best Writers*, trans. Ed. Aston (London: George Eld, 1611), p. 17.

24. Compare Herodotus, *The Histories*, p. 143.

25. Leo Africanus, *The History and Description of Africa*, trans. John Pory, ed. Robert Brown (London: Hakluyt Society, 1896), p. 870.

26. For instance, George Sandys, *A Relation of a Journey begun An: Dom: 1610* (London: W. Barrett, 1615), A6 verso.

27. Sandys, *Relation of a Iourney*, pp. 108–9.

28. Peter Heylyn, *Cosmographie in Four Books. Containing the Chorographie and Historie of the World, and all the principal Kingdoms, Provinces, Seas, and Isles thereof*, 2nd ed. (London: for Henry Seile, 1657), p. 921.

29. Wallerstein, *The Modern World-System*, vol. 1, pp. 40, 168.

30. Abu-Lughod, *Before European Hegemony*, pp. 146, 212–15.

31. Braudel, *The Mediterranean*, pp. 389, 548, 567.

32. Henry Blount, *A Voyage into the Levant*, 2nd ed. (London: for Andrew Crooke, 1637), p. 49.

33. Abu-Lughod, *Before European Hegemony*, p. 363.

34. Wallerstein, *Modern World-System*, vol.1, p. 89.

35. George Abbot, *A Briefe Description of the whole WORLDE. . . . newly augmented and enlarged* (London: John Brown, 1605), K2 recto–verso.

36. William Shakespeare, *Antony and Cleopatra*, ed. M. R. Ridley (London: Arden–Routledge, 1965), 1.1.1–10.

37. On gypsies so-called, properly Roma, in Shakespeare, see Alden T. Vaughan and Virginia Mason Vaughan, *Shakespeare's Caliban: A Cultural History* (Cambridge: Cambridge University Press, 1991), pp. 33–36.

38. Walter Ralegh, *The History of the World*, Book 1 (London: Walter Burre, 1614), pp. 85, 96.

39. Thomas Browne, *Religio Medici*, in *The Prose of Sir Thomas Browne*, ed. Norman Endicott (New York: New York University Press, 1967), p. 69.

40. Gillies, *Shakespeare*, p. 119.

41. Plutarch, *The Morals*, p. 1308.

42. Cited in Shakespeare, *Antony and Cleopatra*, ed. Ridley, p. 212 note.

43. For a general discussion of the play's mythological background, see Janet Adelman, *The Common Liar: An Essay on Antony and Cleopatra* (New Haven, Conn.: Yale University Press, 1973), pp. 53–101.

44. Plutarch, "The Life of Marcus Antonius," in *Plutarch's Lives of the Noble Grecians and Romans*, vol. 6., trans. Thomas North (London, 1896; rpt. New York: AMS Press, 1967), p. 4.

45. Karl G. Galinsky, *The Herakles Theme: The Adaptations of the Hero in Literature from Homer to the Twentieth Century* (Totowa, N.J.: Rowman and Littlefield, 1972), p. 118.

46. Although he takes the unified "Dorian" origin of the Hercules myth for granted, Eugene M. Waith shows how the very excessiveness associated with its powerful central figure poses a threat to the Graeco-Roman order he supposedly exemplifies in the play: *The Herculean Hero in Marlowe, Chapman, Shakespeare and Dryden* (New York: Columbia University Press, 1962), pp. 113–21. On Hercules, Antony, cross-dressing, and excess, see Adelman, *Common Liar*, pp. 90–91, 116, 135.

47. Cicero, *The Nature of the Gods*, trans. Horace C. P. McGregor (London: Penguin, 1972), pp. 209–10.

48. Bernal, *Black Athena*, 1:113.

49. Richard Lynche, *An Historical Treatise of the Travels of Noah into Europe: Containing the first inhabitation and peopling thereof* (London: Adam Islip, 1601), D1 recto, D4 recto, K1 recto; and see Galinsky, *Herakles Theme*, p. 131 note.

50. On Hercules as a libertine, and the related tradition of the comic Hercules, see Galinsky, *Herakles Theme*, pp. 81–98, and Waith, *Herculean Hero*, p. 19. Gillies (*Shakespeare*, p. 113) thinks that the "historical" Antony deliberately evoked the hero's promiscuity to justify his own cosmopolitanism.

51. See also Waith, *Herculean Hero*, p. 116.

52. Jyotsna Singh, "Renaissance Antitheatricality, Antifeminism, and Shakespeare's *Antony and Cleopatra*," *Renaissance Drama* 20 (1989), 99–21.

53. Loomba, *Gender*, p. 125.

54. Lucy Hughes-Hallett, *Cleopatra: Histories, Dreams and Distortions* (New York: HarperCollins, 1990), pp. 90–91.

55. Bernal, *Black Athena*, 1:79; Homer, *The Iliad*, p. 302.

56. Galinsky, *Herakles Theme*, pp. 81–94.

57. Edmund Spenser, *The Faerie Queene*, ed. Thomas P. Roche (New Haven, Conn.: Yale University Press, 1978), 5.1.2.

58. On Spenser, Hercules, and Isis, see Adelman, *Common Liar*, pp. 67, 81.

59. For the proverb, see Karen Newman, "'And Wash the Ethiop White': Femininity and the Monstrous in *Othello*," in *Shakespeare Reproduced: The Text in History and Ideology*, eds. Jean E. Howard and Marion F. O'Connor (New York: Methuen, 1987), p. 142; Newman cites Geoffrey Whitney, *A Choice of Emblems* (1586).

60. Leo Africanus, *History*, p. 880. Shakespeare either turns the house into a pyramid or uses "pyramid" to signify an obelisk; Lepidus asks about "the Ptolemies'

pyramises" (2.7.33), and Pliny describes the great obelisk Ptolemy I raised at Alexandria: *The Historie of the World. Commonly called, The Natvrall Historie of C. Plinivs Secvndvs*, vol. 1, trans. Philemon Holland (London: Adam Islip, 1601), p. 575. It is possible that Shakespeare's pyramids or pyramises represent a mixture, confused or deliberately multivalent, of obelisks and sepulchers. Herodotus describes how Cheops' pyramids are set on "a small Ilande, through the whyche by a trenche or small draught, he caused the river to have passage"(*Famous Hystory*, p. 104 recto), and this recalls Leo's measuring column in its cistern, which in turn suggests an obelisk.

61. Compare Herodotus, *The Histories*, p. 179.

62. Lloyd, *Consent of Time*, p. 159; Sandys, *Relation of a Iourney*, p. 131; Heylyn, *Cosmographie*, p. 923.

63. William Lithgow, *A most delectable and True Discourse of an admired and painefnll* [sic] *Peregrination from Scotland, to the most Famous Kingdomes in Europe, Asia, and Affrica* (London: Nicholas Okes, 1623), p. 159.

64. She was the lover of Sappho's brother and a fellow-slave with Aesop: Herodotus, *Famous Hystory*, p. 105 recto; Pliny, *Historie*, p. 578; Diodorus, *History*, p. 44; for a variation, see Strabo, *The Geography*, trans. Horace Leonard Jones (London: Loeb Classical Library–Heinemann, 1917), p. 93.

65. Bernal, *Black Athena*, vol. 1, p. 152; Erwin Panofsky, *Meaning in the Visual Arts* (Garden City, N.Y.: Doubleday-Anchor, 1955), pp. 158–59; Jean Seznec, *The Survival of the Pagan Gods*, trans. B. E. Sessions (New York: Pantheon, 1953), pp. 99–103.

66. Walter Benjamin, *The Origin of German Tragic Drama*, trans. John Osborne (London: Verso, 1985), p. 171.

67. Newman, "'And Wash the Ethiop,'" p. 148.

68. Sandys, *Relation of a Iourney*, p. 106; Horace, *Odes* 1.37.21, in *The Odes and Epodes*, trans. C. E. Bennett (Cambridge: Loeb Classical Library–Harvard University Press, 1978), p. 100.

69. Jonathan Dollimore, "Shakespeare, Cultural Materialism, Feminism, and Marxist Humanism," *NLH* 21:3 (1990), 487; Carol Thomas Neely, *Broken Nuptials in Shakespeare's Plays* (New Haven, Conn.: Yale University Press, 1985), pp. 160, 165.

70. Butler, *Gender Trouble*, p. 68.

71. Valerie Traub, *Desire and Anxiety: Circulations of Sexuality in Shakespearean Drama* (New York: Routledge, 1992), pp. 45–46.

72. Butler, *Gender Trouble*, p. 139.

73. Mary Hamer, *Signs of Cleopatra: History, Politics, Representation* (London: Routledge, 1993), pp. xv–xxii, 1–23.

74. Said, *Culture and Imperialism*, pp. 118, 120; and see Mitchell, *Colonising Egypt*, esp. p. 17.

75. John Michael Archer, "Sovereignty and Intelligence in *King Lear*," in *Ideological Approaches to Shakespeare: The Practice of Theory*, eds. Robert P. Merrix and

Nicholas Ranson (Lewiston: Mellen, 1992), pp. 195–96. On sources as propaganda, see Adelman, *Common Liar*, pp. 54–59.

76. Loomba, *Gender*, p. 130.

77. Hamer, *Signs of Cleopatra*, pp. 21–22, 23.

CHAPTER 2

1. I. H. *Paradise Transplanted and Restored, In a Most Artfull and Lively Representation of The several Creatures, Plants, Flowers, and other Vegetables, in their full growth, shape, and colour: Shown at Christopher Whiteheads at the two wreathed Posts in Shooe-Lane, London* (London, 1661; rpt. London: Edwin Pearson, 1871), p. 1.

2. See Maureen Quilligan for a suggestive discussion of the relation between gender and unfree labor in *Paradise Lost*, which I am about to juxtapose with I. H.'s text: "Freedom, Service, and the Trade in Slaves: The Problem of Labor in *Paradise Lost*," in *Subject and Object in Renaissance Culture*, eds. Margreta de Grazia, Maureen Quilligan, and Peter Stallybrass (Cambridge: Cambridge University Press, 1996), pp. 213–34.

3. Walter Benjamin, "Paris, Capital of the Nineteenth Century," in *Reflections: Essays, Aphorisms, Autobiographical Writings*, trans. Edmund Jephcott (New York: Harcourt Brace Jovanovich, 1978), pp. 150, 152.

4. John Milton, *Paradise Lost*, 11:829–38. The Hughes edition is based on the twelve-book version of 1674. Further citations of *Paradise Lost* and other texts by Milton in Chapter 2 are from this edition.

5. This chapter is indebted to David Quint's book *Epic and Empire: Politics and Generic Form from Virgil to Milton* (Princeton, N.J.: Princeton University Press, 1993). My exploration of the ties between *Paradise Lost* and the Old World also complements the detailed discussion of the epic's links with the New in Martin J. Evans, *Milton's Imperial Epic: Paradise Lost and the Discourse of Colonialism* (Ithaca, N.Y.: Cornell University Press, 1996). Evans uncovers a complex and somewhat contradictory combination of attitudes toward New World empire in Milton's poem.

6. *Mandeville's Travels*, vol. 1, ed. Malcolm Letts (London: Hakluyt Society, 1953), pp. 28–29.

7. *Mandeville's Travels*, p. 29.

8. Albert Hourani, *A History of the Arab Peoples* (Cambridge, Mass.: Belknap Press–Harvard University Press, 1991), pp. 33, 85.

9. Henri de Feynes, *An Exact and Curious Svrvey of all the East Indies, euen to Canton*, trans. Loiseau de Tourval (London: Thomas Dawson for William Arondell, 1615), pp. 6–7.

10. Marco Polo, *The Travels of Marco Polo*, trans. Ronald Latham (London: Penguin, 1958), pp. 52–53; *Mandeville's Travels*, pp. 159–60.

11. Herodotus, *Famous Hystory*, pp. 60 recto–verso.

12. Diodorus, *History*, pp. 74–75.

13. Walter Ralegh, *History of the World*, p. 213.

14. Johannes Boemus, *Manners, Lawes, and Customes*, pp. A3 verso–A4 recto.

15. Lodowick Lloyd, *The Consent of Time* (London: George Bishop, 1590), p. 103.

16. George Abbot, *Briefe Description of the whole WORLDE*, pp. G4 verso–H1 recto.

17. Robert Stafford, *A Geographicall and Anthologicall description of all the Empires and Kingdomes, both of Continent and Ilands in this terrestriall Globe* (London: T.C. for Simon Waterson, 1607), p. 44.

18. Pliny, *Historie*, p. 136. Archaeologists now believe that Babylon did not decline relative to Seleucia: *The Oxford Classical Dictionary*, 3rd ed., s.v. "Babylon." The economics of empire Pliny helped found, while materialist, is not necessarily free of fiction. Economic explanations, no less than moral or cultural ones, are models above all else.

19. John Speed, *A Prospect of the Most Famous Parts of the World* (London: John Dawson for George Humble, 1631), p. 3.

20. Abu-Lughod, *Before European Hegemony*, p. 193; Braudel, *Civilization*, pp. 468–69.

21. John Cartwright, *The Preachers Travels* (London: for Thomas Thorpe, 1611), p. 102.

22. Thomas Herbert, *A Relation of Some Yeares Travaile, Begvnne Anno 1626. Into Afrique and the greater Asia, especially the Territories of the Persian Monarchie* (London: William Stansby and Jacob Bloome, 1634), p. 139. Hereafter cited as *Relation*.

23. Thomas Herbert, *Some Yeares Travels into Divers Parts of Asia and Afrique. . . . With a revivall of the first Discoverer of America*, "Revised and Enlarged by the Author" (London: K. Bip. for Iacob Blome and Richard Bishop, 1638), p. 219. Hereafter *Travels*.

24. Cesare Federici, *The Voyage and Trauaile: of M. Caesar Frederick, Merchant of Venice, into the East India* (London: Richard Jones and Edward White, 1588), p. 2 verso.

25. Heylyn, *Cosmographie*, p. 785.

26. Robert Ralston Cawley, *Milton and the Literature of Travel* (Princeton, N.J.: Princeton University Press, 1951), p. 11.

27. Stevie Davies, *Images of Kingship in Paradise Lost: Milton's Politics and Christian Liberty* (Columbia: University of Missouri Press, 1983), p. 40; John Leonard, *Naming in Paradise: Milton and the Language of Adam and Eve* (Oxford: Clarendon, 1990), p. 54.

28. Diodorus, *History*, p. 77; Sandys, *Relation of a Iourney*, p. 141.

29. Quint, *Epic and Empire*, pp. 264–65.

30. See John Guillory, "Dalila's House: *Samson Agonistes* and the Sexual Division of Labor," in *Rewriting the Renaissance: The Discourses of Sexual Difference in Early*

Modern Europe, eds. Margaret W. Ferguson, Maureen Quilligan, and Nancy J. Vickers (Chicago: University of Chicago Press, 1986), p. 340 note.

31. Mary Nyquist, "The Genesis of Gendered Subjectivity in the Divorce Tracts and in *Paradise Lost*," in *Re-membering Milton: Essays on the Texts and Traditions*, eds. Mary Nyquist and Margaret W. Ferguson (New York: Methuen, 1987), p. 120. On Eve and subjection, see Diane K. McColley, *Milton's Eve* (Urbana: University of Illinois Press, 1983) and Christine Froula, "When Eve Reads Milton: Undoing the Canonical Economy," *Critical Inquiry* 10 (1983), 321–47.

32. Northrop Frye, *The Return of Eden: Five Essays on Milton's Epics* (Toronto: University of Toronto Press, 1965), p. 141.

33. Alan H. Gilbert, *A Geographical Dictionary of Milton* (New York: Russell & Russell, 1919), p. 221 recto.

34. Ludovico di Varthema, *The Nauigation and vyages of Lewes Vertomannus*, in Richard Eden and Richard Willes, *The History of Trauayle in the West and East Indies* (London: Richard Iugge, 1577), pp. 378 verso–379 recto.

35. Samuel Purchas, ed., *Hakluytus Posthumus or Purchas His Pilgrimes*, 20 vols. (Glasgow: James MacLehose and Sons, 1905), 10:324.

36. Jean-Baptiste Tavernier, *The Six Voyages of John Baptista Tavernier . . . Through Turkey into Persia and the East Indies, Finished in the Year 1670*, trans. J. Phillips (London: for R. L. and M. P., 1678), 1:255.

37. Joseph E. Duncan, *Milton's Earthly Paradise: A Historical Study of Eden* (Minneapolis: University of Minnesota Press, 1972), p. 220.

38. *Mandeville's Travels*, p. 215.

39. See Mary Irma Corcoran, *Milton's Paradise with Reference to the Hexameral Background* (Washington, D.C.: Catholic University of America Press, 1945); Duncan, *Milton's Earthly Paradise*, pp. 36–66.

40. J.-P. Migne, ed., *Patrologiae cursus completus. Series Latina*, 221 vols. (Paris, 1844–64; rpt. Turnhout: Brepols, 1982), 34:378.

41. Corcoran, *Milton's Paradise*, pp. 17, 20.

42. Tertullian, in Migne, *Patrologiae*, 1:520; Duncan, *Milton's Earthly Paradise*, p. 61. On the poem and its tradition in general, see A. Bartlett Giamatti, *The Earthly Paradise and the Renaissance Epic* (Princeton, N.J.: Princeton University Press, 1966), pp. 70–79.

43. Isidore, in Migne, *Patrologiae*, 82:496; Duncan, *Milton's Earthly Paradise*, pp. 67–68; Curtius, *European Literature*, pp. 23, 192

44. Thomas Aquinas, *Summa Theologiae* (New York: McGraw-Hill, 1964), 1a. 102:1–3.

45. Dante, *Purgatorio*, ed. Charles S. Singleton (Princeton, N.J.: Bollingen–Princeton University Press, 1982), canto 27.

46. Duncan, *Milton's Earthly Paradise*, pp. 84-85; Giamatti, *Earthly Paradise*, p. 105.

47. Duncan, *Milton's Earthly Paradise*, p. 86.

48. The two reappear in Ludovico Ariosto's Dantean earthly Paradise in canto 34 of *Orlando Furioso*: Giamatti, *Earthly Paradise*, pp. 107, 163.

49. Dante, *Purgatorio*, canto 28, lines 49–51.

50. Duncan, *Milton's Earthly Paradise*, pp. 190, 205.

51. Corcoran, *Milton's Paradise*, p. 17 note; Duncan, *Milton's Earthly Paradise*, p. 190.

52. Christopher Columbus, *Four Voyages*, 2:36–38; Walter Ralegh, "The discovery of the large, rich, and beautiful Empire of Guiana," in Richard Hakluyt, *Voyages and Discoveries*, ed. Jack Beeching (London: Penguin, 1972), p. 389.

53. Samuel Purchas, *Purchas His Pilgrimage, or Relations of the World and the Religions Observed in all Ages and places Discovered* (London: William Stansby for Henrie Fetherstone, 1626), p. 15.

54. On Junius, see Duncan, *Milton's Earthly Paradise*, p. 206.

55. James I, "A Premonition to All Most Mightie Monarchies, Kings, Free Princes, and States," in *The Political Works of James I*, ed. C. H. McIlwain (Cambridge, Mass.: Harvard University Press, 1918), p. 136.

56. Merritt Y. Hughes, "Satan and the 'Myth' of the Tyrant," in *Essays in English Literature from the Renaissance to the Victorian Age Presented to A. S. P. Woodhouse*, eds. Millar MacLure and F. W. Watt (Toronto: University of Toronto Press, 1964); Joan S. Bennett, "God, Satan, and King Charles: Milton's Royal Portraits," *PMLA* 93 (1977), 441–47. On Davidic monarchy in England, see Quint, *Epic and Empire*, pp. 325–40.

57. Karl Marx, "The British Rule in India," in *Surveys from Exile*, ed. David Fernbach (New York: Vintage, 1974), p. 306.

CHAPTER 3

1. John Milton, *A Brief History of Moscovia*, ed. George B. Parks, in *The Complete Prose Works of John Milton*, vol. 8, eds. William Alfred et al. (New Haven, Conn.: Yale University Press, 1982), pp. 474–75.

2. Milton's *History of Britain* is the only other comparable work he wrote and may have been intended to parallel the *Brief History of Moscovia*. See George B. Parks, Preface, *Moscovia*, p. 456.

3. Adam Olearius, *The Voyages & Travels of the Ambassadors Sent by Frederick Duke of Holstein, to the Great Duke of Muscovy, and the King of Persia . . . Containing a compleat History of Muscovy, Tartary, Persia, And other adjacent Countries*, trans. John Davies (London: for Thomas Dring and John Starkey, 1662), p. 77.

4. Larry Wolff, *Inventing Eastern Europe: The Map of Civilization on the Mind of the Enlightenment* (Stanford, Calif.: Stanford University Press, 1994), p. 11.

5. We will soon consider the most influential version, but an early-seventeenth-century account that sums up the tradition may be found in Jacques Margeret, *The Russian Empire and the Grand Duchy of Muscovy*, trans. Chester L. Dunning (Pittsburgh: University of Pittsburgh Press, 1983), pp. 3–7.

6. Richard Eden, *The Decades of the newe worlde*, in *The First Three English Books on America*, ed. Edward Arber (Birmingham: Turnbull & Spears, 1895), p. 283.

7. For the Roxolani, see Strabo, pp. 221–23; Pliny, *Historie*, surveys the Scythians and other northern peoples, pp. 117–24. See also Lucan, *The Pharsalia*, 3:262–86, trans. H. T. Riley (London: George Bell, 1903), pp. 106–7.

8. Pliny, *Natural Historie*, pp. 121, 123–24.

9. Herodotus, *The Histories*, pp. 272–73. This modern edition is cited hereafter parenthetically as *Histories*.

10. François Hartog, *The Mirror of Herodotus: The Representation of the Other in the Writing of History*, trans. Janet Lloyd (Berkeley: University of California Press, 1988), pp. 14–18.

11. See Wolff, *Inventing Eastern Europe*, p. 287, who briefly cites Hartog in his excellent discussion of the survival of the Scythian tradition in the eighteenth century.

12. Hartog, *Mirror*, pp. 17–18, 30–31; and Wolff, p. 152, who refers to the mappamundi of Fra Mauro.

13. Hartog, *Mirror*, p. 32.

14. Hartog, *Mirror*, p. 200.

15. One slave blows air into the anus of the mare though a small tube to force down the udder while another slave milks. A circle of blind slaves then stirs the milk in a vat until the best part rises to the top.

16. Hartog, *Mirror*, p. 254. The tension between nomadism and governance within the classical discourse of Scythia must have been particularly tangible for Athenians, whose police force during Herodotus' time was composed of roughly three hundred enslaved Scythian archers: M. I. Finley, *Ancient Slavery and Modern Ideology* (Harmondsworth: Penguin, 1983), p. 85.

17. On the relation of master and king, see Hartog, *Mirror*, pp. 334–35. For a somewhat breezy but useful survey of slavery in *The Histories*, see F. D. Harvey, "Herodotus and the Man-Footed Creature," in Léonie Archer, ed., *Slavery and Other Forms of Unfree Labor* (London: Routledge, 1988), pp. 42–52.

18. Finley, *Ancient Slavery*, pp. 118–19. Hartog, *Mirror*, p. 332, cites other instances in *The Histories* where the whip stands in for the Greek view of despotism as violent and an extension of the master-slave paradigm.

19. Herberstein, *Notes upon Russia [Rerum Moscoviticarum Commentarii]*, trans. R. H. Major (London: Hakluyt Society, 1851–52), pp. 26–27.

20. Giles Fletcher, *Of the Russe Common Wealth. Or Maner of Gouernement by the Russe Emperour, (commonly called the Emperour of Moskouia) with the manners, and fashions of the people of that Countrey* (London: T. D. for Thomas Charde, 1591), pp. 13 recto–verso.

21. Heylyn, *Cosmographie*, p. 513.

22. Richard Hellie, *Slavery in Russia, 1450–1725* (Chicago: University of Chicago Press, 1982), pp. 15–16, 30–33, 46–47, 716.

23. Hellie, *Slavery*, p. 23.

24. Abraham Ortelius, *The Theatre of the Whole World* (London: 1606; rpt. Amsterdam: Theatrum Orbis Terrarum Ltd., 1968), p. 104; the Latin original appeared in 1570.

25. See Maija Jansson and Nikolai Rogozhin, *England and the North: The Russian Embassy of 1613–1614* (Philadelphia: American Philosophical Society, 1994), pp. vi–vii, 1–71. The Russian and American scholars in this volume provide a useful corrective to a British historiography that traditionally underplays the political aspects of Elizabethan links with Russia in favor of the narrowly commercial ones centered on the Muscovy Company. I strive for a balance between the two approaches.

26. E. Delmar Morgan and C. H. Coote, eds., *Early Voyages and Travels in Russia and Persia* (London: Hakluyt Society, 1886), p. 259. The trade in kerseys was thought to be particularly important (see pp. lxiv, 221, and passim), although it may not have been as vital as contemporaries often claimed: see T. S. Willan, *The Early History of the Muscovy Company, 1553–1603* (Manchester: Manchester University Press, 1956), p. 186.

27. The standard work for the sixteenth century is Willan. For a critique of Willan's focus on commerce at the expense of diplomacy, see Jansson and Rogozhin, *England and the North*, pp. vi, 12 note 45, 16–17. For a revised sense of the commercial aims of the Muscovy Company, see Robert Brenner, *Merchants and Revolution: Commercial Change, Political Conflict, and London's Overseas Traders, 1550–1653* (Princeton, N.J.: Princeton University Press, 1993), pp. 13, 20–21.

28. Richard Chancellor, "The First Voyage to Russia," in Lloyd E. Berry and Robert O. Crummey, eds., *Rude and Barbarous Kingdom: Russia in the Accounts of Sixteenth-Century English Voyagers* (Madison: University of Wisconsin Press, 1968), pp. 13, 18, 38.

29. Daryl W. Palmer, "Jacobean Muscovites: Winter, Tyranny, and Knowledge in *The Winter's Tale*," *Shakespeare Quarterly* 46 (1995), 330, 336. A recent discussion of the Muscovy Company and Marlowe's *Tamburlaine* plays is offered in Richard Wilson, "Visible Bullets: Tamburlaine the Great and Ivan the Terrible," *ELH* 62 (1995), 47–68.

30. Anthony Jenkinson, in Berry and Crummey, *Rude and Barbarous Kingdom*, p. 56.

31. Ortelius, *Theatre*, between pp. 104 and 105.

32. Randolph's account is included in Berry and Crummey, *Rude and Barbarous Kingdom*, pp. 65–70. On the circumstances of his ultimately successful embassy, see Willan, *Early History*, pp. 94–111.

33. Turberville, "Verse Letters from Russia," in Berry and Crummey, *Rude and Barbarous Kingdom*, p. 75. The poems were published in *Tragicall Tales* (1587), and again in Hakluyt's *Principall Navigations* (1589).

34. On "sodomy" as the demonic opposite of Christianity, see Alan Bray, *Homosexuality in Renaissance England* (London: Gay Men's Press, 1982), pp. 19–31. He also discusses Turberville's depiction of the Russians on pp. 25 and 75.

35. Lloyd E. Berry, *The English Works of Giles Fletcher, the Elder* (Madison: University of Wisconsin Press, 1964), pp. 150–53.

36. Braudel, *Civilization*, p. 455.

37. On the "new geography" in early modern Europe and the sense of instability it brought with it, see Rabasa, *Inventing America*, pp.180–209, and Gillies, *Shakespeare*, pp. 1–39.

38. Philip Sidney, *Astrophil and Stella* 2:9–11, in *Sir Philip Sidney: Selected Poems*, ed. Katherine Duncan-Jones (Oxford: Clarendon, 1973).

39. Charles Verlinden, "Encore sur les origines de sclavus=esclave," in Verlinden, *L'esclavage dans l'Europe médiévale*, vol. 2 (Gent: Rijksuniversiteit te Gent, 1977).

40. Robin Blackburn, *The Making of New World Slavery: From the Baroque to the Modern, 1492–1800* (London: Verso, 1997), pp. 54–56, 76–79.

41. Morgan and Coote, *Early Voyages*, p. 89.

42. Morgan and Coote, *Early Voyages*, p. 95.

43. Morgan and Coote, *Early Voyages*, p. 211. Until 1627–28, foreigners were in effect permitted to own Russian slaves in Russia. Even after this date the exclusion was based not on nationality but on religion, since only Orthodox masters were henceforth allowed to hold Orthodox slaves. The change in the law was specifically intended to limit Westerners in Russia, however (Hellie, *Slavery*, pp. 73–74).

44. In the seventeenth century, the Commonwealth employed Irish and Scottish slaves in the West Indies, and in at least one instance Parliament justified the use of English Cavaliers in the plantations as well, despite uneasy efforts to differentiate them from Africans. See Quilligan, *Subject and Object*, pp. 216–20.

45. That the play and *Astrophil and Stella* have Russia and slavery in common has been noted by Frances Yates, *A Study of 'Love's Labour's Lost'* (Cambridge: Cambridge University Press, 1936), 133–34, and by R. S. White, "Muscovites in *Love's Labour's Lost*," *Notes and Queries* 33 (1986), 350.

46. William Shakespeare, *Love's Labour's Lost*, ed. Richard David (London: Arden–Methuen, 1956), 5.2.157 SD; italics removed.

47. *Gesta Grayorum*, ed. W. W. Greg (Oxford: Malone Society, 1914), pp. 44–46. The Prince of Purpoole went on a trip to Russia himself, returning later in the Revels ill from his fictional journey at sea and so unable to greet Queen Elizabeth (pp. 54–55); this is often compared with Rosaline's comment that the undisguised Berowne is "Sea-sick, I think, coming from Muscovy" (5.2.393). Earlier in the week a performance of a "Comedy of Errors," probably Shakespeare's, was mounted after a chaotic embassy from the Temple to Gray's Inn (p. 22). For a summary of past scholarship linking *Love's Labour's Lost* to Gray's Inn, see David, Introduction, *Love's Labour's Lost*, pp. xxx–xxxi.

48. *Gesta Grayorum*, pp. 43–44.

49. Morgan and Coote, *Early Voyages*, pp. 51–52, 89.

50. Raphael Holinshed, *Chronicles of England, Scotland, and Ireland* (London, 1587; rpt. London: J. Johnson, 1807–8), 3:805; see Fred Sorensen, "The Masque of the Muscovites in *Love's Labour's Lost,*" *Modern Language Notes* 50 (1935), 499–501.

51. William Shakespeare, *Titus Andronicus,* ed. Jonathan Bate (London: Arden–Routledge, 1995), 2.2.72. Cimmeria, far from the sun, was supposed to be a land of perpetual darkness.

52. See Wolff, *Inventing Eastern Europe,* pp. 345–46.

53. David, Introduction, *Love's Labour's Lost,* p. xxxiii.

54. Gillies, *Shakespeare,* p. 45.

55. Jerome Horsey, "Travels," in Berry and Crummey, *Rude and Barbarous Kingdom,* p. 301. Ivan's insistence on Mary Hastings or some other English bride was cut off by his death in 1584 during the embassy of Jerome Bowes. The marriage business may have added to uneasiness about a commercially expansive England's potential similarity to imperial Russia. Ivan, like Elizabeth's father, Henry VIII, had already been married seven times before this quest for an eighth wife; his seventh was still living. His death was announced to Elizabeth's ambassador with the curious phrase "the English Emperor was dead," meaning, it would seem, the emperor who had favored England. For the negotiations, see Willan, *Early History,* p. 161–66, and Jansson and Rogozhin, *England and the North,* pp. 26–32.

56. On sodomy and other forms of the "preposterous" throughout the play, see Patricia Parker, "Preposterous Reversals: *Love's Labor's Lost,*" *Modern Language Quarterly* 54 (1993), 435–82. Parker discusses the implied reversals of 5.2 without relating the "Muscovites" to sodomy, although the travel material supports her reading of the text here (pp. 466–67). Wilson, "Visible Bullets," p. 62, notes Ivan IV's rumored sexual relationship with his favorite Theodor Basmanov in discussing the Muscovites scene in passing.

57. Berry and Crummey, *Rude and Barbarous Kingdom,* p. 52.

58. LeFebvre, *The Production of Space,* trans. Donald Nicholson-Smith (Oxford: Blackwell, 1991), pp. 71–79. I owe this reference to a suggestion from John Gillies.

59. Braudel, *The Mediterranean,* p. 785.

60. My ideas on this point, and on racial difference throughout this chapter, are deeply indebted to the work of Kim F. Hall. See in particular "Sexual Politics and Cultural Identity in *The Masque of Blackness,*" in *The Performance of Power: Theatrical Discourse and Politics,* eds. Sue-Ellen Case and Jenelle Reinelt (Iowa City: University of Iowa Press, 1991), and recently *Things of Darkness: Economies of Race and Gender in Early Modern England* (Ithaca, N.Y.: Cornell University Press, 1995).

61. See Mies, *Patriarchy,* passim, and Brown, *Ends of Empire,* pp. 44–45. On the "fair" pun, see Hall, *Darkness,* p. 90.

62. For the opinion that Fletcher is typically concerned with sentiment and structure rather than ethics or politics in *The Loyal Subject,* see Kate Watkins Tibbals, ed., Introduction, in Thomas Heywood, *The Royall King and Loyall Subject,* Series in

Philology and Literature, vol. 12 (Philadelphia: University of Pennsylvania, 1906), p. 32. See also Charles L. Squier, *John Fletcher* (Twayne: Boston, 1986), p. 71.

63. William Painter, *The Palace of Pleasure*, tome 2, novel 4, ed. Joseph Jacobs (Dover: New York, 1966), 2:176–208. For summaries and a comparison of the three texts, see Tibbals, Introduction, *The Royall King*, pp. 10–32.

64. As Palmer, "Jacobean Muscovites," p. 327, points out, a proposal that England establish a protectorate over its trading posts in north Russia was floated at court in 1612. See also Chester Dunning, "James I, the Russia Company, and the Plan to Establish a Protectorate Over North Russia," *Albion* 21 (1989), 206–26. But as Jansson and Rogozhin suggest, James may not have taken the scheme seriously or even known much about it (*England and the North*, p. 67). The Russian embassy of 1613–14 that Jansson and Rogozhin describe, which stressed dynastic over commerical concerns, scants the plan; the embassy may have been more topical for Fletcher's audience.

65. For a contrary view, see Tibbals, Introduction, *The Royall King*, p. 27. The play, with its Tartar invasion, its unchecked autocrat, its hardy soldiers, and its suggestions of sodomy, should emerge in the context of this chapter as completely "Russian" in the early modern English sense.

66. John Fletcher, *The Loyal Subject*, in *The Dramatic Works in the Beaumont and Fletcher Canon*, vol. 5, ed. Fredson Bowers (Cambridge: Cambridge University Press, 1982), 1.2.5, 11–12.

67. Fletcher went on to write a play about the Moluccas, in what is now Indonesia, called *The Island Princess* (1620–21); it depicts the islands under the religious sway of the Moors.

68. A possible allusion to poem 11 of *Astrophil and Stella* may show that Fletcher had at least been reading Sidney recently. Young Archas tests his sisters in the guise of Alinda, acting as a fallen court woman who predicts the duke's seduction of them. "Will he play with me too?" Viola asks. "Look babies in your eyes, my prettie sweet one," Alinda replies (3.4.53–54).

69. Fredson Bowers, Introduction to Fletcher, *Loyal Subject*, pp. 152–54.

70. Parks, Preface to Milton, *Moscovia*, p. 461.

71. Milton, *Paradise Lost*, 2:1021–33.

CHAPTER 4

1. According to K. N. Chaudhuri, European trade with Asia, especially India, "was an integral part of a much larger movement of expansion which in time was responsible for forging entirely new forms of economic ties between Europe and the peripheral areas"; the flow of bullion was key here. See *The Trading World of Asia and the East India Company, 1660–1760* (Cambridge: Cambridge University Press, 1978), p. 10. On India and Russia as external to the European economy in the seventeenth century, see Immanuel Wallerstein, *The Modern World-System*, vol. 2, *Mercantilism*

and the Consolidation of the European World-Economy, 1600–1750 (San Diego: Academic Press, 1980), p. 274.

2. Eden, *Decades of the newe worlde*, p. 285.

3. On the early modern European need to link India with the texts of Graeco-Roman antiquity in general, see Cohn, *Colonialism*, p. 79.

4. See John F. Richards, *The Mughal Empire*, New Cambridge History of India, I:5 (Cambridge: Cambridge University Press, 1993). The first part of the New Cambridge History is entitled "The Mughals and Their Contemporaries." I address my differences with a more recent example of work from this important historical school, to which I am indebted, at the chapter's end. In cultural criticism, see the useful opening chapters in Jyotsna G. Singh, *Colonial Narratives/Cultural Dialogues: "Discoveries" of India in the Language of Colonialism* (London: Routledge, 1996). Balachandra Rajan appreciates the European fascination with Hindu India but stresses the Mughals in his chapters on Milton and Dryden's *Aureng-Zebe* in his book *Under Western Eyes: India from Milton to Macaulay* (Durham, N.C.: Duke University Press, 1999).

5. Propertius, "Elegies" 3.13.15–22, in *Propertius*, trans. H. E. Butler (London: Loeb Classical Library–Heinemann, 1976), pp. 222, 223.

6. Gayatri Chakravorty Spivak, "Can the Subaltern Speak?" in *Marxism and the Interpretation of Culture*, eds. Cary Nelson and Lawrence Grossberg (Urbana: University of Illinois Press, 1988), p. 305.

7. Lata Mani, "Contentious Traditions: The Debate on *Sati* in Colonial India," in *The Nature and Context of Minority Discourse*, eds. Abdul R. JanMohamed and David Lloyd (New York: Oxford University Press, 1990), pp. 321–35. The points about feasibility and modernization are made more fully in an earlier article, "Production of an Official Discourse on *Sati* in Early Nineteenth Century Bengal," *Review of Women's Studies* (April 1986), pp. 32–40, included as a supplement to *Economic and Political Weekly* 21, no. 17 (April 26, 1986).

8. Spivak, "Subaltern," p. 298 (author's emphasis). The burden of her now classic analysis pertains to women, will, and claims made about *sati* in Hindu religious texts. Spivak considers a particular historical example and its implications for archival claims past and present in "The Rani of Sirmur: An Essay in Reading the Archives," *History and Theory* 24 (1985), 247–72. This essay and "Can the Subaltern Speak?" have been recontextualized in the third chapter of Spivak, *A Critique of Postcolonial Reason: Toward a History of the Vanishing Present* (Cambridge, Mass.: Harvard University Press, 1999). Here Spivak registers some differences with Mani's account (p. 285, n. 133). For a somewhat oblique criticism of both Mani and Spivak, see Rajeswari Sunder Rajan, *Real and Imagined Women: Gender, Culture and Postcolonialism* (London: Routledge, 1993), pp. 34, 53–55.

9. Mani, "Traditions," p. 351.

10. Mani, "Traditions," pp. 345–46, 348–49.

11. For a similar view, see Spivak, "Subaltern," p. 301.

12. Mani, "Traditions," p. 351 and n. 40. She cites Mary Louise Pratt, "Scratches on the Face of the Country; or, What Mr. Barrow Saw in the Land of the Bushmen," *Critical Inquiry* 12 (1985), 119–43.

13. The earliest exceptions are Henry Lord, *A Discovery of the Sect of the Banians. . . Gathered from their BRAMANES, Teachers of that Sect* (London: Francis Constable, 1630), discussed below, and the Dutch missionary Abraham Rogerius, *De Open Deure* (1651), cited in Partha Mitter, *Much Maligned Monsters: History of European Reactions to Indian Art* (Oxford: Clarendon, 1977), pp. 50–51. I am indebted to Mitter's important book.

14. Cicero, *Tusculan Disputations*, trans. J. E. King (London: Loeb Classical Library–Heinemann, 1971), 5.27.77–78, p. 505.

15. Diogenes Laertius, *Lives of Eminent Philosophers*, vol. 1, trans. R. D. Hicks (London: Loeb Classical Library–Heinemann, 1959), 1.6, pp. 6–8; Strabo, *The Geography*, trans. Horace Leonard Jones (London: Loeb Classical Library–Heinemann, 1917), 16.2.39–40, p. 289.

16. Strabo, *Geography*, 15.1.61, p. 104.

17. Ktesias [Ctesias], *Ancient India as Described by Ktesias the Knidian*, ed. J. W. McCrindle (London: Trubner, 1882), pp. 12, 17.

18. In Diodorus, *History*, p. 94. Other Alexandrian writers on India whose work survives in citation are Aristobulus, Clitarchus, Nearchus, and Onesecritus: see Lionel Pearson, *The Lost Histories of Alexander the Great* (New York: American Philological Society, 1960). Encounters with the wise men of India were apparently featured in all of them.

19. Strabo, 15.1.56–60, p. 99–103.

20. Pomponius Mela, *The Rare and singuler worke of Pomponius Mela, That excellent and worthy cosmographer, of the Situation of the world*, trans. Arthur Golding (London: Thomas Hacket, 1590), p. 82.

21. Pliny, *Historie*, p. 155.

22. Arrian, *Indica*, in *Ancient India as Described by Megasthenes and Arrian*, trans. J. W. McCrindle (London: Trubner, 1877), p. 209.

23. Arrian, *Anabasis*, 7:2–3, in *Arrian*, vol. 2, ed. E. Iliff Robson (London: Loeb Classical Library–Heinemann, 1933), pp. 209–13.

24. Herodotus, *The Histories*, trans. Burn, p. 246. Herodotus also describes the large Indian ants that dig for gold, which are then mentioned by Arrian (*Indica*, p. 217), Pomponius Mela (p. 82), and, interestingly, Propertius at the beginning of Elegy 3:13. The ants were apparently mentioned by Nearchus as well, and François Hartog (*Mirror*, pp. 357–59) uses this and some geographical parallels to argue that India was conceived of on an analogy with Herodotus' Egypt. One might also mention the seven tribes attributed to India as to Egypt by Megasthenes and Arrian. India was in fact something of a mirror to Egypt and its monumental antiquity, as the links through Dionysus, Herakles, and Pythagoras indicate. But it reversed as

well as copied Egyptian culture in Graeco-Roman discourse, undoing monumentality even as it destabilized claims for Egypt's priority.

25. Pseudo-Callisthenes, *The Romance of Alexander the Great by Pseudo-Callisthenes*, trans. from the Armenian version by Albert Mugrdich Wolohojian (New York: Columbia University Press, 1969), p. 121. There is a similar episode in Plutarch's first-century A.D. *Life of Alexander*, without the grave question, an example as well of another early use of the term "gymnosophist": *Plutarch's Lives*, vol. 7, trans. Bernadotte Perrin (London: Loeb Classical Library–Heinemann, 1971).

26. For a comprehensive survey of medieval attitudes toward the subcontinent, see Thomas Hahn, "The Indian Tradition in Western Medieval Intellectual History," *Viator* 9 (1978), 213–34.

27. Friar Jordanus, *Mirabilia Descripta: The Wonders of the East*, trans. Henry Yule (London: Hakluyt Society, 1863), p. 12. Subsequent citations will be included parenthetically in the text.

28. I am not arguing here or in the discussion of Mani's evidence above that conflicts between Hindus and Muslims in India were ever *caused* by European discourse or even, much later, British administration, whatever lines of influence may exist. Two related discussions from decidedly different academic schools of thought each serve as a corrective to such a move: see C. A. Bayly, "The Pre-History of 'Communalism'? Religious Conflict in India, 1700–1860," *Modern Asian Studies* 19 (1985), 177–203, and Gyanendra Pandey, "In Defense of the Fragment: Writing about Hindu-Muslim Riots in India Today," in *A Subaltern Studies Reader, 1986–1995*, ed. Ranajit Guha (Minneapolis: University of Minnesota Press, 1997), pp. 1–33. For a balanced overview that nevertheless gives full weight to European influences on communalism, see Partha Chatterjee, *The Nation and Its Fragments: Colonialism and Postcolonial Histories* (Princeton, N.J.: Princeton University Press, 1993), pp. 102–13, 224–27.

29. Niccolo Conti, as told to Poggio Bracciolini, in R. H. Major, ed., *India in the Fifteenth Century* (London: Hakluyt Society, 1857), p. 4.

30. Ludovico di Varthema, *The Travels of Ludovico di Varthema in Egypt, Syria, Arabia Deserta and Arabia Felix, in Persia, India, and Ethiopia, A.D. 1503 to 1508*, trans. John Winter Jones (London: Hakluyt Society, 1863), pp. 108–9.

31. Mitter, *Monsters*, pp. 17–18.

32. See Mitter, *Monsters*, pp. 19–20, 27, who misses Eden's earlier version in Sebastian Munster, *A treatyse of the newe India*, trans. Richard Eden (London, 1553), rpt. in *The First Three English Books on America*, ed. Edward Arber, p. 17; Varthema, *The Nauigation and vyages*, pp. 387 verso–388.

33. Duarte Barbosa, *The Book of Duarte Barbosa: An Account of the Countries Bordering on the Indian Ocean and their Inhabitants*, 2 vols., trans. Mansel Longworth Dames (London: Hakluyt Society, 1918), 1:115.

34. Domingos Paes, "Narrative of Domingos Paes," in *A Forgotten Empire: Vijayanagar*, ed. Robert Sewell (New Delhi: National Book Trust, 1970), p. 234.

35. Paes' account foreshadows the British attitude toward dancers in the nineteenth century: see Kunal M. Parker, "'A Corporation of Superior Prostitutes': Anglo-Indian Legal Conceptions of Temple Dancing Girls, 1800–1914," *Modern Asian Studies* 32 (1998), 559–633. My thanks to Yumna Siddiqi for this reference.

36. Mitter, *Monsters*, p. 5; Marco Polo, *The Travels of Marco Polo*, trans. Ronald Latham (London: Penguin, 1958), pp. 270–71.

37. Dealing with largely different sources from the ones I address here, Margo Hendricks remarks, "early modern accounts of India are marked by an emerging taxonomy of gender and linguistic difference. It is not unusual for the writer of an English Renaissance narrative to digress from topographical, mercantile, or political description in order to address a culture's sexual practices and behavior, especially the actions of women." See her article "'Obscured by dreams': Race, Empire, and Shakespeare's *A Midsummer Night's Dream*," *Shakespeare Quarterly* 47 (1996), 43.

38. Henry Yule and A. C. Burnell, *Hobson-Jobson: A Glossary of Colloquial Anglo-Indian Words and Phrases, and of Kindred Terms, Etymological, Historical, Geographical, and Discursive*, new edition ed. William Crooke (London, 1903; rpt. New Delhi: Minshiram Manoharlal, 1994), p. ix, and s.v. "Pagoda." "Hobson-Jobson" is a corruption of the chanted Arabic names Hassan and Hosein of the Muharram festival.

39. On the fetish, see William Pietz's classic series of articles entitled "The Problem of the Fetish" in *Res* 9 (1985), 5–17; *Res* 13 (1987), 23–45; and *Res* 16 (1988), 105–23. The word follows a similar Portuguese-Dutch-English trajectory, but a fetish is in some sense the opposite of an idol, as Pietz argues. A connection with the money form, however, persists in the usage of both words. See also Pietz's note on the word "Guinea" in the final article (p. 105 note). *Hobson-Jobson's* entry "Fetish" bears comparison to Pietz's analysis, and includes some Indian examples.

40. *Hobson-Jobson*, s.v. "Pagoda," p. 656b; Fernão Lopez de Castanheda, *The firste Booke of the Historie of the Discouerie and Conquest of the East Indias*, trans. N. L. (London: Thomas East, 1582), pp. 34, 37.

41. Jan Huyghen Van Linschoten, *The Voyage of John Huyghen Van Linschoten to the East Indies*, 2 vols., ed. A. C. Burnell (London: Hakluyt Society, 1885), 1:242.

42. Cited in *Hobson-Jobson*, s.v. "Pagoda," p. 656a.

43. Pietro della Valle, *The Travels of Pietro della Valle in India, From the Old English translation of 1664, by G. Havers*, ed. Edward Grey (London: Hakluyt Society, 1892), p. 306.

44. Linschoten, *Voyage*, 1:1–2.

45. Ralph Fitch in William Foster, ed., *Early Travels in India, 1583–1619* (Oxford: Oxford University Press, 1921), p. 15.

46. In Foster, *Early Travels*, p. 321.

47. William Methwold, "Relations of the Kingdome of Golchonda," in *Relations of Golconda in the Early Seventeenth Century*, ed. W. H. Moreland (London: Hakluyt Society, 1931), p. 13.

48. Odoric of Pordenone, in *Cathay and the Way Thither*, vol. 2, ed. Henry Yule (London: Hakluyt Society, 1913), pp. 144–45.

49. Mandeville, *Mandeville's Travels*, pp. 125–26. Stephen Greenblatt uses Odoric and Mandeville to show how a traditional opposition between the sacred and the demonic was blurred in their idol processions' exotic parallel with the Christian iconography of "holy wounds." Turning to *The Travels of Mendes Pinto* (a text whose concern with parts east of the Indian subcontinent places it outside my purview), Greenblatt shows how a Juggernaut-like ceremony in Laos initiates a new opposition between the natural and unnatural. See "Mutilation and Meaning," in *The Body in Parts: Fantasies of Corporeality in Early Modern Europe* (New York: Routledge, 1997), pp. 225–29.

50. Conti, in Major, ed., *India*, p. 28; for Balbi, see *Hobson-Jobson*, p. 467a.

51. William Bruton, *Newes from the East Indies: Or, A Voyage to Bengalla* (London: I. Okes, 1638), p. 29.

52. Thomas Bowrey, *A Geographical Account of the Countries Round the Bay of Bengal, 1669 to 1679*, ed. R. C. Temple (Cambridge: Hakluyt Society, 1905), p. 10.

53. *Hobson-Jobson*, p. ix.

54. C. T. Onions, *The Oxford Dictionary of English Etymology* (Oxford: Clarendon, 1966), s.v. "garnet[1]." References to meaning, etymology, and dates in the remainder of the paragraph are to this dictionary, and to *Merriam-Webster's Collegiate Dictionary*, 10th ed.

55. Linschoten comments on the number of both garnet stones and shrimp (*garnaeten* in Dutch) in India: 2:140, 11.

56. *Hobson-Jobson*, p. 462.

57. See Singh, *Colonial Narratives*, pp. 7-8.

58. Chaudhuri, *Trade and Civilization*, p. 88.

59. Quoted in William Wilson Hunter, *A History of British India*, vol. 2 (London: Longmans, Green, 1900), p. 273. Capitals tacitly removed.

60. According to Chaudhuri, the leading economic historian of the period, "the use of force whether directly expressed or not was an implicit part of European trade with Asia." The Dutch were ahead of the English here, but the East India Company followed suit during the second half of the seventeenth century (*Trading World*, pp. 111, 115). It is true, however, that Company members advocated the threat of force because they usually saw themselves as Mughal victims rather than aggressors. The Mughals in fact profited in bullion from the trade and encouraged it. The English commanded the seas, one component of an imperial campaign, but had little military power on land; their use of force was thus most successful when it was only implicit, as Child found out (pp. 461–62). For all this, several elements of a possible, if hardly inevitable, colonial strategy were already in place, and the subject of some controversy in England itself. Adapting a theoretical concept from Karl Polanyi, Chaudhuri sees the East India Company's presence on the subcontinent as "redistributive," the centralized exploitation of the local division of labor, rather than a matter of "purely reciprocal exchanges" (*Trading World*, p. 114).

61. Bernier, *A Continuation of the Memoires of Monsieur Bernier, Concerning the Great Mogol*, trans. H. O. (London: Moses Pitt, 1672), p. 110.

62. Pierre d'Avity, *The Estates, Empires, & Principalities of the World. Represented by description of Countries, maners of Inhabitants, Riches of Provinces, forces, Gouernment, Religion; and the Princes that haue gouerned in euery Estate*, trans. Edward Grimstone (London: Adam Islip for Matthew Lownes and John Bill, 1615), p. 774.

63. Lord, *Discovery*, p. 71.

64. Heylyn, *Cosmographie*, p. 878. Compare Jean-Baptiste Tavernier, *Six Voyages*, p. 161: "The first *Caste* is that of the *Brammins*, who are the successors of the ancient *Brachmans*, or *Indian* Philosophers, that study'd Astrology."

65. Bernier, *Continuation*, pp. 131, 133–34. Tavernier provides several descriptions of the different kinds of fakirs, who are followers of Islam in his account (*Six Voyages*, pp. 160, 165–66).

66. Fryer, *A New Account of East India and Persia. Being Nine Years' Travels, 1672–1681*, 3 vols., ed. William Crooke (London: Hakluyt Society, 1904), 1:256: "Here are many Monuments of their misled Zeal; the most dreadful to remember, is an extraordinary one erected by the River side, where they Burn their Dead, in Honour of a Woman who Burnt her self with her dead Husband." See also 2:18.

67. Strabo, 15.1.30, p. 53.

68. Diodorus, 19:33, in *Diodorus of Sicily*, vol. 9, trans. Russell M. Geer (London: Loeb Classical Library–Heinemann, 1962), pp. 319–21.

69. Diodorus, *Sicily*, 19:34, p. 323.

70. Withington, in Foster, *Early Travels*, p. 219. Withington also preserves the story that widows were first made to burn themselves by law to stop them from murdering their husbands: "then they were forced unto yt; but nowe they have gotte such a custome of yt that they doe yt most willinglye" (p. 221).

71. Terry, in Foster, *Early Travels*, p. 323.

72. See Valle, *Travels*, pp. ii–iv, and *Viaggi di Pietro della Valle, Il Pelegrino*, vol. 2 (Turin: G. Gancia, 1843), pp. 308–15.

73. Michel de Montaigne, "Of custom, and not easily changing an accepted law," in *The Complete Essays of Montaigne*, trans. Donald Frame (Stanford, Calif.: Stanford University Press, 1958), p. 80. In his essay "Of Virtue," Montaigne provides a second-hand *sati* account, quoting Propertius and stressing the widow's voluntary involvement (pp. 534–35). In the essay "A Custom of the Island of Cea," he tells of a Juggernaut-like procession somewhere in the "new regions" (p. 261).

74. Peter Mundy, *The Travels of Peter Mundy in Europe and Asia, 1608–1667*, vol. 2, *Travels in Asia, 1628–1634*, ed. R. C. Temple (London: Hakluyt Society, 1914), p. 35.

75. Cohn, *Colonialism*, pp. 9–10, 96–97.

76. Bernier was another, only he tells of a woman rescued by disreputable men; they frequent the pyres of women who are guarded by a small number of attendants, presumably with rape in mind. "Some *Portugueses* living in Sea-ports," he adds, "have

sometimes carried away some of them" (*Continuation*, p. 127). Stories such as these undermine the heroic myths of rescue and protection at the source.

77. It is unclear whether Bernier really was acting with the authority of the Agah, who had commanded the parents to prevent the burning, or whether he was pretending to at their request. He immediately reported his interview with the woman to the Agah (p. 119).

78. Mani traces an "ideal typical representation" of *sati* in the early nineteenth century to British extrapolations from the pundits' accounts of scripture, an abstract narrative dissociated from particular events. Some elements of this narrative were already part of the early modern genre of widow burning accounts, however, and their classical precursors. See Mani, "Production of an Official Discourse," p. 38.

79. As Balachandra Rajan has recently argued in his illuminating discussion of *Aureng-Zebe*, "Bernier is not the source of Dryden's play. But his book may be its indispensable background. Dryden is not ignoring Bernier's text; he is writing a critique of it," from an English point of view that appropriates Mughal history for exemplary purposes (*Under Western Eyes*, p. 70).

80. John Dryden, *Aureng-Zebe*, in *The Works of John Dryden*, vol. 12, ed. Vinton A. Dearing (Berkeley: University of California Press, 1994), 3.1.325, 479. Later citations are from this edition.

81. For instance, see Singh, *Colonial Narratives*, pp. 29–40, for a compelling discussion of Roe. On Mughal court society during this period, see Richards, *Mughal Empire*, pp. 94–118.

82. Thomas Roe, *The Embassy of Sir Thomas Roe to India, 1615–19*, 2nd ed., ed. William Foster (Oxford: Oxford University Press, 1926), pp. 82–83.

83. For an account of the historical events on which the play is based, see Dearing, ed., *Works of John Dryden*, pp. 383–85.

84. On the critical debate over Aureng-Zebe's character, see the useful summary by Dearing, ed., *Works of John Dryden*, pp. 392–94.

85. There may be a partial recollection of Juggernaut in Arimant's complaint of his hopeless love, for which he will finally sacrifice his life in battle:

My Virtue, Prudence, Honour, Interest, all
Before this Universal Monarch fall.
Beauty, like Ice, our footing does betray;
Who can tread sure on the smooth, slippery way? (2.1.33–36)

86. François Bernier, *The History of the Late Revolution of the Empire of the Great Mogul* (London: Moses Pitt, 1671), pp. 18, 131. On the historical Aureng-Zebe's reputation for piety, see Richards, *Mughal Empire*, p. 153.

87. On reincarnation see, for instance, the "Bachali" of Conti's account. According to Tavernier, "the *Bramins* make them believe, that in dying after that manner, they shall revive again with him in another World, with more honour and more advantages than they enjoy'd before" (*Six Voyages*, p. 169). Bernier records of a *sati*, "it was said, that she had been heard to pronounce with great force these two

words, *Five, Two*, to signifie, according to the Opinion of those that hold the Soul's Transmigration, that this was the *Fifth* time she had burn't her self with the same Husband, and that there remain'd but *two* times for perfection" (*Continuation*, pp. 120–21). For the association of India with dreams and dreaming, see Inden, *Imagining India*, pp. 55–56, 95–96.

88. It is at this point that the equation of woman with tradition in the early modern travel and colonial discourses perhaps blends with the different, modern syndrome by which woman becomes the nation. See Chatterjee, *Nation*, pp. 116–57, and the essays in Nira Yuval-Davis and Floya Anthias, eds., *Woman, Nation, State* (Basingstoke: Macmillan, 1989). I have profited from Rajan's somewhat different account of "the feminization of India" in the play (*Under Western Eyes*, p. 77).

89. In *Amboyna* (1673), which concerns the torture of several East India Company servants by the Dutch VOC in 1623, Dryden's imaginary heroine Ysabinda determines to starve herself after her beloved Towerson is killed (5.1.420–33, in Dearing, ed., *Works of John Dryden*). *Amboyna* is set in the Moluccas (Indonesia), the initial theater of Anglo-Dutch cooperation and rivalry in the East Indies.

90. There is little textual evidence to support the "back-story" for Melesinda that Dearing conjectures: "Dryden seems to have conceived of Melesinda as a Hindu princess who had been forcibly married to Morat" (*Works of John Dryden*, p. 436, line 613 note). A Hindu Melesinda, whether a convert or apostate from Islam in grief, still does not explain why the Mughal prince Morat is to be burnt despite his brother's emphatic command to prepare the family sepulchre.

91. Bernier, *Continuation*, pp. 119, 121, 123; Bowrey, *Geographical Account*, p. 35. See also Gabriel Dellon, *A Voyage to the East-Indies*, trans. J. C. (London: D. Brown, 1698), pp. 47, 49–50.

92. C. A. Bayly, *Empire and Information: Intelligence Gathering and Social Communication, 1780–1870* (Cambridge: Cambridge University Press, 1996), p. 48. Niccolao Manucci was a late-seventeenth-century traveler in Mughal India; William Hawkins was ambassador to the Mughal court, 1608.

93. Inden's *Imagining India* is split between a European nineteenth-century and an eighth-to-tenth-century Hindu "imperial formation." In the rather different case of nineteenth-century Egypt, Timothy Mitchell's *Colonising Egypt* does not deal with the modeling of pharaonic Egypt at all, despite its fascination for Europeans. I am indebted to both of these studies.

94. Cohn, *Colonialism*, pp. 17–18, 112–13.

95. Cohn, *Colonialism*, p. 78.

96. Cohn, *Colonialism*, p. 79.

97. There is a slight tendency toward a similar elevation of the uncolonized body in Mitchell, *Colonizing Egypt*, pp. 154–55.

Works Cited

Abbot, George. *A Briefe Description of the whole WORLDE. . . . newly augmented and enlarged.* London: John Brown, 1605.

Abu-Lughod, Janet L. *Before European Hegemony: The World System A.D. 1250–1350.* New York: Oxford University Press, 1989.

Adelman, Janet. *The Common Liar: An Essay on Antony and Cleopatra.* New Haven, Conn.: Yale University Press, 1973.

Amin, Samir. *Eurocentrism.* Trans. Russell Moore. New York: Monthly Review Press, 1989.

———. "The Ancient World Systems versus the Modern Capitalist World System." *Review: Fernand Braudel Center* 14:3 (1991), 349–85.

———. *Capitalism in the Age of Globalization: The Management of Contemporary Society.* London: Zed Books, 1997.

Andrea, Bernadette. "Columbus in Istanbul: Ottoman Mappings of the 'New World.'" *Genre* 30 (1997), 135–65.

Appadurai, Arjun. *Modernity at Large: Cultural Dimensions of Globalization.* Minneapolis: University of Minnesota Press, 1996.

Apollodorus. *The Library.* Trans. J. G. Frazer. London: Loeb Classical Library–Heinemann, 1921.

Archer, John Michael. "Sovereignty and Intelligence in *King Lear.*" In *Ideological Approaches to Shakespeare: The Practice of Theory.* Eds. Robert P. Merrix and Nicholas Ranson. Lewiston: Mellen, 1992.

Arrian. *Indica.* In *Ancient India as Described by Megasthenes and Arrian.* Trans. J. W. McCrindle. London: Trubner, 1877.

———. *Anabasis.* In *Arrian.* Vol. 2. Ed. E. Iliff Robson. London: Loeb Classical Library-Heinemann, 1933.

Avity, Pierre d'. *The Estates, Empires, & Principalities of the World. Represented by description of Countries, maners of Inhabitants, Riches of Provinces, forces, Gouernment, Religion; and the Princes that haue gouerned in euery Estate.* Trans. Edward Grimstone. London: Adam Islip for Matthew Lownes and John Bill, 1615.

Barbosa, Duarte. *The Book of Duarte Barbosa: An Account of the Countries Bordering on the Indian Ocean and their Inhabitants*. 2 vols. Trans. Mansel Longworth Dames. London: Hakluyt Society, 1918.

Bayly, C. A. "The Pre-History of 'Communalism'? Religious Conflict in India, 1700–1860." *Modern Asian Studies* 19 (1985), 177–203.

———. *Empire and Information: Intelligence Gathering and Social Communication, 1780–1870*. Cambridge: Cambridge University Press, 1996.

Benjamin, Walter. "Theses on the Philosophy of History." In *Illuminations*. Trans. Harry Zohn. New York: Schocken Books, 1969.

———. "Paris, Capital of the Nineteenth Century." In *Reflections: Essays, Aphorisms, Autobiographical Writings*. Trans. Edmund Jephcott. New York: Harcourt Brace Jovanovich, 1978.

———. [*Passagen-Werk*] "N." Trans. Leigh Hafrey and Richard Sieburth. *Philosophical Forum* 15:1–2 (1983–84), 1–40.

———. *The Origin of German Tragic Drama*. Trans. John Osborne. London: Verso, 1985.

———. "Eduard Fuchs: Collector and Historian." In *The Essential Frankfurt School Reader*. Eds. Andrew Arato and Eike Gebhardt. New York: Continuum, 1987.

Bennett, Joan S. "God, Satan, and King Charles: Milton's Royal Portraits." *PMLA* 93 (1977), 441–47.

Bernal, Martin. "Black Athena Denied: The Tyranny of Germany over Greece." *Comparative Criticism* 8 (1986), 3–69.

———. *Black Athena: The Afroasiatic Roots of Classical Civilization*. Vol. 1, *The Fabrication of Ancient Greece, 1785–1985*. New Brunswick, N.J.: Rutgers University Press, 1987.

———. *Black Athena: The Afroasiatic Roots of Classical Civilization*. Vol. 2, *The Archaeological and Documentary Evidence*. New Brunswick, N.J.: Rutgers University Press, 1991.

Bernier, François. *The History of the Late Revolution of the Empire of the Great Mogul*. London: Moses Pitt, 1671.

———. *A Continuation of the Memoires of Monsieur Bernier, Concerning the Great Mogol*. Trans. H. O. London: Moses Pitt, 1672.

Berry, Lloyd E. *The English Works of Giles Fletcher, the Elder*. Madison: University of Wisconsin Press, 1964.

Berry, Lloyd E., and Robert O. Crummey, eds. *Rude and Barbarous Kingdom: Russia in the Accounts of Sixteenth-Century English Voyagers*. Madison: University of Wisconsin Press, 1968.

Blackburn, Robin. *The Making of New World Slavery: From the Baroque to the Modern, 1492–1800*. London: Verso, 1997.

Blaut, J. M. *The Colonizer's Model of the World: Geographical Diffusionism and Eurocentric History*. New York: Guilford Press, 1993.

Blount, Henry. *A Voyage into the Levant.* 2nd ed. London: for Andrew Crooke, 1637.

Boemus, Johannes. *The Manners, Lawes, and Customes of All Nations, Collected out of the Best Writers.* Trans. Ed Aston. London: George Eld, 1611.

Bowrey, Thomas. *A Geographical Account of the Countries Round the Bay of Bengal, 1669 to 1679.* Ed. R. C. Temple. Cambridge: Hakluyt Society, 1905.

Braudel, Fernand. *The Mediterranean and the Mediterranean World in the Age of Philip II.* Trans. Siân Reynolds. New York: Harper & Row, 1976.

———. *Civilization and Capitalism, 15th–18th Century.* Vol. 2, *The Perspective of the World.* Trans. Siân Reynolds. New York: Harper & Row, 1984.

Bray, Alan. *Homosexuality in Renaissance England.* London: Gay Men's Press, 1982.

Brenner, Robert. *Merchants and Revolution: Commercial Change, Political Conflict, and London's Overseas Traders, 1550–1653.* Princeton, N.J.: Princeton University Press, 1993.

Brown, Laura. *Ends of Empire: Women and Ideology in Early Eighteenth-Century English Literature.* Ithaca, N.Y.: Cornell University Press, 1993.

Browne, Thomas. *Religio Medici.* In *The Prose of Sir Thomas Browne.* Ed. Norman Endicott. New York: New York University Press, 1967.

Bruton, William. *Newes from the East Indies: Or, A Voyage to Bengalla . . . With the state and magnificence of the Court of Malcandy, kept by the Nabob Viceroy . . . Also their detestable Religion, mad and foppish rites, and Ceremonies, and wicked Sacrifices and impious Customes used in those parts.* London: I. Okes, 1638.

Butler, Judith. *Gender Trouble: Feminism and the Subversion of Identity.* New York: Routledge, 1990.

———. *Bodies That Matter: On the Discursive Limits of "Sex".* New York: Routledge, 1993.

Cartwright, John. *The Preachers Travels.* London: for Thomas Thorpe, 1611.

Castanheda, Fernão Lopez de. *The firste Booke of the Historie of the Discouerie and Conquest of the East Indias.* Trans. N. L. London: Thomas East, 1582.

Cawley, Robert Ralston. *Milton and the Literature of Travel.* Princeton, N.J.: Princeton University Press, 1951.

Chartier, Roger. *The Order of Books: Readers, Authors, and Libraries in Europe between the Fourteenth and Eighteenth Centuries.* Trans. Lydia G. Cochrane. Stanford, Calif.: Stanford University Press, 1994.

Chatterjee, Partha. *The Nation and Its Fragments: Colonialism and Postcolonial Histories.* Princeton, N.J.: Princeton University Press, 1993.

Chaudhuri, K. N. *The Trading World of Asia and the East India Company, 1660–1760.* Cambridge: Cambridge University Press, 1978.

———. *Trade and Civilization in the Indian Ocean: An Economic History of the Rise of Islam to 1750.* Cambridge: Cambridge University Press, 1985.

———. *Asia before Europe: Economy and Civilization of the Indian Ocean from the Rise of Islam to 1750.* Cambridge: Cambridge University Press, 1990.

Chew, Samuel C. *The Crescent and the Rose: Islam and England During the Renaissance.* New York, 1937. Rpt. New York: Octagon Press, 1974.

Cicero. *Tusculan Disputations.* Trans J. E. King. London: Loeb Classical Library-Heinemann, 1971.

———. *The Nature of the Gods.* Trans. Horace C. P. McGregor. London: Penguin, 1972.

Clifford, James. *The Predicament of Culture: Twentieth-Century Ethnography, Literature, and Art.* Cambridge, Mass.: Harvard University Press, 1988.

Cohn, Bernard S. "Representing Authority in Victorian India." In *An Anthropologist among the Historians and Other Essays.* Delhi: Oxford University Press, 1990.

———. *Colonialism and Its Forms of Knowledge: The British in India.* Princeton, N.J.: Princeton University Press, 1996.

Columbus, Christopher. *The Four Voyages of Columbus.* 2 vols. Ed. Cecil Jane. London, 1930, 1933. Rpt., with corrections, New York: Dover, 1988.

Corcoran, Mary Irma. *Milton's Paradise with Reference to the Hexameral Background.* Washington, D.C.: Catholic University of America Press, 1945.

Curtius, Ernst Robert. *European Literature and the Latin Middle Ages.* Trans. Willard R. Trask. Princeton, N.J.: Princeton University Press, 1953.

D'Amico, Jack. *The Moor in English Renaissance Drama.* Tampa: University of South Florida Press, 1991.

Dante Alighieri. *The Divine Comedy.* Vol. 2, *Purgatorio.* Ed. John D. Sinclair. Princeton, N.J.: Bollingen-Princeton University Press, 1982.

Danby, John F. *Poets on Fortune's Hill: Studies in Sidney, Shakespeare, Beaumont and Fletcher.* London: Faber and Faber, 1952.

Davies, Stevie. *Images of Kingship in Paradise Lost: Milton's Politics and Christian Liberty.* Columbia: University of Missouri Press, 1983.

Dellon, Gabriel. *A Voyage to the East-Indies.* Trans. J. C. London: D. Brown, 1698.

Diodorus Siculus. *The History of Diodorus Siculus. Containing all that is Most Memorable and of greatest Antiquity in the first Ages of the World until the Fall of Troy.* Trans. H.[enry] C[ogan]. London: John Macock for Giles Calvert, 1653.

———. *Diodorus of Sicily.* Vol. 9. Trans. Russell M. Geer. London: Loeb Classical Library-Heinemann, 1962.

Diogenes Laertius. *Lives of Eminent Philosophers.* Vol. 1. Trans. R. D. Hicks. London: Loeb Classical Library-Heinemann, 1959.

Dollimore, Jonathan. "Shakespeare, Cultural Materialism, Feminism, and Marxist Humanism." *NLH* 21:3 (1990), 471–93.

Dryden, John. *Aureng-Zebe.* In *The Works of John Dryden.* Vol. 12. Ed. Vinton A. Dearing. Berkeley: University of California Press, 1994.

———. *Amboyna.* In *The Works of John Dryden.* Vol. 12. Ed. Vinton A. Dearing. Berkeley: University of California Press, 1994.

Duncan, Joseph E. *Milton's Earthly Paradise: A Historical Study of Eden.* Minneapolis: University of Minnesota Press, 1972.

Dunning, Chester. "James I, the Russia Company, and the Plan to Establish a Protecorate over North Russia." *Albion* 21 (1989), 206–26.

Eden, Richard. *The Decades of the newe worlde.* In *The First Three English Books on America.* Ed. Edward Arber. Birmingham: Turnbull & Spears, 1895.

Edwards, Ruth B. *Kadmos the Phoenician: A Study in Greek Legends and the Mycenaean Age.* Amsterdam: Adolph M. Hakkert, 1979.

Evans, Martin J. *Milton's Imperial Epic: Paradise Lost and the Discourse of Colonialism.* Ithaca, N.Y.: Cornell University Press, 1996.

Fabian, Johannes. *Time and the Other: How Anthropology Makes Its Object.* New York: Columbia University Press, 1983.

Federici, Cesare. *The Voyage and Trauaile: of M. Caesar Frederick, Merchant of Venice, into the East India.* London: Richard Jones and Edward White, 1588.

Feynes, Henri de. *An Exact and Curious Svrvey of all the East Indies, euen to Canton.* Trans. Loiseau de Tourval. London: Thomas Dawson for William Arondell, 1615.

Finley, M. I. *Ancient Slavery and Modern Ideology.* Harmondsworth: Penguin, 1983.

Fletcher, Giles. *Of the Russe Common Wealth. Or Maner of Gouernement by the Russe Emperour, (commonly called the Emperour of Moskouia) with the manners, and fashions of the people of that Countrey.* London: T. D. for Thomas Charde, 1591.

Fletcher, John. *The Loyal Subject.* In *The Dramatic Works in the Beaumont and Fletcher Canon.* Vol. 5. Ed. Fredson Bowers. Cambridge: Cambridge University Press, 1982.

Foster, William, ed. *Early Travels in India, 1583–1619.* Oxford: Oxford University Press, 1921.

Foucault, Michel. *The History of Sexuality.* Vol. 1, *An Introduction.* Trans. Robert Hurley. New York: Vintage, 1980.

Froula, Christine. "When Eve Reads Milton: Undoing the Canonical Economy." *Critical Inquiry* 10 (1983), 321–47.

Frye, Northrop. *The Return of Eden: Five Essays on Milton's Epics.* Toronto: University of Toronto Press, 1965.

Fryer, John. *A New Account of East India and Persia. Being Nine Years' Travels, 1672–1681.* 3 vols. Ed. William Crooke. London: Hakluyt Society, 1904.

Galinsky, G. Karl. *The Herakles Theme: The Adaptations of the Hero in Literature from Homer to the Twentieth Century.* Totowa, N.J.: Rowman and Littlefield, 1972.

Gesta Grayorum. Ed. W. W. Greg. Oxford: Malone Society, 1914.

Giamatti, A. Bartlett. *The Earthly Paradise and the Renaissance Epic.* Princeton, N.J.: Princeton University Press, 1966.

Gilbert, Allan H. *A Geographical Dictionary of Milton.* New York: Russell & Russell, 1919.

Gillies, John. *Shakespeare and the Geography of Difference.* Cambridge: Cambridge University Press, 1994.

Gilmore, Myron P. "The New World in French and English Historians of the Sixteenth Century." In *First Images of America: The Impact of the New World on the Old.* Ed. Fredi Chiappelli. Berkeley: University of California Press, 1976.

Gilroy, Paul. *The Black Atlantic: Modernity and Double Consciousness.* London: Verso, 1993.

Greenblatt, Stephen. *Marvelous Possessions: The Wonder of the New World.* Chicago: University of Chicago Press, 1991.

———. "Mutilation and Meaning." In *The Body in Parts: Fantasies of Corporeality in Early Modern Europe.* New York: Routledge, 1997.

Greene, Jody. "New Historicism and Its New World Discoveries." *Yale Journal of Criticism* 4:2 (1991), 163–98.

Grosrichard, Alain. *The Sultan's Court: European Fantasies of the East.* Trans. Liz Heron. London: Verso, 1998.

Guillory, John. "Dalila's House: *Samson Agonistes* and the Sexual Division of Labor." In *Rewriting the Renaissance: The Discourses of Sexual Difference in Early Modern Europe.* Eds. Margaret W. Ferguson, Maureen Quilligan, and Nancy J. Vickers. Chicago: University of Chicago Press, 1986.

Hahn, Thomas. "The Indian Tradition in Western Medieval Intellectual History." *Viator* 9 (1978), 213–34.

———. "Indians East and West: Primitivism and Savagery in English Discovery Narratives of the Sixteenth Century." *Journal of Medieval and Renaissance Studies* 8 (1978), 77–114.

Hall, Kim F. "Sexual Politics and Cultural Identity in *The Masque of Blackness.*" In *The Performance of Power: Theatrical Discourse and Politics.* Eds. Sue-Ellen Case and Jenelle Reinelt. Iowa City: University of Iowa Press, 1991.

———. "'I Rather Would Wish to Be a Black-Moor': Beauty, Race, and Rank in Lady Mary Wroth's *Urania.*" In *Women, "Race," and Writing in the Early Modern Period.* Eds. Margo Hendricks and Patricia Parker. London: Routledge, 1994.

———. *Things of Darkness: Economies of Race and Gender in Early Modern England.* Ithaca, N.Y.: Cornell University Press, 1995.

Halpern, Richard. *The Poetics of Primitive Accumulation: English Renaissance Culture and the Genealogy of Capital.* Ithaca, N.Y.: Cornell University Press, 1991.

Hamer, Mary. *Signs of Cleopatra: History, Politics, Representation.* London: Routledge, 1993.

Hartog, François. *The Mirror of Herodotus: The Representation of the Other in the Writing of History.* Trans. Janet Lloyd. Berkeley: University of California Press, 1988.

Harvey, F. D. "Herodotus and the Man-Footed Creature." In Léonie Archer, ed. *Slavery and Other Forms of Unfree Labor.* London: Routledge, 1988.

Heliodorus. *An Aethiopian History.* Trans. Thomas Underdowne. London: David Nutt, 1895.

————. *An Ethiopian Romance.* Trans. Moses Hadas. Ann Arbor: University of Michigan Press, 1957.

Hellie, Richard. *Slavery in Russia, 1450–1725.* Chicago: University of Chicago Press, 1982.

Hendricks, Margo. "'Obscured by dreams': Race, Empire, and Shakespeare's *A Midsummer Night's Dream.*" *Shakespeare Quarterly* 47 (1996), 37–60.

Herberstein, Sigismund von. *Notes upon Russia [Rerum Moscoviticarum Commentarii].* 2 vols. Trans. R. H. Major. London: Hakluyt Society, 1851–52.

Herbert, Thomas. *A Relation of Some Yeares Travaile, Begvnne Anno 1626. Into Afrique and the greater Asia, especially the Territories of the Persian Monarchie.* London: William Stansby and Jacob Bloome, 1634.

————. *Some Yeares Travels into Divers Parts of Asia and Afrique. . . . With a revivall of the first Discoverer of America.* Revised and enlarged by the author. London: K. Bip. for Iacob Blome and Richard Bishop, 1638.

Herodotus. *The Famous Hystory of Herodotus.* Trans. B. R. London: Thomas Marshe, 1584.

————. *The Histories.* Trans. A. R. Burn and Aubrey de Sélincourt. London: Penguin, 1972.

Heylyn, Peter. *Cosmographie in Four Books. Containing the Chorographie and Historie of the World, and all the principal Kingdoms, Provinces, Seas, and Isles thereof.* 2nd ed. London: for Henry Seile, 1657.

Hirsch, Rudolph. "Printed Reports on the Early Discoveries and Their Reception." In *First Images of America: The Impact of the New World on the Old.* Ed. Fredi Chiappelli. Berkeley: University of California Press, 1976.

Holinshed, Raphael. *Chronicles of England, Scotland, and Ireland.* London, 1587. Rpt. London: J. Johnson, 1807–1808.

Homer. *The Iliad.* Trans. Richmond Lattimore. Chicago: University of Chicago Press, 1951.

————. *The Odyssey.* Trans. Richmond Lattimore. New York: HarperCollins, 1975.

Horace. *The Odes and Epodes.* Trans. C. E. Bennett. Cambridge, Mass.: Loeb Classical Library-Harvard University Press, 1978.

Hornblower, Simon, and Antony Spawforth, eds. *The Oxford Classical Dictionary.* 3rd ed. Oxford: Oxford University Press, 1996.

Hourani, Albert. *A History of the Arab Peoples.* Cambridge, Mass.: Belknap Press-Harvard University Press, 1991.

Hughes, Merritt Y. "Satan and the 'Myth' of the Tyrant." In *Essays in English Literature from the Renaissance to the Victorian Age Presented to A. S. P. Woodhouse.* Eds. Millar MacLure and F. W. Watt. Toronto: University of Toronto Press, 1964.

Hughes-Hallett, Lucy. *Cleopatra: Histories, Dreams and Distortions.* New York: HarperCollins, 1990.

Hunter, William Wilson. *A History of British India.* Vol. 2. London: Longmans, Green, 1900.

I. H. *Paradise Transplanted and Restored, In a Most Artfull and Lively Representation of The several Creatures, Plants, Flowers, and other Vegetables, in their full growth, shape, and colour: Shown at* Christopher Whiteheads *at the two wreathed Posts in Shooe-Lane, London.* London, 1661. Rpt. London: Edwin Pearson, 1871.

Inden, Ronald. *Imagining India.* Oxford: Basil Blackwell, 1990.

James I, King of England. "A Premonition to All Most Mightie Monarchies, Kings, Free Princes, and states." In *The Political Works of James I.* Ed. C. H. McIlwain. Cambridge, Mass.: Harvard University Press, 1918.

Jansson, Maija and Nikolai Rogozhin. *England and the North: The Russian Embassy of 1613–1614.* Philadelphia: American Philosophical Society, 1994.

Johnson-Odim, Cheryl, Gerda Lerner, Ann N. Michelini, Margaret Washington, Madeline C. Zilfi, and Martin Bernal. "Comment: The Debate over Black Athena." *Journal of Women's History* 4 (1993), 84–135.

Jones, Eldred. *Othello's Countrymen: Africans in English Renaissance Drama.* Oxford: Oxford University Press, 1965.

Friar Jordanus. *Mirabilia Descripta: The Wonders of the East.* Trans. Henry Yule. London: Hakluyt Society, 1863.

Katz, David S. *Philo-Semitism and the Readmission of the Jews to England, 1603–1655.* Oxford: Clarendon, 1982.

Knapp, Jeffrey. *An Empire Nowhere: England, America, and Literature from Utopia to the The Tempest.* Berkeley: University of California Press, 1992.

Ktesias [Ctesias]. *Ancient India as Described by Ktesias the Knidian.* Ed. J. W. McCrindle. London: Trubner, 1882.

Lach, Donald F. *Asia in the Making of Europe.* Vol. 1, *The Century of Discovery.* Chicago: University of Chicago Press, 1965.

———. *Asia in the Making of Europe.* Vol. 2, *A Century of Wonder.* Book 1, *The Visual Arts.* Chicago: University of Chicago Press, 1970.

LeFebvre, Henri. *The Production of Space.* Trans. Donald Nicholson-Smith. Oxford: Blackwell, 1991.

Leo Africanus. *The History and Description of Africa.* Trans. John Pory. Ed. Robert Brown. 3 vols. London: Hakluyt Society, 1896.

Leonard, John. *Naming in Paradise: Milton and the Language of Adam and Eve.* Oxford: Clarendon, 1990.

Linschoten, John Huyghen Van. *The Voyage of John Huyghen Van Linschoten to the East Indies.* 2 vols. Ed. A. C. Burnell. London: Hakluyt Society, 1885.

Lithgow, William. *A most delectable and True Discourse of an admired and painefull [sic] Peregrination from Scotland, to the most Famous Kingdomes in Europe, Asia, and Affrica.* London: Nicholas Okes, 1623.

Lloyd, Lodowick. *The Consent of Time.* London: George Bishop, 1590.

Loomba, Ania. *Gender, Race, Renaissance Drama.* Manchester: Manchester University Press, 1989.

Lord, Henry. *A Discovery of the Sect of the Banians . . . Gathered from their BRA-MANES, Teachers of that Sect.* London: Francis Constable, 1630.

Lucan. *The Pharsalia.* Trans. H. T. Riley. London: George Bell, 1903.

Lynche, Richard. *An Historical Treatise of the Travels of Noah into Europe: Containing the first inhabitation and peopling thereof.* London: Adam Islip, 1601.

Major, R. H., ed. *India in the Fifteenth Century.* London: Hakluyt Society, 1857.

Mandeville, John. *Mandeville's Travels.* Vol. 1. Ed. Malcolm Letts. London: Hakluyt Society, 1953.

Mani, Lata. "Production of an Official Discourse on *Sati* in Early Nineteenth Century Bengal." *Review of Women's Studies* (April 1986), 32–40; supplement to *Economic and Political Weekly* 21:17 (April 26, 1986).

———. "Contentious Traditions: The Debate on *Sati* in Colonial India." In *The Nature and Context of Minority Discourse.* Eds. Abdul R. JanMohamed and David Lloyd. New York: Oxford University Press, 1990.

Margeret, Jacques. *The Russian Empire and the Grand Duchy of Muscovy.* Trans. Chester L. Dunning. Pittsburgh: University of Pittsburgh Press, 1983.

Marx, Karl. "The British Rule in India." In *Surveys from Exile.* Ed. David Fernbach. New York: Vintage, 1974.

Matar, Nabil. *Islam in Britain, 1558–1685.* Cambridge: Cambridge University Press, 1998.

———. *Turks, Moors, and Englishmen in the Age of Discovery.* New York: Columbia University Press, 1999.

McColley, Diane K. *Milton's Eve.* Urbana: University of Illinois Press, 1983.

Methwold, William. "Relations of the Kingdome of Golchonda." In *Relations of Golconda in the Early Seventeenth Century.* Ed. W. H. Moreland. London: Hakluyt Society, 1931.

Mies, Maria. *Patriarchy and Accumulation on a World Scale: Women in the International Division of Labour.* London: Zed Books, 1986.

Migne, J.-P., ed. *Patrologiae cursus completus. Series Latina.* Paris, 1844–64. Rpt. Turnhout: Brepols, 1982.

Milton, John. *The Complete Poems and Major Prose.* Ed. Merritt Y. Hughes. Indianapolis: Odyssey, 1957.

———. *A Brief History of Moscovia . . . Gather'd from the Writings of several Eye-witnesses.* Ed. George B. Parks. In *The Complete Prose Works of John Milton.* Vol. 8. Eds. William Alfred et al. New Haven, Conn.: Yale University Press, 1982.

Mitchell, Timothy. *Colonising Egypt.* Berkeley: University of California Press, 1991.

Mitter, Partha. *Much Maligned Monsters: History of European Reactions to Indian Art.* Oxford: Clarendon, 1977.

Montaigne, Michel de. *The Complete Essays of Montaigne.* Trans. Donald Frame. Stanford, Calif.: Stanford University Press, 1958.

Morgan, E. Delmar, and C. H. Coote, eds. *Early Voyages and Travels in Russia and Persia.* London: Hakluyt Society, 1886.

Mudimbe, V. Y. *The Idea of Africa*. Bloomington: Indiana University Press, 1994.

Mullaney, Steven. *The Place of the Stage: License, Play, and Power in Renaissance England*. Chicago: University of Chicago Press, 1988.

Mundy, Peter. *The Travels of Peter Mundy in Europe and Asia, 1608–1667*. Vol. 2, *Travels in Asia, 1628–1634*. Ed. R. C. Temple. London: Hakluyt Society, 1914.

Munster, Sebastian. *A treatyse of the newe India*. Trans. Richard Eden. London, 1553. Rpt. in *The First Three English Books on America*. Ed. Edward Arber. Birmingham: Turnbull & Spears, 1895.

Neely, Carol Thomas. *Broken Nuptials in Shakespeare's Plays*. New Haven, Conn.: Yale University Press, 1985.

Newman, Karen. "'And Wash the Ethiop White': Femininity and the Monstrous in *Othello*." In *Shakespeare Reproduced: The Text in History and Ideology*. Eds. Jean E. Howard and Marion F. O'Connor. New York: Methuen, 1987.

Nyquist, Mary. "The Genesis of Gendered Subjectivity in the Divorce Tracts and in *Paradise Lost*." In *Re-membering Milton: Essays on the Texts and Traditions*. Eds. Mary Nyquist and Margaret W. Ferguson. New York: Methuen, 1987.

Olearius, Adam. *The Voyages & Travels of the Ambassadors Sent by Frederick Duke of Holstein, to the Great Duke of Muscovy, and the King of Persia . . . Containing a compleat History of Muscovy, Tartary, Persia, And other adjacent Countries*. Trans. John Davies. London: for Thomas Dring and John Starkey, 1662.

Odoric of Pordenone. In *Cathay and the Way Thither*. Vol. 2. Ed. Henry Yule. London: Hakluyt Society, 1913.

Onions, C. T. *The Oxford Dictionary of English Etymology*. Oxford: Clarendon, 1966.

Ortelius, Abraham. *The Theatre of the Whole World*. London, 1606. Rpt. Amsterdam: Theatrum Orbis Terrarum Ltd., 1968.

Oz, Avraham. *The Yoke of Love: Prophetic Riddles in The Merchant of Venice*. Newark: University of Delaware Press, 1995.

Paes, Domingos. "Narrative of Domingos Paes." In *A Forgotten Empire: Vijayanagar*. Ed. Robert Sewell. New Delhi: National Book Trust, 1970.

Painter, William. *The Palace of Pleasure*. Ed. Joseph Jacobs. New York: Dover, 1966.

Palmer, Daryl W. "Jacobean Muscovites: Winter, Tyranny, and Knowledge in *The Winter's Tale*." *Shakespeare Quarterly* 46 (1995), 323–39.

Pandey, Gyanendra. "In Defense of the Fragment: Writing about Hindu-Muslim Riots in India Today." In *A Subaltern Studies Reader, 1986–1995*. Ed. Ranajit Guha. Minneapolis: University of Minnesota Press, 1997.

Panofsky, Erwin. *Meaning in the Visual Arts*. Garden City, N.Y.: Doubleday-Anchor, 1955.

Parker, Kunal M. "'A Corporation of Superior Prostitutes': Anglo-Indian Legal Conceptions of Temple Dancing Girls, 1800-1914." *Modern Asian Studies* 32 (1998), 559–633.

Parker, Patricia. *Literary Fat Ladies: Rhetoric, Gender, Property.* New York: Methuen, 1987.

——. "Preposterous Reversals: *Love's Labor's Lost.*" *Modern Language Quarterly* 54 (1993), 435–82.

Pearson, Lionel. *The Lost Histories of Alexander the Great.* New York: American Philological Society, 1960.

Pietz, William. "The Problem of the Fetish." *Res* 9 (1985), 5–17; *Res* 13 (1987), 23–45; *Res* 16 (1988), 105–23.

Pliny. *The Historie of the World. Commonly called, The Natvrall Historie of C. Plinivs Secvndvs.* Vol. 1. Trans. Philemon Holland. London: Adam Islip, 1601.

Plutarch. *The Philosophie, commonlie called, The Morals written by the learned Philosopher Plutarch of Chaeronea.* Trans. Philemon Holland. London: Arnold Hatfield, 1603.

——. "The Life of Marcus Antonius." In *Plutarch's Lives of the Noble Grecians and Romans.* Vol. 6. Trans. Thomas North. London, 1896. Rpt. New York: AMS Press, 1967.

——. "Life of Alexander." In *Plutarch's Lives.* Vol. 7. Trans. Bernadotte Perrin. London: Loeb Classical Library-Heinemann, 1971.

Polo, Marco. *The Travels of Marco Polo.* Trans. Ronald Latham. London: Penguin, 1958.

Pomponius Mela. *The Rare and singuler worke of Pomponius Mela, That excellent and worthy cosmographer, of the Situation of the world.* Trans. Arthur Golding. London: Thomas Hacket, 1590.

Pratt, Mary Louise. "Scratches on the Face of the Country; or, What Mr. Barrow Saw in the Land of the Bushmen." *Critical Inquiry* 12 (1985), 119–43.

Propertius. *Propertius.* Trans. H. E. Butler. London: Loeb Classical Library–Heinemann, 1976.

Prösler, Martin. "Museums and Globalization." In *Theorizing Museums: Representing Identity and Diversity in a Changing World.* Eds. Sharon Macdonald and Gordon Frye. Oxford: Blackwell, 1996.

Pseudo-Callisthenes. *The Romance of Alexander the Great by Pseudo-Callisthenes.* Trans. from the Armenian version by Albert Mugrdich Wolohojian. New York: Columbia University Press, 1969.

Purchas, Samuel. *Purchas His Pilgrimage, or Relations of the World and the Religions Observed in all Ages and places Discovered.* London: William Stansby for Henrie Fetherstone, 1626.

Purchas, Samuel, ed. *Hakluytus Posthumus or Purchas His Pilgrimes.* 20 vols. Glasgow: James MacLehose and Sons, 1905.

Quilligan, Maureen. "Freedom, Service, and the Trade in Slaves: The Problem of Labor in *Paradise Lost.*" In *Subject and Object in Renaissance Culture.* Eds. Margreta de Grazia, Maureen Quilligan, and Peter Stallybrass. Cambridge: Cambridge University Press, 1996.

Quint, David. *Epic and Empire: Politics and Generic Form from Virgil to Milton.* Princeton, N.J.: Princeton University Press, 1993.

Rabasa, José. *Inventing America: Spanish Historiography and the Formation of Eurocentrism.* Norman: University of Oklahoma Press, 1993.

Rajan, Balachandra. *Under Western Eyes: India from Milton to Macaulay.* Durham, N.C.: Duke University Press, 1999.

Ralegh, Walter. *The History of the World.* Book 1. London: Walter Burre, 1614.

———. "The discovery of the large, rich, and beautiful Empire of Guiana." In Richard Hakluyt, *Voyages and Discoveries.* Ed. Jack Beeching. London: Penguin, 1972.

Relihan, Constance C. "Erasing the East from *Twelfth Night.*" In Joyce Green MacDonald, ed. *Race, Ethnicity, and Power in the Renaissance.* Madison, N.J.: Fairleigh Dickinson University Press, pp. 80–94.

Richards, John F. *The Mughal Empire.* New Cambridge History of India, I:5. Cambridge: Cambridge University Press, 1993.

Roe, Thomas. *The Embassy of Sir Thomas Roe to India, 1615–19.* 2nd ed. Ed. William Foster. Oxford: Oxford University Press, 1926.

Rosen, Alan. "The Rhetoric of Exclusion: Jew, Moor, and the Boundaries of Discourse in *The Merchant of Venice.*" In *Race, Ethnicity, and Power in the Renaissance.* Ed. Joyce Green MacDonald. Madison, N.J.: Fairleigh Dickinson University Press, 1997.

Said, Edward W. *Orientalism.* New York: Vintage, 1979.

———. *Culture and Imperialism.* New York: Knopf, 1993.

Sandys, George. *A Relation of a Iourney begun An: Dom: 1610.* London: W. Barrett, 1615.

Seznec, Jean. *The Survival of the Pagan Gods.* Trans. B. E. Sessions. New York: Pantheon, 1953.

Shakespeare, William. *Love's Labour's Lost.* Ed. Richard David. London: Arden-Methuen, 1956.

———. *Antony and Cleopatra.* Ed. M. R. Ridley. London: Arden-Routledge, 1965.

———. *Twelfth Night.* Eds. J. M. Lothian and T. W. Craik. London: Arden-Routledge, 1975.

———. *Titus Andronicus.* Ed. Jonathan Bate. London: Arden-Routledge, 1995.

Shapiro, James. *Shakespeare and the Jews.* New York: Columbia University Press, 1996.

Sidney, Philip. *Sir Philip Sidney: Selected Poems.* Ed. Katherine Duncan-Jones. Oxford: Clarendon, 1973.

Singh, Jyotsna G. "Renaissance Antitheatricality, Antifeminism, and Shakespeare's *Antony and Cleopatra.*" *Renaissance Drama* 20 (1989), 99–21.

———. *Colonial Narratives/Cultural Dialogues: "Discoveries" of India in the Language of Colonialism.* London: Routledge, 1996.

Smith, Paul. *Millennial Dreams: Contemporary Culture and Capital in the North.* London: Verso, 1997.

Sorensen, Fred. "The Masque of the Muscovites in *Love's Labour's Lost.*" *Modern Language Notes* 50 (1935), 499–501.

Spenser, Edmund. *The Faerie Queene.* Ed. Thomas P. Roche. New Haven, Conn.: Yale University Press, 1978.

Speed, John. *A Prospect of the Most Famous Parts of the World.* London: John Dawson for George Humble, 1631.

Spivak, Gayatri Chakravorty. "The Rani of Sirmur: An Essay in Reading the Archives." *History and Theory* 24 (1985), 247–72.

———. "Can the Subaltern Speak?" In *Marxism and the Interpretation of Culture.* Eds. Cary Nelson and Lawrence Grossberg. Urbana: University of Illinois Press, 1988.

———. *A Critique of Postcolonial Reason: Toward a History of the Vanishing Present.* Cambridge, Mass: Harvard University Press, 1999.

Stafford, Robert. *A Geographicall and Anthologicall description of all the Empires and Kingdomes, both of Continent and Ilands in this terrestriall Globe.* London: T.C. for Simon Waterson, 1607.

Stagl, Justin. *A History of Curiosity: The Theory of Travel, 1550–1800.* Chur, Switzerland: Harwood Academic, 1995.

Strabo. *The Geography.* Trans. Horace Leonard Jones. London: Loeb Classical Library–Heinemann, 1917.

Squier, Charles L. *John Fletcher.* Boston: Twayne, 1986.

Sunder Rajan, Rajeswari. *Real and Imagined Women: Gender, Culture and Postcolonialism.* London: Routledge, 1993.

Tavernier, Jean-Baptiste. *The Six Voyages of John Baptista Tavernier . . . Through Turkey into Persia and the East Indies, Finished in the Year 1670.* Trans. J. Phillips. London: for R. L. and M.P., 1678.

Thomas Aquinas. *Summa Theologiae.* New York: McGraw-Hill, 1964.

Tibbals, Kate Watkins, ed. "Introduction." In Thomas Heywood. *The Royall King and Loyall Subject.* University of Pennsylvania Series in Philology and Literature, vol. 12. Philadelphia, 1906.

Traub, Valerie. *Desire and Anxiety: Circulations of Sexuality in Shakespearean Drama.* New York: Routledge, 1992.

Valle, Pietro della. *Viaggi di Pietro della Valle, Il Pelegrino.* Vol. 2. Turin: G. Gancia, 1843.

———. *The Travels of Pietro della Valle in India, From the Old English translation of 1664.* Trans. G. Havers. Ed. Edward Grey. London: Hakluyt Society, 1892.

Vaughan, Alden T., and Virginia Mason Vaughan. *Shakespeare's Caliban: A Cultural History.* Cambridge: Cambridge University Press, 1991.

Vaughan, Virginia Mason. *Othello: A Contextual History.* Cambridge: Cambridge University Press, 1994.

Varthema, Ludovico di. *The Nauigation and vyages of Lewes Vertomannus.* In Richard Eden. *The History of Trauayle in the West and East Indies.* London: Richard Iugge, 1577.

———. *The Travels of Ludovico di Varthema in Egypt, Syria, Arabia Deserta and Arabia Felix, in Persia, India, and Ethiopia, A.D. 1503 to 1508.* Trans. J. W. Jones. London: Hakluyt Society, 1863.

Vespucci, Amerigo. *The Letters of Amerigo Vespucci.* Trans. Clements R. Markham. London: Hakluyt Society, 1894.

Verlinden, Charles. "Encore sur les origines de sclavus=esclave." In Verlinden, *L'esclavage dans l'Europe médiévale.* Vol. 2. Gent: Rijksuniversiteit te Gent, 1977.

Vitkus, Daniel J. "Turning Turk in *Othello:* The Conversion and Damnation of the Moor." *Shakespeare Quarterly* 48 (1997), 145–76.

Vitkus, Daniel J. "Introduction." In *Three Turk Plays from Early Modern England: Selimus, A Christian Turned Turk, and the Renegado.* Ed. Vitkus. New York: Columbia University Press, 2000.

Waith, Eugene M. *The Herculean Hero in Marlowe, Chapman, Shakespeare and Dryden.* New York: Columbia University Press, 1962.

Wallerstein, Immanuel. *The Modern World-System.* Vol. 1, *Capitalist Agriculture and the Origins of the European World-Economy in the Sixteenth Century.* San Diego: Academic Press, 1974.

———. *The Modern World-System.* Vol. 2, *Mercantilism and the Consolidation of the European World-Economy, 1600–1750.* San Diego: Academic Press, 1980.

———. *Historical Capitalism.* London: Verso, 1983.

———. *Unthinking Social Science: The Limits of Nineteenth-Century Paradigms.* Cambridge: Polity Press, 1991.

———. "The Construction of Peoplehood." In Etienne Balibar and Immanuel Wallerstein. *Race, Nation, Class: Ambiguous Identities.* London: Verso, 1991.

———. *Geopolitics and Geoculture: Essays on the Changing World System.* Cambridge: Cambridge University Press, 1991.

White, R. S. "Muscovites in *Love's Labour's Lost.*" *Notes and Queries* 33 (1986), 350.

Willan, T. S. *The Early History of the Muscovy Company, 1553–1603.* Manchester: Manchester University Press, 1956.

Wilson, Richard. "Visible Bullets: Tamburlaine the Great and Ivan the Terrible." *ELH* 62 (1995), 47–68.

Wolff, Larry. *Inventing Eastern Europe: The Map of Civilization on the Mind of the Enlightenment.* Stanford, Calif.: Stanford University Press, 1994.

Yates, Frances. *A Study of "Love's Labour's Lost."* Cambridge: Cambridge University Press, 1936.

Yule, Henry, and A. C. Burnell. *Hobson-Jobson: A Glossary of Colloquial Anglo-Indian Words and Phrases, and of Kindred Terms, Etymological, Historical, Geographical, and Discursive.* New edition ed. William Crooke. London, 1903. Rpt. New Delhi: Minshiram Manoharlal, 1994.

Yuval-Davis, Nira, and Floya Anthias, eds. *Woman, Nation, State.* Basingstoke: Macmillan, 1989.

Index